WOODCUT OF JONATHAN EDWARDS

BY FRANK FLINN

JONATHAN EDWARDS:

BIBLIOGRAPHICAL SYNOPSES

BY

NANCY MANSPEAKER

THE EDWIN MELLEN PRESS
NEW YORK AND TORONTO

Library of Congress Cataloging in Publication Data

Manspeaker, Nancy.
    Jonathan Edwards, bibliographical synopses.

    (Studies in American Religion; v. 3)
    Includes bibliographical references.
    1. Edwards, Jonathan, 1703-1758--Bibliography.
I. Title. II. Series.
Z8255.5.M35 [BX7260.E3]   016.2858'092'4   81-9491
ISBN 0-88946-907-5   AACR2

Studies in American Religion ISBN 0-88946-992-X

Printed in the United States of America

To the memory of
Claude R. Leetham
and Arthur G. Gibson

ACKNOWLEDGEMENTS

It is not possible to acknowledge the many people who provided generous assistance during the course of this project, but special thanks must be given to Mrs. Paul McGrath of the University of St. Michael's College Library, Toronto, to Jayne Confer of the Clifford E. Barbour Library, Pittsburgh Theological Seminary, and to Judith Mistichelli of the Library of Congress, Washington, D. C. I am also much indebted to Mrs. Jennie L. Celko for many varieties of help and support.

CONTENTS

INTRODUCTION

Two centuries ago, Jonathan Edwards (1703-1758) seemed fated to be buried amid the ruins of a religion that was rapidly becoming a cultural anachronism. "Calvinism," said William Ellery Channing, "we are persuaded, is giving place to better views. It has passed its meridian, and is sinking to rise no more."[1] Jonathan Edwards, whom Leslie Stephen once described as having "excited little attention during his lifetime, except amongst the sharers of his own religious persuasions,"[2] did not seem likely to survive, as fewer found themselves able to share his vision. His death, in 1758, received little public notice.[3] When Samuel Hopkins came to prepare a volume of Edwards' sermons for publication, together with a biography of Edwards, the response was less than overwhelming. In 1762, Hopkins reported the printer "waiting for subscriptions, very few of which come in."[4] Hopkins devoted his labors to editing other of Edwards' writings for the press, but he soon "became satisfied that they would not be sold, and...turned his mind to other projects."[5] Within his own generation, Jonathan Edwards was no longer marketable, and Ezra Stiles, President of Yale College, thought the handwriting was on the wall. In 1787, President Stiles predicted that in another generation, the writings of Jonathan Edwards would fade into oblivion; and, said Stiles, "when Posterity occasionally comes across them in the Rubbish of Libraries, the rare Characters who may read & be pleased with them, will be looked upon as singular & whimsical...."[6]

Prophecy has always been a perilous enterprise even when the signs appear conclusive, and President Stiles has fared no better than most who have felt similarly inspired. Jonathan Edwards never quite receded into the obscurity

that Stiles predicted, though one suspects for reasons not
yet fully appreciated by current scholars who are frequently
amused by Stiles' apparent lack of foresight. In a variety
of images, as theologian, preacher, poet, metaphysician,
maniac, mystic, artist, saint, and perhaps most importantly,
as "the virtual embodiment of the sulphurous side of
Calvinism,"[7] Jonathan Edwards continued to capture the imagination of successive generations. When the last extensive
inventory of biography and criticism of Jonathan Edwards was
undertaken by John J. Coss, in 1917, a formidable body of
literature had already developed. It is only in recent
years, however, that those who would read and be pleased
with Edwards have ceased to be haunted by the thought that
they may be accounted singular or whimsical. Presumably,
they have been reassured by the conviction that there is
safety in numbers.

Since the appearance of Perry Miller's seminal study of
Edwards, in 1949, and the concurrent resurgence of interest
in colonial studies and the Puritan tradition in America,
scholarly interest in Jonathan Edwards has reached unprece-
dented proportions. The frequent references to a veritable
"renaissance" of Edwards scholarship now in progress are not
essentially misleading, as books, articles, and doctoral
dissertations on Jonathan Edwards continue to proliferate at
a rate unparalleled in its history. Dissertations completed
a quarter of a century ago are being revised for publication
as Edwards beomes increasingly topical and marketable.
There is scarcely a work now appearing in the areas of
American theology, the history of American philosophy,
psychology, religion, literature and culture that does not
have something to say about Jonathan Edwards. What is said
is not always new, or interesting, or well-considered; but
Jonathan Edwards has now become established as a figure who
must be taken into account in any work of substance in

these several areas, and a writer knowingly leaves himself
open to criticism for failure to address the life or work
or influence of Jonathan Edwards.

With the lesson of the unfortunate Stiles in view one
hesitates to wax prophetic, and the day may again come when
it is no longer quite as fashionable to read and be pleased
with Jonathan Edwards. The Yale edition of Edwards' works
now in progress, in itself perhaps the most significant
testimony to the hold that Jonathan Edwards has on the imagination of the present generation, may well help put Edwards
back on the path to obscurity. Charles Reynolds Brown once
remarked that one fortunate result of Edwards' untimely
death was that posterity was thereby spared the completion
of Edwards' *History of the Work of Redemption*. The Yale
editors intend to spare us little, but promise "a full and
complete exposure of his ideas in a manner never before
possible."[8] Thus exposed, Jonathan Edwards may command less
of an audience. The current renaissance of scholarly interest in Jonathan Edwards, however, shows no present signs of
abating; and a new inventory of the literature on Jonathan
Edwards has long been overdue. It is hoped that the following bibliography may not simply serve to preserve the
record, but may be of use to those currently involved in the
critical task of interpretation of Jonathan Edwards.

———————————————

Not long after the process of compiling this bibliography had begun, I ran across the following observation by
William S. Morris. "The history of appraisal and interpretation of Edwards," said Morris, "discloses hardly fewer
vagaries than does that of the manuscripts and editions."[9]

Familiar with the history of the Edwards manuscripts, a
history in which, as Stein has observed, survival was something of a miracle in itself,[10] I found Morris' comment
somewhat unnerving. At the outset of a project that would
require reviewing nearly two and a half centuries of scholarship, a project bound to be tedious at the best of times,
it was disconcerting to think that I would be embarking
upon a sea of "vagaries." Steeled with the thought that
perhaps Morris had overstated his case, I persevered. As
my familiarity with the material increased, however, the
quality of much of this material forced serious questions
concerning the present usefulness of any near complete
bibliography of biography and criticism of Jonathan
Edwards.

     One may inevitably expect studies of marginal value in
the literature that develops around any figure, as the skill
and enthusiasm of interpreters prove inadequate to the
subject. One cannot help suspecting, however, that the literature on Jonathan Edwards is marked by more than its fair
share of material that could safely be ignored by current
interpreters, and this not simply for want of skill—and
certainly not for want of enthusiasm—on the part of the
writers.

     In the early literature on Jonathan Edwards one finds,
for example, that Edwards was adopted by a generation of
eugenists who discoursed at seemingly interminable length on
the worthiness of his "germ plasm." Disquisitions were
written as to whether the example of this Great Progenitor
and his illustrious descendants did not suggest that "the
tendency to be a college president may run in the blood."[11]
In the opinion of one would-be eugenist, Edwards' greatest
contribution to posterity was, in fact, his genetic structure:

> The theology of Jonathan Edwards may be
> dead, and his books unread, but the man
> was greater than the theologian.   In
> leaving to his children...the legacy
> that he gave, he did the best a man can
> do for the world. [12]

One is tempted to pause to explore the many implications of
this statement, but that will be left to the imagination of
the reader.

Other writers concluded that "there was more in
[Edwards] than the seeds of a famous family;"[13] and what
they found was "a distorted or diseased mind,"[14] a victim of
"delusional insanity,"[15] a "rabid theologian"[16] who exhibited discernible marks of the sadist. [17]

Are such insights likely to help one to a fuller understanding of the works of Edwards, or are they not, as Clyde
A. Holbrook once observed concerning the work of Edwards'
"detractors," destined from the outset to reveal more about
the critics themselves than they reveal about Edwards?[18]
Rightly or wrongly, by the end of the nineteenth century,
Jonathan Edwards had become a symbol of all that more
enlightened generations found repellent in their "Calvinist"
or "Puritan" heritage; and many of the jugular criticisms
of Edwards that have appeared are more properly read, not as
scholarly estimates of the historical Edwards, but as thinly
veiled revolts against those concepts for which Edwards had
proven an undeniably effective spokesman.   This is to
suggest no more than the more articulate of Edwards' detractors have themselves admitted.   As Charles Angoff argued in
the course of his lively caricature of Edwards: "There is
no more devastating argument against Calvinism and all it
means than the life and deeds of Jonathan Edwards."[19] One
would only have thought that those enlightened enough to
perceive Edwards' message as "worse than heathen," or horri-

ble and barbarous,[20] could have resisted the somewhat
unenlightened impulse to kill the messenger.

The literature on Jonathan Edwards is liberally salted
with the work of his "detractors," not all of which borders
on the directly abusive; but Edwards has never wanted for
equally uncritical "admirers" who have chosen to extol the
excellencies of Edwards the man in virtual abstraction from
the content of his thought, thus bypassing the interesting
question of whether the messenger was a maniac. Witness the
numerous panegyrics published in 1903, in celebration of the
two hundredth anniversary of Edwards' birth, and the eulo-
gies of his descendants who warmed themselves with the
thought that "even piety is, to a certain extent, an inheritance."[21] With the notable exception of the eager eugenists, Edwards' uncritical "admirers" rarely provide one with
readings as entertaining as those provided by his "detractors;" but with a little application one can find such
suggestive insights as that Edwards "breathes an atmosphere
of his own; his soul is like a star and dwells apart."[22]
Or one can discover that this "precious paragon" was
"unequalled in intellect and unsurpassed in virtue;" that
"Doubtless, he was born regenerated."[23]

Nor have writers confined themselves to prose in
expressing their righteous indignation or veneration (not to
be confused with interpretation) of Jonathan Edwards.
Edwards has inspired poems of both esteem and ridicule
which, unlike the writings of Edwards himself, will never
find their way into anthologies of American literature. He
has been criticized, analyzed, and popularized by those who
admit to having read his works "rather casually,"[24] and, one
suspects, by many more who have read them even less.

There is no question but that the record of appraisal
and interpretation of Jonathan Edwards is worth preserving
in its entirety. At more than one point, however, I was

tempted to leave the task of assembling this record to
another, and compile instead a bibliography of selected
items that those currently involved in the critical task of
interpretation of Jonathan Edwards would find invaluable, or
at least useful. And lest now the present reader be
unnerved, it should be observed that this selected bibliography would have been of substantial length. In the end,
however, the decision was made to include the chaff along
with the grain, with annotations that suggest the distinction, and this for one basic reason: if many of the studies
identified on the following pages are all but useless to the
serious student of Edwards' thought, they disclose the elements of a story that I think worth writing—the story of
the image of Jonathan Edwards in American culture.

Why has Jonathan Edwards consistently inspired such
passionate "scholarship," exalted by one generation and
damned by the next? Why did the two hundredth anniversary
of the birth of this "terrible theologian" assume something
of the proportions of a national holiday? How did this
"poor, departed enthusiast" become the model for those
would-be eugenists who sought to purify the germ plasm of
America? Why does Charles Angoff now "feel a kinship" with
a man he once dismissed as "a pathetic, befuddled, sickly,
angry, Puritan," and "the most bitter hater of man the
American pulpit ever had?"[25] What is the impetus behind the
current renaissance of interest in Jonathan Edwards?[26]

Obviously, not all of the less than marginal items
included in this bibliography will be of use to one who
would write such a story. But, assuming the story worth
writing, I included works written by those who read Edwards
"rather casually;" and having done so, there seemed little
justification in deliberately excluding any item devoted to
Jonathan Edwards.

This bibliography includes all of the items cited in
the two most extensive previously published bibliographies
of literature on Jonathan Edwards: that published by John
J. Coss, in 1917, and Stephen S. Webb's 1962 revision of the
annotated bibliography prepared by Faust and Johnson. Both
Coss and Webb, however, have identified studies whose reference to Edwards is so circumspect or incidental that I
would not have included them had I run across these items
independently. These items have been included only for the
sake of completeness (relative to Coss and Webb), and this
accounts for the apologetic tone of some of the annotations.
A number of other minor bibliographies have appeared over
the years, and I have not always included every item cited
in these bibliographies. As a general rule I have attempted
to exclude fugitive references, and the annotations for
these bibliographies will indicate if such exclusions have
been made.

For the rest, this bibliography attempts to include all
published books, chapters in books, articles, and monographs
on Jonathan Edwards, and all works in which Edwards' thought
or influence is given more than incidental consideration.
Current encyclopedias of general knowledge were not consul-
ted, the only exception being the *Britannica* whose several
articles on Edwards are of some significance for the history
of interpretation of Jonathan Edwards. Some selectivity was
exercised with regard to book reviews, particularly reviews
of twentieth century publications. Book reviews have been
listed in the bibliography following the volume under
review; of these, only titled reviews or review articles
have also been given an independent entry under the author's
name.

Editions of writings by Jonathan Edwards have been
included only if the editor's introduction has, should, or
is likely to become an important or influential secondary
source. Editions selected for inclusion are listed under
the editor's name.

The attempt was made to include all doctoral dissertations on Edwards. Attention should be drawn, however, to
the list of dissertations recently published by Richard S.
Sliwoski. Sliwoski identifies a number of dissertations
that I had not discovered which "devote considerable
attention to Jonathan Edwards as part of a study of a
problem or theme...."[27] Sliwoski's article appeared too late
for these items to be included in this bibliography. No
direct effort was made to identify theses on Jonathan
Edwards submitted for other degrees; the few such theses
that are included in this bibliography are those that have
already been cited elsewhere in the literature on Edwards.

About the poetry. I did not set out and search the
libraries for any poetry that Jonathan Edwards may have
inspired over the years. Thus the pieces by Robert Lowell
are noticeably absent. However, I felt a certain responsibility to spare others the frustration experienced when I
found a reference to an item on Jonathan Edwards and, often
after a great deal of time and effort had been spent in
locating the item, it turned out to be a poem—and generally
a bad one at that.

Whenever I have quoted a text, I have reproduced the
original spelling and grammar. Over a period of two hundred years, stylistic conventions change. I have not introduced any comments on these. Especially obvious is the
lack of agreement whether to say Edwardsean or Edwardean.

FOOTNOTES

[1] Joseph G. Haroutunian, *Piety Versus Moralism: The Passing of the New England Theology* (1932; rpt. New York, 1970), xxv.

[2] Leslie Stephen, "Jonathan Edwards," *Littell's Living Age*, 120 (1874), 219-220.

[3] Ola E. Winslow, *Jonathan Edwards, 1703-1758: A Biography* (1940; rpt. New York, 1961), 321.

[4] Edwards Amasa Park, "Memoir [of Samuel Hopkins]," in *The Works of Samuel Hopkins* (Boston, 1854), I, 217.

[5] *Ibid.*, 219.

[6] Ezra Stiles, *The Literary Diary of Ezra Stiles*, ed. F. B. Dexter (New York, 1901), III, 275.

[7] I. W. Riley, "The Real Jonathan Edwards," *Open Court*, 22 (1908), 705.

[8] *The Works of Jonathan Edwards* (New Haven, 1977), V, x.

[9] William S. Morris, "The Reappraisal of Edwards," *New England Quarterly*, 30 (1957), 515.

[10]Stephen J. Stein, "A Notebook on the Apocalypse by Jonathan Edwards," *William and Mary Quarterly*, s.3, 29 (1972), 627.

[11]D. O. S. Lowell, "The Descendants of Jonathan Edwards," *Munsey's Magazine*, 35 (1906), 264.

[12]Edith A. Winship, "The Human Legacy of Jonathan Edwards," *World's Work*, 6 (1903), 3894.

[13]Philip G. Nordell, "Jonathan Edwards and Hell Fire," *Forum*, 75 (1926), 860.

[14]Clarence Darrow, "The Edwardses and the Jukeses," *American Mercury*, 6 (1925), 153.

[15]Joseph H. Crooker, "Jonathan Edwards: A Psychological Study," *New England Magazine*, n.s., 2 (1890), 167.

[16]Charles Angoff, *A Literary History of the American People* (1931; rpt. New York, 1935), 298.

[17]Henry Bamford Parkes, *Jonathan Edwards: The Fiery Puritan* (New York, 1930), 102.

[18]See Holbrook, "Jonathan Edwards and his Detractors," *Theology Today*, 10 (1953), 384-396.

[19]Charles Angoff, *A Literary History of the American People*, 289.

[20]Oliver Wendell Holmes, "Jonathan Edwards," in his *Pages from an Old Volume of Life* (Boston, 1891), 396.

[21]Remarks by George Woodbridge, in *The Memorial Volume of the Edwards Family Meeting*, ed. Jonathan E. Woodbridge (Boston, 1871), 149.

[22]W. Frothingham, "Jonathan Edwards and the Old Clergy," *The Continental Monthly*, 1 (1862), 269.

[23]Kate M. Cone, "Jonathan Edwards," *Outlook*, 75 (1903), 260; Rufus W. Griswold, *Prose Writers of America, 1706-1870*, rev. ed. (Philadelphia, 1847), 53; Griffith H. Humphrey, *Jonathan Edwards* (n.p., 1903), 13.

[24]Don C. Seitz, "Jonathan Edwards: Consistent Theologian," *Outlook*, 143 (1926), 316.

[25]Charles Angoff, ed., *Jonathan Edwards: His Life and Influence* (Rutherford, New Jersey, 1975), 15; and *A Literary History of the American People*, 290, 299.

[26]One important contribution to this story has already been made by Donald L. Weber in his doctoral dissertation, "The Image of Jonathan Edwards in American Culture."

[27]Richard S. Sliwoski, "Doctoral Dissertations on Jonathan Edwards," *Early American Literature*, 14 (1979-80), 318.

BIBLIOGRAPHICAL SYNOPSES

"[An Account of a] Loan Exhibition [of the Possessions of
Jonathan Edwards]." In *Exercises Commemorating the 200th
Anniversary of the Birth of Jonathan Edwards.* Andover,
1904, pp. 61-65.
Partial list of the Edwards memorabilia exhibited at
Andover at the anniversary celebration.

Ahlstrom, Sydney E. *A Religious History of the American
People.* New Haven, 1972.
Includes a brief, general introduction to Edwards'
thought. Ahlstrom comments on the 'five different
Edwardses' that have been revealed to his interpreters
through the continuing publication of his writings.

Ahlstrom, Sydney E. "The Romantic Religious Revolution and
the Dilemmas of Religious History." *Church History,*
46 (1977), 149-170.
Ahlstrom presents Edwards as a precursor of the romantic
religious revolution: "In Edwards the rising age of
science found an American interpreter who showed an
astonishing awareness of its implications for true
religion. Before his busy pen was stilled he had refor-
mulated the faith of his fathers and placed it in the
context of a modern philosophy of nature."

Aijan, Paul Misak. "The Relation of the Concepts of Being
and Value in Calvinism to Jonathan Edwards." Doctoral
dissertation, University of Southern California, 1950.

Aldridge, Alfred Owen. "Benjamin Franklin and Jonathan
Edwards on Lightning and Earthquakes." *Isis,* 31 (1950),
162-164.
Noting a striking similarity in the explanations of
lightning offered by Franklin and Edwards, I. Bernard

Cohen (*Benjamin Franklin's Experiments*, Cambridge,
1941), raised the question as to whether they derived
from the same source. Aldridge argues that the "essay"
in question by Franklin is actually a transcript of an
article from Ephraim Chamber's *Cyclopedia*, and he
suggests the probability that Edwards' discussion of
lightning and earthquakes in the *Notes on Natural
Science* also derives from this source.

Aldridge, Alfred Owen. "Edwards and Hutcheson." *Harvard
Theological Review*, 44 (1951), 35-53.
Aldridge analyzes the influence of Hutcheson on Edwards'
doctrine of virtue, suggesting that *The Nature of True
Virtue* is "literally a commentary on Hutcheson."

Edwards' discussion of the relation of beauty to
virtue, Aldridge argues, "was designed as a refutation
of Hutcheson, or at least as a retracing of Hutcheson's
ground from a Calvinistic viewpoint. Yet Edwards was
subconsciously so sympathetic toward the Hutchesonian
concepts of a benevolent universe that he finally went
even further than Hutcheson in visualizing a universe
almost pantheistic."

Aldridge, Alfred Owen. *Jonathan Edwards*. New York, 1964.
A lengthy biography of Edwards and detailed exposition
of his thought. Written by one well-versed in the
eighteenth century context of Edwards' thought, this
otherwise reliable study is marred by an often cavalier
approach to Edwards' theology and a frequent lack of
theological insight. At the age of twenty, Aldridge
observes, Edwards "had organized in capsule form the
theology of his lifetime. In essence, it was traditional Calvinism modified by new doctrines of affection
and benevolence. It could be summarized as gloomy

optimism."

Review

Winslow, Ola E. *American Literature,* 38 (1966),
127-128.

Aldridge, Alfred Owen. "Jonathan Edwards and William Godwin
on Virtue." *American Literature,* 18 (1947), 308-318.
Aldridge examines the similarities between the views of
Edwards and Godwin on virtue, and recounts the dispute
between Godwin and Samuel Parr concerning Godwin's
interpretation of Edwards.

Alexander, Archibald. *Outlines of Moral Science.* New York,
1852.
This rather unimpressive volume includes a brief
critique of Edwards' treatise on *The Nature of True
Virtue,* a work, Alexander observes, that "has surprised
all his admirers." While Alexander reveals a less than
fragile grasp of Edwards' doctrine of virtue (finding
it "not essentially different" from that of Cumberland),
the volume was of some significance in the nineteenth
century controversy over *The Nature of True Virtue.*

Alexis, Gerhard T. "Calvinism and Mysticism in Jonathan
Edwards." Doctoral dissertation, University of
Minnesota, 1947.
In twentieth century scholarship Edwards' intellectual
history is often interpreted in terms of a conflict
between a native "mysticism" and Calvinistic theology.
The result of this supposed conflict is variously
described as a repudiation of the mystic vision of
Edwards' youth in favor of the hard logic of Calvinism,
a victory for the mystical element that was clothed in
the verbal forms of Calvinism, or some manner of uneasy

alliance between the two. Alexis' study is an attempt
to clarify the relation between Calvinism and mysticism
in Edwards' thought, and he argues that Edwards' great
achievement lay in the manner in which he united these
elements.

"At the beginning of his ministry in Northampton
Edwards knew the joy of the mystic but had no theory to
account for it; he knew the theories of Calvinism but
had little joy in them. The formulation of principles
which would combine mysticism and Calvinism, in a way
superior to any thus far falteringly attempted, principles which could bring peace to the heart and satisfac-
tion to the mind, was to be the great work of his mature
years." For Edwards, Alexis argues, mystical experience
was made both reasonable and acceptable theologically
in terms of saving grace and the divine and supernatural
light.

Alexis, Gerhard T. "Jonathan Edwards and the Theocratic
    Ideal." *Church History*, 35 (1966), 328-343.
    "Do we find in Jonathan Edwards an advocate and conveyor
    of a theocratic ideal?" Alexis answers this question in
    the negative: "Not unless we so change the original
    terms that we are no longer talking about the same prin-
    ciple. Or perhaps we can say that the terms as such
    appear in Edwards but not in the necessary conjunction."
    In Edwards, Alexis argues, "the vital link in the theo-
    cratic ideal is missing: the agency of the saints in
    expressing God's will for the whole of culture."

Allen, Alexander Viets Griswold. *Life and Writings of
    Jonathan Edwards*. Boston, New York, and Edinburgh, 1889.
    The single most important study of Edwards prior to the
    publication of Perry Miller's *Jonathan Edwards* in 1949.

Allen's intention in this volume was to present a
portrait of Edwards' life, what he thought, and most
importantly, how he came to think as he did. His
starting point was Edwards' early philosophical
writings.

Allen contends that Edwards was essentially a
mystic, whose acceptance of his Calvinistic heritage
was real but less than wholehearted: "There are traces
of an inward rebellion which was suppressed." Throughout his life, Allen argues, Edwards' thinking was
polarized between the mystic vision of his youth and
traditional Calvinistic theology, symbolized in Edwards'
"Augustinian idea of God as absolute and arbitrary will."

"Like Augustine he abandoned philosophy for the
absorbing devotion to Divine and arbitrary will, which
better suited his practical career as a reformer,
concerned mainly with the well-being of the churches.
But the other element of his thought, though subordinated, was not annihilated. It appears in all his
writings, —an element seemingly incongruous, and difficult to reconcile with his other teaching. It
reappeared in his later years with something of the
beauty which had fascinated the vision of his youth."

Allen provides a thorough, critical analysis of
Edwards' major writings then published. Inspired by
Edwards' reputedly "secretive" nature, however, and the
suggested polarity in his thought, Allen frequently
succumbs to the temptation "to distinguish what he may
have meant to affirm from what he actually teaches."
In many respects scholars have yet to go beyond Allen's
basic insights, methods, and conclusions in their interpretation of Edwards.

Reviews

Fisher, George Park. "Professor Allen's Life of
     Jonathan Edwards." *New Englander and Yale Review*,
     52 (1890), 85-88.
Richards, C. A. "An American Religious Leader." *Dial*,
     10 (1889), 166-167.
Smyth, Egbert C. "Professor Allen's Jonathan Edwards,
     With Extracts from Copies of Unpublished
     Manuscripts." *Andover Review*, 13 (1890), 285-304.
Wellman, J. W. "A New Biography of Jonathan Edwards."
     Our Day, 5 (1890), 195-219; 288-307. Also, *A
     Review of Dr. A. V. G. Allen's Biography of Jonathan
     Edwards*. Boston, 1890.
"Jonathan Edwards." *Nation*, 49 (1889), 314-315.
"Jonathan Edwards." *The Spectator*, 64 (1890), 58-59.

Allen, Alexander Viets Griswold. "The Place of Edwards in
     History." In *Jonathan Edwards: A Retrospect*, ed. Harry
     Norman Gardiner. Boston, 1901, pp. 1-31.
     "The deepest affinity of Edwards was not that with
     Calvin, or with Augustine, but with the great Florentine
     poet."

          Allen draws a lengthy parallel between Edwards and
     Dante, attempting to show that "in constitution and
     temperament he [Edwards] was a different man from
     Augustine or from Calvin, that he is not, paradoxical
     as it may seem to say it, ──he is not really so great a
     theologian as he is when viewed as a poetic interpreter
     of life. He never wrote, so far as we know, a line of
     poetry. But he had the poet's imagination, and tender-
     ness, and insight combined with an unsurpassed gift for
     spiritual speculation."

Allen, Alexander Viets Griswold. "The Transition in New
    England Theology." *Atlantic Monthly*, 68 (1891),
    767-780.
    An insightful study of the work of Samuel Hopkins viewed
    in relation to the theology of Edwards. Hopkins, Allen
    argues, marks a transition in the New England Theology:
    he was more "humane" than Edwards.

Allen, William. *An Address, Delivered at Northampton, Mass.,*
    on the Evening of October 29, 1854, in Commemoration of
    the Close of the Second Century Since the Settlement of
    the Town. Northampton, 1855.
    An historical review of the early years of the town of
    Northampton. Edwards is merely mentioned in a brief
    biographical note.

Allibone, S. Austin, ed. "Jonathan Edwards." In *A Critical*
    Dictionary of English Literature and British and
    American Authors. Philadelphia, 1858; rpt. 1891.
    Vol. I, pp. 545-547.
    A brief biographical sketch, a list of Edwards'
    published writings, and a collection of testimonies to
    Edwards' prowess as a metaphysician and theologian. Not
    all sources quoted by Allibone are included in this
    bibliography.

Allison, Oscar Ethan. "Jonathan Edwards: A Study in
    Puritanism." Doctoral dissertation, Boston University,
    1916.

Anderson, Wallace Earl. "Immaterialism in Jonathan Edwards'
    Early Philosophical Notes." *Journal of the History of*
    Ideas, 25 (1964), 181-200.
    A valuable study of the concept of solidity in Edwards'

early philosophical writings, examined in relation to
his apparent sources. Anderson demonstrates the
influence of Newton, Locke, and the Cambridge Platonist
Henry More in the development of Edwards' discussions;
but he concludes that while "it is possible to mark out
the predominant influences of Newton, More, and Locke,
neither Edwards' concepts nor the immaterialism they
allowed him to formulate were directly adopted from
these sources." No attempt is made to assess the
influence of this early "immaterialism" on Edwards'
later thought.

Anderson, Wallace Earl. "Mind and Nature in the Early
    Philosophical Writings of Jonathan Edwards." Doctoral
    dissertation, University of Minnesota, 1961. In
    Dissertation Abstracts, 22 (1961), 2029.
    Anderson traces the development of Edwards' early
    idealism from its beginnings in the essay *Of Atoms* to
    its most explicit statement in *The Mind*. "The evaluation
    of the sources of Edwards' early thought rests upon a
    detailed discussion of his reading and reading interests
    up to the time when his notes were composed. The stages
    of the development of his thought were established in
    part by a study of the extant manuscripts of the *Notes
    on Natural Science*, and by a reconstruction of the
    original order of the entries as they appeared in the
    lost manuscript of *The Mind*. The reconstruction appears
    in an appendix to the dissertation."
        Anderson's reconstruction of *The Mind* should be
    compared with that suggested by Leon Howard.

Anderson, Wilbert L. "The Preaching Power of Jonathan
    Edwards." *Congregationalist and Christian World*, 88
    (1903), 463-466.

An uncritical attempt to explain Edwards' effectiveness in promoting the Great Awakening.

"This poet-theologian has a habit of ecstacy. He is a Dante never far from the heights of beatific vision.... What Edwards beheld as a poet he declared as a preacher. The unity of his spirit and his work was complete. Such was his concern for the glory of God and the salvation of men that he used his visions as seer to move the congregations to which he preached."

Angoff, Charles. "Jonathan Edwards." In his *A Literary History of the American People*. New York, 1931; rpt. 1935, pp. 289-310.
Angoff offers a brief biographical sketch of Edwards, an unrelenting criticism of Edwards as a thinker, and a decidedly negative estimate of Edwards' role in the history of American culture. In Angoff's estimation: "There is no more devastating argument against Calvinism and all it means than the life and deeds of Jonathan Edwards."

Angoff's caricature of Edwards offers little to the serious student of Edwards' thought, but it provides an excellent illustration of Edwards' image in the 1920s and the early years of the next decade. Angoff depicts Edwards as a pathetic, "sickly, angry, Puritan," a "rabid theologian," and "the most bitter hater of man the American pulpit ever had." Edwards, Angoff suggests, "made of his intellectual life a compromise, and he paid the price of all compromisers: intellectual paralysis in his lifetime and oblivion after his death.... He left nothing for posterity that is in the least vitalizing."

Angoff, Charles, ed. *Jonathan Edwards: His Life and Influence*. Rutherford, New Jersey, 1975.

Volume arising out of the 1973 Leverton Lecture Series at Fairleigh Dickinson University. In the introduction to this volume, written some forty years after his bitter condemnation of Edwards, Angoff admits: "I do feel a kinship with Jonathan Edwards."

Contents

Introductory Remarks, by Charles Angoff, pp. 15-18.

Imagery and Analysis: Jonathan Edwards on Revivals of Religion, by C. Conrad Cherry, pp. 19-28.

The Brazen Trumpet: Jonathan Edwards's Conception of the Sermon, by Wilson H. Kimnach, pp. 29-44.

Proceedings of a Symposium in which the major participants were Charles Angoff, C. Conrad Cherry, Wilson H. Kimnach, Charles Wetzel, Donald Jones, Edward Cook, pp. 45-65.

Atwater, Lyman H. "Dr. Taylor's Lectures on the Moral Government of God." *Biblical Repertory and Princeton Review*, 31 (1859), 489-538.

An extensive critique of the theology of Nathaniel Taylor. Atwater trusts that his analysis of Taylor's system makes "sufficiently evident, why, since it first flowered out in a sudden promise of triumph, it has been steadily withering and dying out of the theological life of the country." In the course of his discussion of Taylor, Atwater briefly comments on Edwards' doctrine of virtue, the supposed keystone of Taylor's "new divinity." See Atwater's article on "Successive Forms of New Divinity" for a more elaborate critique of Edwards' doctrine of virtue.

Atwater, Lyman H. "The Great Awakening of 1740."
Presbyterian Quarterly and Princeton Review, new series,
5 (1876), 676-689.
A general discussion of the origins, attendant errors,
and long term results of the revival. Little direct
discussion of Edwards.

[Atwater, Lyman H.] "Jonathan Edwards and the Successive
Forms of New Divinity." *Biblical Repertory and*
Princeton Review, 30 (1858), 585-620.
This influential article was apparently prompted by
George Park Fisher's 1858 *Discourse* delivered at Yale.
Fisher's *Discourse,* in Atwater's estimation, had done
much to lend credence to the view that "Edwards was the
father and leader of that theological party which
includes Hopkins, Emmons, and Taylor, and that the
various peculiarities of these and other men, which have
had currency in the country under the assumed title of
New England theology, are developments of Edwards's
system, and may lawfully protect themselves with the
shield of his mighty name." It is quite time, insists
Atwater that this claim be investigated and settled.
     Seeking to divorce Edwards from the New England
Theology, Atwater attempts to demonstrate that Edwards
"held and devoted his labours to prove the doctrines
commonly known as Old Calvinism," with but two excep-
tions: he taught "Stapfer's scheme of the mediate
imputation of Adam's sin," and he held an "eccentric
philosophical theory of the nature of virtue." While
these two "peculiarities" were seminal in the development of the new divinity, Atwater insists that they
were external to the main course of Edwards' thought,
and neither "was allowed to act upon or modify other
parts of his theology."

Atwater, Lyman H. "Modern Explanations of the Doctrine of
    Inability." *Biblical Repertory and Princeton Review*,
    26 (1854), 217-246.
    Atwater briefly notes Edwards' views on natural and
    moral necessity and inability, insisting that Edwards
    "did not regard himself as introducing any novel
    doctrines or discoveries on the subject." The discus-
    sion of Edwards is incidental and superficial.

Atwater, Lyman H. "The Power of Contrary Choice." *Biblical
    Repertory and Princeton Review*, 12 (1840), 532-549.
    On the occasion of the appearance of a new edition of
    Edwards' *Freedom of the Will* (New York, 1840), Atwater
    attempts to clarify and refute two arguments that were
    frequently appealed to in critiques of Edwards' work:
    that man has a power of contrary choice, and that such a
    power is requisite to moral agency and accountability.
    There is no direct discussion of Edwards' treatise, and
    no historical account of Edwards' later antagonists who,
    for the most part, go unnamed.

Austin, Samuel, ed. "Memoirs of the Late Reverend Jonathan
    Edwards." In *The Works of President Edwards*. Worcester,
    1808. Vol I, pp. 9-99.

B., A. "Edwards on the Imputation of Original Sin." *The
    Christian Advocate*, 9 (1831), 131-134.

Bacon, Benjamin Wisner. *The Theological Significance of
    Jonathan Edwards*. Proceedings at the Dedication of the
    Memorial Gateway to Jonathan Edwards at the Old Burying
    Ground, South Windsor, 25 June 1929. [New Haven, 1929].
    "The significance of Edwards for theology is that he
    took Paul and Calvin in deadly earnest in the midst of

a generation that did not. The fruit of his labor was a
Great Awakening of the Puritan church, an awakening not
only of its sentiments, but of its intellect as well."
Brief, largely biographical account of Edwards,
appropriate to the occasion.

Bacon, Edwin M. *The Connecticut River*. New York, 1906.
Includes brief remarks on the house of Timothy Edwards
and the Edwards family.

Bacon, Edwin M. "Jonathan Edwards." In his *Literary
Pilgrimages in New England to the Homes of Famous Makers
of American Literature*. New York, 1902, pp. 432-440.

Baird, Samuel J. "Edwards and the Theology of New England."
Southern Presbyterian Review, 10 (1858), 574-592.
Reprinted in *British and Foreign Evangelical Review*,
7 (1858), 544-562.
An analysis of Edwards' theories of causation and
identity and his speculations on the nature of virtue;
in these notions, Baird suggests, are to be found the
root of the New England Theology. "We are well aware,"
notes Baird, "that it is impossible to reconcile these
opinions, with doctrines which are maintained by Edwards,
in other parts of his works. Inconsistency is the
common characteristic of error. And we are not so much
interested in these, as the sentiments of Edwards; so
much, as that they are the principles which, put forth
with the authority of his great name, have revolu-
tionized the theology of New England."

Baird, Samuel J. *A History of the New School, and of the
Questions Involved in the Disruption of the Presbyterian
Church in 1838*. Philadelphia, 1868.

Includes a summary discussion of the relation of the New
England Theology to the theology of Edwards.

"Prior to the rise of Edwards, the theology of New
England had always been strictly conformed to that of
the body of the Reformed Churches. His own theological
views, as to the doctrines of the Reformed confessions,
were in general harmony with the Westminster divines.
In two respects, however, he must be recognized as the
spring, whence have flowed many heresies, to plague the
Church of God, which he loved; —in the nature of some
of his opinions; and in the mode of discussion which he
introduced." In the article noted above Baird examines
in more detail those "peculiarities" of Edwards' thought
that gave rise to the New England Theology.

Baker, Nelson B. "Anthropological Roots of Jonathan
    Edwards' Doctrine of God." Doctoral dissertation,
    University of Southern California, 1952.

Bancroft, George. "Jonathan Edwards." In *The New American
    Cyclopaedia: A Popular Dictionary of General Knowledge,*
    ed. George Ripley and Charles A. Dana. New York,
    1858-63. Vol. VII, pp. 11-20.
    An excellent biographical sketch with a brief discussion
    of Edwards' characteristics as a thinker and a
    popularized account of his theology. Particular
    attention is given to Edwards' doctrine of virtue which,
    in Bancroft's estimation, marks a turning point in the
    intellectual (or spiritual) history of New England.

"Edwards sums up the old theology of New England,
    and is the fountain head of the new. The toils of a
    century turned the wilderness, to which men had been
    driven for liberty to say their prayers, into a garden
    of plenty, peace, and joyous activity; he that will

trace the corresponding transition of Calvinism from a
haughty self-assertion of the doctrine of election
against the pride of oppression to its adoption of love
as the central point of its view of creation and the
duty of the created; he that will know the workings of
the mind of New England in the middle of the last
century, and the throbbings of its heart, must give his
days and nights to the study of Jonathan Edwards."

Barnett, Das Kelley. "The Doctrine of Man in the Theology
of Jonathan Edwards (1703-1758)." Doctoral dissertation,
Southern Baptist Theological Seminary, 1943.

Bastaki, Shafikah A. A. "A Reconstruction of Jonathan
Edwards' Volitional Theory in the Context of Contemporary
Action Theory: An Examination of *Freedom of the Will*."
Doctoral dissertation, University of Pittsburgh, 1972.
In *Dissertation Abstracts International*, 33 (1973),
6961A-6962A.
This study "has two major objectives: First, to elicit
Jonathan Edwards' position on the metaphysical status
of actions and volitions, and secondly, to reconstruct
the elicited concepts into a comprehensive theory of
action. The reconstruction is carried out in the
context of the contemporary post-Wittgensteinian
discussions of actions, volitions and their causes."

Batschelet, Margaret Susan. "Jonathan Edwards' Use of
Typology: A Historical and Theological Approach."
Doctoral dissertation, University of Washington, 1977.
In *Dissertation Abstracts International*, 38 (1977),
3493A-3494A.

Bauer, Charles G. "Jonathan Edwards and his Relation to the
    New England Theology." Doctoral dissertation, Temple
    University, 1912.

Baumgartner, Paul R. "Jonathan Edwards: The Theory behind
    his Use of Figurative Language." *PMLA*, 78 (1963),
    321-325.
    Baumgartner argues that for Edwards, figurative language
    was not used simply for its emotional effectiveness, it
    was not simply "a way of pointing out accidental
    similarities between things, or a way of accomodating
    spiritual truths to fallen man's understanding or
    emotions." Rather, grounded in his doctrine of analogy,
    for Edwards "figurative language is a skillful device
    of human truth."

Bayley, Frank W. *Five Colonial Artists of New England*.
    Boston, 1929.

Beach, Waldo. "The Recovery of Jonathan Edwards." *Religion
    in Life*, 27 (1958), 286-289.
    Review of *Freedom of the Will* (New Haven, 1957), edited
    by Paul Ramsey.

Becker, William Hartshorne. "The Distinguishing Marks of
    the Christian Man in the Thought of Jonathan Edwards."
    Doctoral dissertation, Harvard University, 1964.

Berner, Robert L. "Grace and Works in America: The Role
    of Jonathan Edwards." *Southern Quarterly*, 15 (1977),
    125-134.
    Berner views Edwards' dismissal from Northampton as "a
    symptom of a coming revolution." What Edwards was
    resisting, suggests Berner, "might be described as the

democratization of Northampton within the institution
of the church."

Blakey, Robert. "Dr. Jonathan Edwards." In his *History of
the Philosophy of Mind: Embracing the Opinions of All
Writers on Mental Science from the Earliest Period to
the Present Time*. London, 1848. Vol. IV, pp. 492-519.
Blakey briefly rehearses the causal argument of Edwards'
Freedom of the Will and attempts to provide "as full a
view as possible of the chief bearings which Edwards's
metaphysics have on the science of theology" by applying
Edwards' theory of cause and effect to a number of
theological principles. The point of this exercise,
oddly enough, is to evaluate Edwards as a philosopher.
Edwards, Blakey concludes, "was an acute, but not a
great philosopher."
    "Dr. Edwards had a peculiarly constituted mind:
—a mind capable of pursuing, with incomparable stead-
iness and clearness, the longest and most intricate
chain of reasoning; but a mind, withal, by no means
endowed with the loftiest powers of logical comprehen-
sion."

Blau, Joseph L. *Men and Movements in American Philosophy*.
New York, 1952.
Includes a brief and somewhat superficial discussion of
the impact of Newton and Locke on the young Edwards,
and Edwards' later use of these thinkers in his attempt
to construct "a solid philosophical foundation for
Calvinism." Blau concludes that "there is little
vitality left in Edwards' thought. Strong as his system
seemed, like the deacon's 'one hoss shay' it fell to
pieces all at once, leaving scarcely a trace behind."

Bledsoe, Albert Taylor. *An Examination of President
    Edwards' Inquiry into the Freedom of the Will.*
    Philadelphia, 1845.
    "If I have come to the conclusion, that the whole scheme
    of moral necessity which Edwards has laboured to estab-
    lish, is founded in error and delusion; this has not
    been because I came to the examination with any precon-
    ceived opinion." Thus Bledsoe opens his study, and he
    was wise to so advise his readers, for the spirit of
    such a disinterested seeker of truth is not transparent
    in the body of the work.
        The critical question, argues Bledsoe, is whether
    Edwards' basic premise is correct, whether volition is
    really the correlative of an efficient cause. Edwards,
    Bledsoe insists, holds that "volitions are not merely
    caused to be thus, and not otherwise, by motives; they
    are 'caused to arise and come forth into existence.'
    This is the great doctrine for which Edwards contends;
    and this is the very doctrine which I deny." Bledsoe's
    avowed interest is not religious orthodoxy but psycho-
    logical orthodoxy; and he contends that Edwards'
    fundamental error was his confounding of the will (a
    faculty by which the mind acts), with the affections (in
    which the mind is passive). "It is in this confusion
    of things, in this false psychology, that he laid the
    foundation of his system."
        Beyond his criticisms of Edwards, Bledsoe also
    maintains a running commentary on the "pseudo
    disciples," or "pretended followers and blind admirers
    of President Edwards," and the younger Edwards provokes
    the harshest of Bledsoe's criticisms. "Let those who
    do fondly imagine that they are the only men who under-
    stand the Inquiry, and that the most elaborate replies
    to it may be sufficiently refuted by raising the cry of

'misconstruction;' let them, I say, take some pains to
understand the work themselves, instead of merely giving
echo to the blunders of the younger Edwards."

Bledsoe, Albert Taylor. "An Examination of President
Edwards' Inquiry into the Freedom of the Will." *The
Southern Review*, new series, 22 (1877), 376-404.
A reprint of the introduction and the first three
sections of Bledsoe's *Examination*. The *Examination* was
eventually reprinted in its entirety through subsequent
issues of *The Southern Review*: 23 (1878), 5-33;
338-389; 24 (1878), 64-93; 344-372.

Bledsoe, Albert Taylor. "Foreknowledge and Free Will."
The Southern Review, 15 (1874), 91-109.
A reprint of section XI of the *Examination*.

Bledsoe, Albert Taylor. "The Relation of the Will to the
Feelings." *The Southern Review*, new series, 17 (1875),
435-448.
A reprint of section VIII of the *Examination*.

"Bledsoe's Examination of Edwards's Inquiry." *New
Englander*, 5 (1847), 337-347.
A highly unsympathetic review, obviously written by one
of the "followers of Edwards" who had received such
short, or, in the reviewer's words, "contemptuous"
treatment at Bledsoe's hands. The reviewer challenges
Bledsoe's interpretation of Edwards and attempts to
dissect the "principal curiosity" of Bledsoe's study,
his theory of the nature of volition.

Blight, James George. "Gracious Discoveries: Toward an
    Understanding of Jonathan Edwards' Psychological Theory,
    and an Assessment of his Place in the History of
    American Psychology." Doctoral dissertation, University
    of New Hampshire, 1974.

Boardman, George Nye. *A History of New England Theology*.
    New York, 1899.
    A systematic study of the theology of Edwards and the
    various schools of new divinity to which it gave rise.
        "Edwards wrote in response to the demands of his
    day, without any presentiment of the fact that he was
    opening the way for Hopkinsianism and yet other and
    later doctrinal schemes. Still it was his freedom of
    thought, his philosophical principles, his religious
    fervor and his anxiety to see new life infused into the
    churches of the country, that gave the impulse to that
    thinking, which after a slow development appeared as
    the New England scheme."
        Boardman offers little in the way of interpretation
    but is content, for the most part, to detail the views
    of the various schools of new divinity on a number of
    central issues through a series of brief quotations from
    the primary works. The theology of Edwards is not
    considered extensively or in any depth. Valuable as a
    guide to the sources.

Bogue, Carl W. *Jonathan Edwards and the Covenant of Grace*.
    Cherry Hill, New Jersey, 1975. (Doctoral dissertation,
    Free University of Amsterdam, 1975.)
    A systematic study of the covenant of grace in the
    theology of Edwards. The value of this study goes
    beyond Bogue's extensive, theological analysis of
    Edwards' doctrine of the covenant of grace and its

place in his theological system. Bogue carries out his
study in close conversation with Edwards' modern interpreters and in the process provides a critical examination and evaluation of modern Edwards scholarship.

Bogue is particularly critical of those who would
attempt to make Edwards something other than a biblical
theologian. "Many in this age would deem it unfortunate
that any first-rate mind would operate under the
'medieval' notion that theology is the queen of the
sciences. If the form of the theology is Calvinism,
such a critic may change his judgment from unfortunate
to tragic. But that is where Jonathan Edwards stood....
By inclination, by training, by preaching and writing,
Jonathan Edwards gave his whole life to the service of
the Christ of Scripture."

Boorman, John Arthur. "A Comparative Study of the Theory
of Human Nature as Expressed by Jonathan Edwards, Horace
Bushnell, and William Adams Brown: Representative
American Protestant Thinkers of the Past Three
Centuries." Doctoral dissertation, Columbia University,
1954. In *Dissertation Abstracts*, 14 (1954), 1467-1468.

Brady, Gertrude V. "Basic Principles of the Philosophy of
Jonathan Edwards." Doctoral dissertation, Fordham
University, 1951.

[Brazer, J.] "Essay on the Doctrine of the Divine
Influence." *Christian Examiner*, 18 (1835), 50-83.
Includes a brief critique of Edwards' position in
Religious Affections concerning the influence of the
Holy Spirit in conversion. "We feel compelled to reject
it altogether. We find no authority for it in reason,
in human experience, in the philosophy of the human mind,

or in the Scriptures."

Breck, Robert, *et al.* *An Account of the Council which
    Dismissed the Reverend Mr. Edwards*. Boston, 1750.
    The letter by Hobby and his confederates is countered
    by a more elaborate account of the proceedings of the
    council and a detailed response to the objections made
    to Edwards' dismissal. The importance of the contro-
    versy between Edwards and his congregation, argues Breck,
    is evident in the fact that the doors of the Northampton
    church had been closed for many years and would have
    remained so for many more years were Edwards not dis-
    missed. The people, Breck insists, have a "right of
    private judgment" on the question of qualifications for
    communion.

Breck, Robert, *et al.* *A Letter to the Reverend Mr. Hobby,
    in Answer to his Vindication of the Protest, against the
    Result of an Ecclesiastical Council met at Northampton*.
    Boston, 1751.
    A second reply to Hobby.

Bridgman, S. E. "Northampton." *New England Magazine,* new
    series, 21 (1900), 581-604.

Brown, Charles Reynolds. "Jonathan Edwards." In
    Encyclopedia Britannica. 14th edition. Vol VIII,
    pp. 18-20.
    A popularized, superficial, and decidedly unsympathetic
    portrait of Edwards' life and thought. Brown finds
    Edwards "sadly lacking in the humanities. The human
    qualities were obscured by his passion for metaphysics
    in his ambitious theological treatises. He had little
    feeling for poetry or for the beauties of the natural

world." Edwards, Brown suggests, "seemed to find more
joy in battering the strongholds of Arminianism and in
rearing the stought defenses of his own Calvinistic
theology than in preaching good tidings to the poor, or
binding up the broken-hearted."

Brown, E. Francis. "Jonathan Edwards, Theologian and
  Philosopher." *New York Times*, 24 April 1932, p. 2.
  Review of Arthur C. McGiffert's *Jonathan Edwards* (New
  York, 1932).

Brumm, Ursala. *American Thought and Religious Typology*,
  trans. John Hoaglund. New Brunswick, New Jersey, 1970.
  A study of the origins and growth of American religious
  typology and its relation to literary symbolism. Brumm
  underscores the future orientation of Edwards' typology:
  "the early theological version of that nineteenth-
  century American view of history which looked rather to
  the future than to the past... [and] written in the
  conviction that all human events were developing toward
  the fulfillment of man's aspirations in America."

Bryant, Marcus Darrol. "America as God's Kingdom." In
  Religion and Political Society, edited and translated
  in the Institute of Christian Thought. New York, 1974,
  pp. 54-94.
  A study of the eschatological thought of Jonathan
  Edwards. Bryant affirms the received tradition that
  millenial expectations served as a ground for a revolutionary critique of the old order and as a dynamic for
  social change. He suggests, however, that "the
  assumption that the millenial impulse gains fulfillment
  in the American Republic is unwarranted, at least in
  relation to Jonathan Edwards."

"Though Edwards was complicit in this initial
confusion of the millenium with America, a careful
reading of his work will not allow the American tradition to claim him as tutor. For Edwards, America did
have a vocation within the work of Redemption; but
America's vocation was spiritual, not political.
Moreover, Edwards saw the spiritual pride implicit in a
'millenial America' and sought to exorcise the demon."
In the course of his study, Bryant attempts to demonstrate a substantive development in Edwards' thoughts
concerning the millenium.

Bryant, Marcus Darrol. "History and Eschatology in Jonathan
    Edwards: A Critique of the Heimert Thesis." Doctoral
    dissertation, Institute of Christian Thought, University
    of St. Michael's College, 1976. In *Dissertation
    Abstracts International,* 38 (1978), 6180A.
    Bryant challenges the thesis of Alan Heimert's *Religion
    and the American Mind* as it relates to the thought of
    Edwards. Where Heimert suggests that Edwards' activities
    and writings were instrumental in providing pre-Revolu-
    tionary America with a social and political ideology
    embodying a thrust toward American nationalism, Bryant
    argues that Edwards "forges a complex of symbols which
    press towards a transcendent Kingdom rather than a
    worldly kingdom. Thus the constellation of symbols and
    beliefs found in Edwards' work does not provide an
    ideology for American nationalism, but a commentary on
    and critique of formative elements in the American
    tradition."

Buckham, John Wright. "The New England Theologians."
    American Journal of Theology, 24 (1920), 19-29.
    A simplistic and somewhat misleading account of the

relation of the New England Theology to the theology of Edwards.

Buckingham, Willis J. "Stylistic Artistry in the Sermons of Jonathan Edwards." *Papers on Language and Literature*, 6 (1970), 136-151.
Buckingham discusses Edwards as a literary stylist, attempting to revise the estimate of Edwards "as an instinctive writer, competent but 'plain'...."
"His sermons are not always so exhaustive and spectacular as *Sinners* in their range of rhetorical devices; nevertheless, their consistent dignity, tact, and strength lend them the enduring vitality of art."

Buranelli, Vincent. "Colonial Philosophy." *William and Mary Quarterly*, series 3, 16 (1959), 343-362.
An excellent bibliographical essay on colonial philosophy. Includes a brief, general review of Edwards scholarship.

Burggraaff, Winfield J. "Jonathan Edwards: A Biblio-graphical Essay." *Reformed Review*, 18 (1965), 19-33.
Burggraaff examines the recent "rehabilitation" of Edwards by reviewing the interpretations proposed by A. V. G. Allen, Vernon L. Parrington, Henry Bamford Parkes, Ola E. Winslow, and Perry Miller.

Burggraaff, Winfield J. *The Rise and Development of Liberal Theology in America*. New York, 1928. (Doctoral disser-tation, Free University of Amsterdam, 1928.)
"At more than one point Arminianism conquered over Calvinism in the theology of the Edwardeans."
Burggraaff examines those features of the New

England Theology which were in themselves deviations
from Calvinism, or else contained the seed-thoughts for
later deviations in the direction of liberal theology.
These features, Burggraaff suggests, are a shift of
emphasis from the objective to the subjective, the wrong
solution to the problem of free will, and the New
England theory of the Atonement, all of which are traced
to their genesis in the writings of Edwards. "History,"
Burggraaff suggests, "has not justified Edwards' modifi-
cation of Calvinism."

Burnham, Richard. "Mr. Jonathan Edwards." In his *Pious
   Memorials*. London, 1789, pp. 416-433.

Burr, Nelson, R. *A Critical Bibliography of Religion in
   America*. New York, 1971.
   Includes (II, pp. 976-987) biography and criticism of
   Edwards.

Burt, Struthers. "Jonathan Edwards and the Gunman." *North
   American Review*, 207 (1929), 712-718.
   This article has nothing to do with Edwards as such and
   is included here merely to save others the task of
   retrieving it. "Are we becoming the most immoral nation
   in the world?" With little success, Burt searches for
   the roots of crime in the American streets in its
   "puritan" heritage.

Bushman, Richard L. "Jonathan Edwards and Puritan
   Consciousness." *Journal for the Scientific Study of
   Religion*, 5 (1966), 383-396.
   Drawing largely upon Edwards' autobiographical writings,
   "reconstructing Edwards' dominant states of mind," and
   "following his will's struggle to regulate the powers

of heaven and self circulating in his soul," Bushman
attempts to "recover much of the Puritan consciousness,
making it available for translation into modern terms
for our better understanding."

Bushman provides a valuable analysis of the Edwards
who appears in the *Diary, Resolutions,* and the *Personal
Narrative.* Edwards' conversion experience is analyzed
in terms of the resolution of an oedipal complex.

Bushman, Richard L. "Jonathan Edwards as Great Man:
Identity, Conversion, and Leadership in the Great
Awakening." *Soundings,* 52 (1969), 15-46.
An excellent study of Edwards on the model of Erikson's
Young Man Luther. Bushman suggests that Edwards'
influence during the Great Awakening arose from the
emotional congruities of his own life and that of his
people: "Circumstances converged to generate tensions
whose psychological structure happened to coincide with
that which life in the Edwards household formed in
Jonathan."

Bushnell, Horace. *Christ in Theology.* Hartford, 1851.
Bushnell, in the Preface to this work, was the first to
call public attention to Edwards' unpublished, and
supposedly heterodox, tract on the Trinity.

"I very much desired in my exposition of the
Trinity, to present illustrations from a manuscript
dissertation of President Edwards on that subject. Only
a few months ago, I first heard of the existence of such
a manuscript. It was described to me as 'an a priori
argument for the Trinity,' the 'contents of which would
excite a good deal of surprise,' if communicated to the
public. The privilege of access to the manuscript is
declined to me, as I understand, on the ground of 'The

nature of the contents." See article by Richard C.
Pierce below.

Byington, Ezra Hoyt. "Jonathan Edwards, and the Great
    Awakening." *Bibliotheca Sacra,* 55 (1898), 114-127.
    "He is spoken of most frequently as a hard logician, a
    metaphysician, a Calvinistic theologian. If that had
    been all, the revival would not have begun in his
    parish."
        A popularized discussion of Edwards' role in the
    Great Awakening and the general results of the revival.
    Superficial.

Byington, Ezra Hoyt. *The Puritan as a Colonist and a
    Reformer.* Boston, 1899.
    Includes an expanded version of the above article.

Cady, Edwin H. "The Artistry of Jonathan Edwards." *New
    England Quarterly,* 22 (1949), 61-72.
    Cady examines the Enfield sermon as a literary work,
    with particular attention to the imagery employed.
    "By all the ordinary tests, *Sinners in the Hands of
    an Angry God* is a genuine work of literary art and
    testifies to Jonathan Edwards' right to the name of
    artist."

Cairns, Earle E. "Jonathan Edwards, Challenge for
    Evangelism Today." *Moody Monthly,* 66 (1966), 60-62.
    Cairns suggests that modern evangelists learn from the
    example and experience of Jonathan Edwards: "Large
    scale awakening will come again in our day both in
    churches and mass meetings when pastors as well as
    evangelists link life and preaching by a vital
    experience with their God."

Canby, Henry Seidel. "Jonathan Edwards." In his *Classic
    Americans: A Study of Eminent American Writers from
    Irving to Whitman*. New York, 1931; rpt. 1959, pp. 9-22.
    Primarily a biographical study. Canby presents Edwards
    as a "delicate, yet powerful spirit... trapped by
    practical necessity. He believed that he had to use
    every ounce of energy to demonstrate the nature and the
    necessity of righteousness by cold and convincing logic.
    He had to take his place in the succession of God's
    ministers whose duty it was to make a holy land of New
    England." Canby suggests but does not elaborate a
    theory of Edwards' intellectual development, a develop-
    ment precipitated by the turmoil at Yale over the
    defection of the college rector and others from the
    Congregational ministry. Worth reading.

Carpenter, Frederic Ives. "The Radicalism of Jonathan
    Edwards." *New England Quarterly*, 4 (1931), 629-644.
    Carpenter argues for the essential modernity of Edwards,
    citing parallels between Edwards and moderns such as
    Robinson Jeffers.
        "Calvinism," Carpenter suggests, "was merely an
    inherited cloak for his thinking, and often an ill-
    fitting one at that. In his youth he was innocent of
    it, and in his mature life he outgrew it, but always
    he thought it decent to wear in absence of a better."
    For Carpenter, Edwards appears as "the first, if not
    the greatest, of a royal line of modern American
    mystics."

Carse, James Pearce. "The Christology of Jonathan Edwards."
    Doctoral dissertation, Drew University, 1966. In
    Dissertation Abstracts, 27 (1967), 2594A-2595A.
    "In his 1731 sermon, *God Glorified in the Work of*

Redemption, Jonathan Edwards explains that all the good
that the redeemed have 'is in and through Christ.' It
is the premise of this dissertation that the centrality
of Christ in Edwards' theology cannot be adequately
described by means of the orthodox categories of the
person, work, and states of Christ. Edwards was
familiar with the orthodox Reformed literature, but he
rarely made use of such categories in his discussion of
the nature of Christ and his place in the life of the
believer. Edwards' own understanding of Christ is
suggested in the 1731 sermon where he appeals to the
Pauline phrase that Christ is our wisdom, righteousness,
sanctification, and redemption."

Carse, James Pearce. "Incarnation and Atonement in the
     Theology of Jonathan Edwards." S.T.M. thesis, Yale
     Divinity School, 1963.

Carse, James Pearce. *Jonathan Edwards and the Visibility
     of God*. New York, 1967.
     Certainly the most intriguing study of Edwards since
     that of Perry Miller. Carse finds a central key to
     Edwards' thought, and the thesis of his study, in
     Edwards' early critique of Locke. Edwards' fundamental
     insight, Carse argues, was his denial of any distinction
     between appearance and reality. For Edwards, "things
     are what they appear to be," or, "appearances are all
     there are." This insight, Carse suggests, is of key
     importance in understanding Edwards' life and thought.
         "Once Edwards had seen that things are truly what
     they seem to be, and that we can now speak in the old
     way as properly and as truly as ever, he knew that the
     task of reason was not to carry him beyond what the eyes
     can see and the ears can hear, because beyond what is

visible there is nothing at all." Thus, argues Carse, Edwards became the preacher of the visibility of God. Carse re-examines Edwards' major writings from this perspective with some interesting results.

Reviews

Akers, Charles. *New England Quarterly,* 41 (1968), 302-305.

Goetz, Ronald. *Christian Century,* 85 (1968), 844.

Grabo, Norman S. *Early American Literature,* 4 (1969), 45-46.

Winslow, Ola E. *American Literature,* 40 (1968), 400-401.

Carse, James Pearce. "Mr. Locke's Magic Onions and an Unboxed Beetle for Young Jonathan." *Journal of Religion,* 47 (1967), 331-339.

The key chapter from Carse's *Jonathan Edwards,* examining Edwards' youthful conversation with Locke and his epistemological and psychological conclusions.

Caskey, Edwin. "If They Were Alive Today. Jonathan Edwards: The First American Philosopher." *Thinker,* 4 (1931), 34-35.

Caskey, James S. "Jonathan Edwards' *Catalogue of Books.*" B.D. thesis, Chicago Theological Seminary, 1931. Includes the only edited version of Edwards' manuscript *Catalogue.*

Cattell, J. McKeen. "Jonathan Edwards on Multidimensional Space and the Mechanistic Conception of Life." *Science,* new series, 52 (1920), 409-410.

This article is barely longer than its title. "If the Einstein conception of space is multidimensional

and inclusive of the essential conceptions of time and
place, then Jonathan Edwards... may prove to be the
spiritual father of this geometry." Citing excerpts
from the *Notes on Natural Science* Cattell exclaims,
"Einstein, Conklin; Behold your King!"

Chalmers, Thomas. *The Christian and Civic Economy of Large
   Towns*. 3 vols. Glasgow, 1821.
   Includes (I, pp. 318-322) a brief discussion of Edwards
   as theologian.

Chandler, P. W. "Jonathan Edwards." *New Jerusalem
   Magazine*, 43 (1871), 593-602.
   "The whole system of Jonathan Edwards is the best
   possible illustration of the danger of a theological
   faith which rests upon the intellectual powers alone."
       Chandler discusses Edwards, Swedenborg, and Horace
   Field on human freedom and responsibility and the divine
   permission of evil. Chandler is less interested in
   examining the substance of Edwards' thought than in
   attempting to demonstrate the "metaphysical legerdemain"
   by which Edwards maintains and expounds contradictory
   positions: "the reader, if he relies upon reason alone,
   is carried away or is lost in the fog and refuses to
   believe in anything at all." Superficial.

Channing, William H. "Edwards and the Revivalists."
   Christian Examiner, 43 (1847), 374-394.
   A generalized discussion of Edwards' theology within the
   context of a critique of the revival, or, that "outbreak
   of enthusiasm" known as the Great Awakening. While
   extremely critical of Edwards' conclusions, Channing is
   quite sympathetic to Edwards the man: "A little more

hope or a little less fear would have completely
remoulded his theology, and made him a teacher of
universal good-will."

Chauncy, Charles. *Five Dissertations on the Scripture
Account of the Fall; and its Consequences.* Boston,
1785.
Includes an unfavorable critique of Edwards' treatise
on *Original Sin.*

Chauncy, Charles. *Seasonable Thoughts on the State of
Religion in New England, A Treatise in Five Parts.*
Boston, 1743.
A lengthy critique of Edwards and the revival by the
leader of the opposition among the Congregational
ministry. More than three quarters of this study is
devoted to a report of the many private excesses and
social disorders which marked the revival. Chauncy
considered the fundamental error of the movement to lie
in its excessive emotionalism: "There is the Religion
of the Understanding and Judgment, and Will, as well as
of the Affections; and if little Account is made of
the former, while great Stress is laid upon the latter,
it can't be but People should run into Disorders."
Chauncy's volume was a calculated response to Edwards'
*Some Thoughts concerning the Present Revival of
Religion in New England.*

Cheever, George. "The Manuscripts of President Edwards."
The Independent, 23 December 1852, n.p. Reprinted in
British and Foreign Evangelical Review, 2 (1853),
259-261; and in *Littell's Living Age,* 36 (1853),
181-182.
A brief discussion of the Edwards manuscripts then

(1852) in the possession of Tryon Edwards. Cheever was
less interested in detailing the manuscript collection
than in relating how the manuscripts reveal Edwards'
thoroughness in the study of Scripture, his habits of
study, powers of intellect, and lack of paper. Includes
brief fragments from the unpublished manuscripts.

Cherry, Charles Conrad. "Imagery and Analysis: Jonathan
Edwards on Revivals of Religion." In *Jonathan Edwards:
His Life and Influence*, ed. Charles Angoff. Rutherford,
New Jersey, 1975, pp. 19-28.
Cherry stresses Edwards' appeal to both reason and
emotion in his revival preaching. Unlike the revivalists of a later America, argues Cherry, "Edwards avoided
the sanctimonious conclusion that religious intuition
is sufficient unto itself and that theology is a waste
of time." Edwards "chose to promote the revivals
through an imagery that evoked an act of the understanding as well as stirred the emotions," and assumed
the "two-fold task of imaginatively promoting the
revivals and of subjecting those same revivals to
analytical scrutiny."

Cherry, Charles Conrad. *Nature and the Religious
Imagination: From Edwards to Bushnell*. Philadelphia,
1980.
Cherry demonstrates how Edwards' use of language and
his theory of religious knowledge accounted the
perception of "the divine meaning of the natural world"
in a symbolic manner that grew out of the Puritan
tradition of typology. Edwards' insights, Cherry
argues, were eclipsed by the rise of moral understandings
of nature in both Unitarianism and the emerging schools
of new divinity. Bushnell is shown recovering Edwards'

"symbolic view of religious truth" under the influence of Coleridge.

Cherry, Charles Conrad. "The Nature of Faith in the Theology of Jonathan Edwards." Doctoral dissertation, Drew University, 1965. In *Dissertation Abstracts,* 26 (1965), 3506-3507.
"This treatment of Jonathan Edwards' doctrine of faith seeks to accomplish two tasks: (1) analyze the various dimensions of the doctrine (here also many elements of Edwards' theology as a whole are seen to converge on his doctrine of faith, and Edwards' relation to his theological harbingers emerges); (2) demonstrate how Edwards' understanding of faith was instrumental for his stance within the American religious situation of his day."

Cherry, Charles Conrad. "Promoting the Cause and Testing the Spirits: Jonathan Edwards on Revivals of Religion." *Journal of Presbyterian History,* 51 (1973), 327-337.
A review of *The Great Awakening* (New Haven, 1972), edited by C. C. Goen.

Cherry, Charles Conrad. "The Puritan Notion of the Covenant in Jonathan Edwards' Doctrine of Faith." *Church History,* 34 (1965), 328-341.
Cherry takes Perry Miller to task for his assertion that Edwards "threw over the whole covenant scheme," and "declared God unfettered by any covenant or obligation." On the contrary, Cherry argues that Edwards "definitely adhered to some of the basic features of his fore-fathers' Covenant Theology." Cherry elaborates Edwards' use of the categories of the Covenant Theology in the context of his doctrine of faith. "Far from over-

throwing the Covenant Theology," Cherry concludes,
"Edwards was quite dependent upon it—in fact, there
is every indication that he had difficulty freeing
himself from its categories even at points where he
discerned their shortcomings. What is of more importance, however, is that in his doctrine of faith Edwards
was clearly a covenant theologian. For Edwards, the
relation of faith was a covenant-relation."

Cherry, Charles Conrad. *The Theology of Jonathan Edwards:
A Reappraisal*. Garden City, 1966.
This study is not as general as its title would
indicate. A revision of Cherry's doctoral dissertation,
it is a scholarly study of Edwards' theology from the
perspective of his notion of faith, and written "under
the conviction that Edwards was first and last a
Calvinist theologian, and that his thought can still be
meaningfully understood by one two centuries removed
from it."

Therein consist Cherry's "reappraisal" of Edwards.
Historically the sulphuric Edwards has been rehabili-
tated, but largely by a process of highlighting those
features of Edwards' thought where he appears to
"transcend" his Calvinism or to pre-figure the post
Puritan era of American thought. "Perhaps such a
procedure would not be totally inappropriate," argues
Cherry, "if Edwards had not so obviously addressed himself to problems in his eighteenth century or if he had
not consciously chosen Puritan Calvinism as the framework for so much of his thought." "For good or ill,"
Cherry insists, "Edwards was a Calvinist theologian;
and, as a Calvinist theologian, he claimed the heritage
of his New England forefathers."

Chrisman, Lewis. "Jonathan Edwards." In his *John Ruskin,*
    Preacher, and Other Essays. New York, [1921], pp. 25-45.

Christian, Curtis Wallace. "The Concept of Life after Death
    in the Theology of Jonathan Edwards, Friedrich
    Schleiermacher, and Paul Tillich." Doctoral dissertation,
    Vanderbilt University, 1965. In *Dissertation Abstracts,*
    26 (1965), 2347-2348.
    "The purpose of this thesis is the examination of the
    concept of life after death in the thought of Jonathan
    Edwards, Friedrich Schleiermacher, and Paul Tillich,
    representative theologians of the last three centuries,
    with special attention to problems for such belief which
    have been created by the modern world view, and with the
    intention of determining whether the theologians under
    discussion provide insights useful in projecting a
    meaningful understanding of life after death."

Christie, Francis A. "Jonathan Edwards." In *Dictionary of
    American Biography.* New York, 1931. Vol. VI, pp. 30-37.
    Biographical sketch of Edwards with a concise and
    reliable summary of the substance of his major publi-
    cations. Christie finds in Edwards' youthful discussion
    of the nature of excellence "the master idea of his
    whole career." Still the best article of its kind about
    Edwards.

*Circular Letters, containing an Invitation to the Ministers
    and Churches of every Christian Denomination in the
    United States, to unite in Their Endeavours to carry
    into Execution the "Humble Attempt" of President
    Edwards.* Concord, 1798.
    Ministers are urged to publicly endorse the Invitation
    and take definite steps to "promote explicit agreement

and visible union of God's people, in extraordinary
prayer, for the revival of religion and the advancement
of Christ's Kingdom on Earth."

Clap, Thomas. *A Letter from the Reverend Mr. Clap, Rector
of Yale-College in New-Haven, to the Rev. Mr. Edwards
of North-Hampton, Expostulating with Him for his
injurious Reflections in his late Letter to a Friend.*
Boston, 1745.
Clap responds to Edwards' pamphlet, *Copies of the Two
Letters.* See next entry.

Clap, Thomas. *A Letter from the Reverend Mr. Thomas Clap,
Rector of Yale-College at New-Haven, To a Friend in
Boston.* Boston, 1745.
Clap sets forth the reasons "why the world ought to give
credit to what he declared when in Boston last; viz.
that the Rev. Mr. Edwards of Northampton told him, that
the Rev. Mr. Whitefield said in his hearing, that it was
his design to turn the generality of the ministers in
the country out of their places, and re-settle them with
ministers from England, Scotland and Ireland."
     This letter touched off a short-lived pamphlet
controversy between Edwards and Clap. Edwards responded
with *Copies of the Two Letters.* This last provoked
Clap's *Letter* cited in the previous entry, to which
Edwards finally responded with *An Expostulatory Letter.*

Clark, George. *A Vindication of the Honor of God, and of
the Rights of Men. In a Letter to the Rev. Mr.
DeCoetlogon occasioned by the Publication of Mr.
Edwards's Sermon on the Eternity of Hell Torments.*
London, 1789.

Clark, Irene Woodbridge. "A Wifely Estimate of Edwards:
    An Unpublished Letter by Edwards's Wife."
    Congregationalist and Christian World, 88 (1903),
    472-473.
    Clark presents a hitherto unpublished letter written by
    Sarah Edwards to the council that met at Northampton to
    examine the difficulties that had arisen between
    Edwards and his congregation. The letter concerns
    Edwards' position on qualifications for communion and
    insists that what might seem a sudden caprice on
    Edwards' part was in reality merely the first public
    action based on a conviction long held.

Clark, Solomon. *Historical Catalogue of the Northampton
    First Church*. Northampton, 1891.
    Includes (pp. 40-67) a review of Edwards' Northampton
    ministry.

Clebsch, William A. *American Religious Thought: A History*.
    Chicago, 1973.
    Edwards, Emerson, and William James provide the forms of
    this history. Clebsch suggests that these three
    thinkers "resisted the moralistic spirituality which
    America's chief religious heritage, Puritanism, almost
    inevitably tends. They resisted not only by denouncing
    moralism but by exploring and affirming another kind of
    spirituality, which is here called aesthetic."
        Clebsch provides an excellent analysis of the
    "sensible spirituality" of Edwards: "To be sure,
    Edwards honored the Founding Fathers of New England,
    cultivated religion of the heart, defended Calvinism.
    But no such part of his work constitutes the central
    legacy: to be grasped by God, not to grasp God, is
    spiritual beauty. The religious life equals the good

life equals the beautiful life—a life made propor-
tionate and proper and harmonious by the divine artist,
a life lived at home in the universe."

Clift, Arlene Louise. "Rhetoric and the Reason-Revelation
Relationship in the Writings of Jonathan Edwards."
Doctoral dissertation, Harvard University, 1969.

Colacurcio, Robert Eugene. "The Perception of Excellency
as the Glory of God in Jonathan Edwards: An Essay
Towards the Epistemology of Discernment." Doctoral
dissertation, Fordham University, 1972. In
Dissertation Abstracts International, 33 (1973), 4468A,
"This thesis tries to faithfully recover Jonathan
Edwards' epistemology of discernment. By 'discernment'
is meant the discrimination of the active, saving
presence of the living God in the heart of the believer.
The thesis concerns itself primarily with the epistemological locus of the operation of God's sovereignty.
For the heart of Edwards' thought is precisely this:
the 'sense of the heart' which is referred to as the
'nodal point of God's saving action in the world.' One
way, therefore, of conceiving the overall intent of this
paper as it bears upon substantive philosophical issues
is to view it as an exploration into the meaning and
validity of knowing with the heart."

Cole, Samuel Valentine. "A Witness to the Truth." In
*Exercises Commemorating the 200th Anniversary of the
Birth of Jonathan Edwards*. Andover, 1904, pp. 95-103.
Reprinted in *New England Magazine*, new series,
29 (1904), 583-586.
A poem.

Collmer, Robert G. "Two Antecedents for a Metaphor from
Jonathan Edwards." *Notes and Queries,* new series,
3 (1956), 396.
Collmer cites precedents for Edwards' dangling spider
image.

Cone, Kate M. "Jonathan Edwards." *Outlook,* 75 (1903),
254-266.
A biographical study of Edwards, written largely in the
subjunctive mood. Cone pays particular attention to the
women in Edwards' life: "With his mother's milk
Jonathan Edwards drew in the life of the mind and the
heart which was common to them both. As he lay, a rosy
baby on her breast, we can readily believe that she
measured the heights which he was indeed destined to
attain...." Or, referring to the revival of religion
that stirred Northampton in 1734-35 under the leadership
of Edwards Cone asks, "What, we wonder, did Grandmother
Stoddard, minister's wife and widow in Northampton for
seventy years think of it all?" These excerpts provide
a fair indication of what Cone is about in this article.
    Note that the portrait that heads the article is
not that of President Edwards but Jonathan Edwards the
Younger.

The Congregationalist and Christian World, 88 (October 3,
1903).
This issue of the *Congregationalist* was devoted
exclusively to articles on Edwards, in commemoration of
the two hundredth anniversary of his birth.
Contents
Our Edwards Number [Editorial], p. 451.
Why Revive Edwards? [Editorial], p. 454.

Tributes to Jonathan Edwards from Careful Students of
his Writings, by [Egbert C. Smyth], p. 458.

The Human Side of Edwards, by George Perry Morris,
pp. 461-462.

The Preaching Power of Jonathan Edwards, by Wilbert L.
Anderson, pp. 463-466.

Jonathan Edwards: His Influence in Scotland, by James
Orr, pp. 467-468.

The Value of Edwards for Today, by George Park Fisher,
pp. 469-471.

Edwards's Habits and Tastes, as Portrayed by a
Contemporary, p. 471.

A Wifely Estimate of Edwards: An Unpublished Letter by
Edwards's Wife, by Irene Woodbridge Clark,
pp. 472-473.

[Notes on] The Pictures in this Number, p. 473.

Conkin, Paul K. "Jonathan Edwards: Theology." In his
*Puritans and Pragmatists: Eight Eminent American
Thinkers*. New York, 1968, pp. 39-72.

A perceptive analysis of Edwards' thought, focusing on
"the twin problems of Edwards' lifetime—defining true
religion and refuting the Arminians."

"As a brilliant Christian theologian, Edwards tried
to use the latest and, for the time, most convincing
scientific and philosophical ideas in defense of a
religious faith which, for him, was vindicated by reason
and even more by immediate and inescapable experience.
In this, he fulfilled the perennial role of theologians.
Edwards' thought grew from his own struggles with the
forces of his time and place. Working in virtual
isolation, with less astute critics and slavish
disciples, his intellectual achievement was a highly
original and very personal work of art.... Into a vast

intellectual homage to an overwhelming God that men were
ever less inclined to treat as God, Edwards poured all
of himself. His biography is almost entirely a
biography of the mind."

Conrad, Leslie, Jr. "Jonathan Edwards' Pattern for
   Preaching." *Church Management,* 33 no. 12 (1957), 45-47.

"A Contemporaneous Account of Jonathan Edwards." *Journal of
   the Presbyterian Historical Society,* 2 (1903), 125-135.
   A reprint of the lengthy account of Edwards that introduced the first edition of Edwards' treatise on *Original
   Sin* in 1758. The account appeared anonymously, but was
   referred to by Sereno E. Dwight as the "testimony of an
   eye-witness," written by "a gentleman connected with the
   college at Princeton, probably Dr. Finley." In this
   Journal the account is presented as "Princeton's
   estimate of the man chosen as head of the college."
   See, however, Donald L. Weber's dissertation where
   Finley's authorship of this piece is disputed. Drawing
   upon manuscript sources, Weber also recounts Samuel
   Hopkins' condemnation of this piece and his attempt to
   have it suppressed.

[Cooke, Parsons]. "Edwards on the Atonement." *American
   Theological Review,* 2 (1860), 97-120. Reprinted in
   British and Foreign Evangelical Review, 9 (1860),
   613-632.
   A highly critical review of "The Rise of the Edwardean
   Theory of the Atonement," by Edwards Amasa Park. Cooke
   challenges the right of the New England theologians to
   claim the banner of Edwards.
      Park's essay, Cooke asserts, "goes far to enucleate
   the paradox of Edwardeanism against Edwards, that

lately developed system which is claimed to be most in
accordance with Edwards, and yet is made vastly more
consistent and improved by positions in conflict with
him." Park should be praised, Cooke continues, for
freely admitting what others had attempted to prove:
"That is, that what he calls the Edwardean System is the
opposite of the system which Jonathan Edwards held."
Cooke insists that "Every application of the term
Edwardean" to the doctrine of the atonement held by his
so-called successors "is an abuse of Edwards's good
name, as well as a perversion of the truth of history."

Coss, John J. "Jonathan Edwards [A Bibliography]." In
Cambridge History of American Literature. New York,
1917. Vol. I, pp. 426-438.
Main headings are Manuscripts, Collected works, Separate
works, and Biography and Criticism. All items cited by
Coss under Biography and Criticism have been included
in this bibliography.

Cowan, James C. "Jonathan Edwards' Sermon Style: *The
Future Punishment of the Wicked Unavoidable and
Intolerable*." *South-Central Bulletin,* 29 (1969),
119-122.

Crabtree, Arthur Bamford. *Jonathan Edwards' View of Man:
A Study in Eighteenth Century Calvinism*. Wallington,
England, 1948. (Doctoral dissertation, University of
Zurich, 1948.)
A systematic analysis of Edwards' doctrines of creation,
the fall, sin, his conception of the understanding and
the will, his anthropology, and his evangelism.

Crook, Isaac. *Jonathan Edwards*. New York, 1903.

Crooker, Joseph H. "Jonathan Edwards: A Psychological
    Study." *New England Magazine*, new series, 2 (1890),
    159-172.
    Still worth reading. Crooker presents a devastating
    analysis of Edwards, suggesting that if a man today
    exhibited some of Edwards' symptoms he would be "put
    under the care of a skillful neurologist." Edwards,
    Crooker argues, "was a theological monomaniac. He was
    afflicted with a species of delusional insanity, which
    took possession of him in his early youth, and which
    had its centre in the dogma of 'Divine sovereignty.'"
        "Delusional monomania," observes Crooker, usually
    assumes the characteristics of its environment, "so that
    the similarity between his general doctrine and the
    creed of his age proves nothing against the position
    here taken, but rather illustrates it." What is
    peculiar about Edwards, insists Crooker, is his "intense
    devotion to the dogma of 'Divine Sovereignty' in its
    most extreme form, to the neglect or contradiction of
    everything else. It absorbed his thought and energy;
    it ruled his life and distorted his judgment; in short,
    it became the centre of a delusional monomania."

Crybbace, Thomas Tully. *An Essay on Moral Freedom: To
    which is Attached a Review of the Principles of Dr.
    Whitby and President Edwards on Free Will*. Edinburgh,
    1829.

Cunsolo, Ronald S. "The Return of Jonathan Edwards: A
    Bicentennial Reflection." *Nassau Review*, 13 (1976),
    86-94

Curti, Merle. *The Growth of American Thought*.   New York,
1943.
Contains a brief, superficial discussion of Edwards'
place in the history of American thought.
"What gives Edwards a highly significant place...
is that he made many concessions to the newer currents
challenging Calvinism, and yet in his final analysis he
subordinated all of these to an amazingly logical
defense of the essentials of the Genevan master as they
had been developed by subsequent Calvinists."

Curtis, Mattoon M.   "Kantean Elements in Jonathan Edwards."
In *Festschrift für Heinze*.   Berlin, 1906, pp. 34-62.
"Not only did Edwards write the first treatise on Ethics
in America, but he shows clearly that the ethical is his
main interest in all his writings.   Ultimately his
theories are always theories of value."
In exploring the "Kantean" elements in Edwards'
thought, Curtis provides an excellent critical analysis
of Edwards' philosophical method.   This piece is still
worth consulting.

Curtis, Mattoon M.   "An Outline of Philosophy in America."
Western Reserve Bulletin, 2 (1896), 3-18.
Includes a brief sketch of Edwards' philosophy.

Curtis, Mattoon M.   "Philosophie in Nord-Amerika."   In
Überweg's *Grundriss der Geschicte der Philosophie*.
Berlin, 1901-06.   Vol. IV, pp. 540-545.

Dana, James.   *An Examination of the late Reverend President
Edwards's "Enquiry on Freedom of Will"; More
especially the Foundation Principles of his Book, with
the Tendency and Consequences of the Reasoning therein*

Contained. Boston, 1770.

An elaborate critique of Edwards' *Freedom of the Will.*
Dana has "no manner of doubt but the foundation
principles of the book... are false," and "of a most
dangerous tendency."

One of Dana's primary objections to Edwards' scheme,
and the stated reason why he chose to pursue the
examination, is that Edwards had made God the efficient
cause of moral evil. Dana finds fault, however, not
only with apparent doctrinal implications of Edwards'
treatise, but with the psychology of the will that it
presumes: "Let a man look into his own breast, and he
cannot but perceive inward freedom—*inward freedom*—
For if freedom be not in the mind, it is no where. And
liberty in the mind implies self-determination."

Dana, James. *The Examination of the late Rev'd President
Edwards's "Enquiry on Freedom of Will," Continued. To
which are subjoined strictures on the Rev'd Mr. West's
"Essay on Moral Agency".* New Haven, 1773.
A continuation of Dana's examination, prompted by
Stephen West's *Essay on Moral Agency.*

"The examiner begs the reader to keep in mind this
single question, *Whether Mr. Edwards's doctrine makes
God the efficient cause of all moral wickedness?* He is
himself clear in the affirmative of this question."

Darrow, Clarence. "The Edwardses and the Jukeses."
American Mercury, 6 (1925), 147-157.
Darrow effectively satirizes the methods and conlusions
of eugenists who, in attempting to demonstrate that
"blood always tells," often point to the illustrious
progeny of President Edwards, who are seen to stand in
marked contrast to the less reputable line of one Max

Jukes. In the course of his criticisms of the eugenists, Darrow makes clear his own estimate of Edwards.

"The amazing thing to me," exclaims Darrow, "is why
anyone of this generation or any other should *want* to
be traced to Jonathan Edwards. Why should any eugenist
resort to the devious ways that have been used in this
genealogy for the purpose of linking even his worst
enemies to Jonathan? Who was Jonathan Edwards? Except
for his weird and horrible theology, he would have
filled no place in American life. His main business was
scaring silly women and children and blaspheming the God
he professed to adore. Nothing but a distorted or
diseased mind could have produced his *Sinners in the
Hands of an Angry God*."

Davenport, Charles B. *Heredity in Relation to Eugenics*.
New York, 1911.
Attempting to demonstrate the importance of the "germ
plasm" of a single individual to the future of the race,
Davenport cites the example of Elizabeth Tuttle,
Edwards' paternal grandmother, and her notable descen-
dants: "These constitute a glorious galaxy of America's
great educators, students, and moral leaders of the
Republic." Davenport concludes that "had Elizabeth
Tuttle not been this nation would not now occupy the
position in culture and learning that it now does."
The unintentional ambiguity of Davenport's conclusion
is only increased upon closer acquaintance with Ms.
Tuttle.

Davidson, Clifford. "Jonathan Edwards and Mysticism."
College Language Association Journal, 11 (1967),
149-156.

Davidson, Edward H. "From Locke to Edwards." *Journal of the History of Ideas,* 24 (1963), 355-372.
A study of epistemology and the philosophy of language in Edwards and Locke.

Davidson, Edward H. *Jonathan Edwards: The Narrative of a Puritan Mind.* Boston, 1966.
An intellectual biography. This study has had mixed reviews. It has been praised as a "brilliantly conceived analysis" of Edwards, a "solid intellectual biography, lucidly presented, far more credible and satisfying than the series of dramatic confrontations and startling paradoxes which characterize the best known previous intellectual biography of Edwards—that of Perry Miller." Another critic finds Davidson perceptive in some places, obscure in others, and often simply incorrect. The book has no discernible thesis.
Reviews
Aldridge, Alfred O. *Seventeenth Century News,* 27 (1969), 32ff.
Winslow, Ola E. *American Literature,* 38 (1966), 388-389.

Davidson, Frank. "Three Patterns of Living." *Bulletin of the American Association of University Professors,* 34 (1948), 364-374.
A popularized discussion of the approaches to life of Edwards, Franklin, and John Woolman.

Day, Jeremiah. *An Examination of President Edwards's Inquiry on the Freedom of the Will.* New Haven, 1841.
"Among the causes of the lamentable dissensions with which, at the present day, the American churches are agitated, a place has been assigned to President Edwards's Treatise on the Freedom of the Will. It is

alleged, that the differences of opinion respecting the
principles and influence of this great work, have occasioned jealousy and alienation of feeling, among those
who ought to be closely united, in the bonds of
Christian affection. If the fact really be so, it is
high time to inquire, whether the fault is in the work
itself, or in those who read it, or in those who,
without having read it, undertake to pronounce authori-
tatively upon its merits."

Day's *Examination* is actually a lengthy statement,
restatement, and elaboration of the substance of
Edwards' treatise. Throughout this volume Day is
involved in answering specific criticisms of *Freedom of
the Will* and evaluating the responses of Edwards'
defenders; however, Day has chosen not to name the
protagonists.

Day, Martin S. *History of American Literature from the
Beginning to 1910.* New York, 1970.
Brief, superficial remarks on Edwards.

Dean, Lloyd F. "Salvation and Self-Interest: Edwards'
Concept of Love and its Relevance to Modern Evangelism."
Gordon Review, 9 (1966), 101-110.
Dean asserts that "it is about time that evangelicals
discover the real Edwards." Unlike the many Edwardses
lately discovered, the "real Edwards" of whom Dean
speaks is an Edwards well known to his contemporaries.
In critique of modern evangelicals who appear to have
forgotten the lesson, Dean elaborates a conviction basic
to Edwards, America's "greatest native revivalist":
that self-love has no determining part in the work of
regeneration. Superficial.

DeJong, Peter Y. *The Covenant Idea in New England Theology,*
1620-1847. Grand Rapids, 1945.
DeJong examines the substance and result of Edwards'
"attack" on the Halfway Covenant system.
"... [I]nstead of restoring the covenant conception
to its true and legitimate place in the church on the
basis of its original confessions after having successfully attacked the false theories prevalent in his days,
Edwards did perhaps more than anyone else toward
preparing for the complete and final eradication of this
idea from New England religious life. He was chiefly
responsible for completely 'Congregationalizing' the
Congregational church, since his ideas on revivalism and
qualifications for church membership signalled the
ultimate triumph of religious individualism and
voluntarism in New England."

Delattre, Roland Andre. "Beauty and Politics: A
Problematic Legacy of Jonathan Edwards." In *American*
Philosophy from Edwards to Quine, ed. Robert W. Shahan
and Kenneth R. Merrill. Norman, Oklahoma, 1977,
pp. 20-48.

Delattre, Roland Andre. "Beauty and Sensibility in the
Thought of Jonathan Edwards: An Essay in Aesthetics and
Ethics." Doctoral dissertation, Yale University, 1966.
In *Dissertation Abstracts,* 27 (1967), 2596A.
"A major achievement of recent Edwards scholarship has
been the recognition of the importance of the aesthetic
dimension of his thought. However, of the twin
aesthetic concepts of beauty and sensibility, much has
been written about the *sense* of beauty, while not nearly
as careful attention has been given to the *object* of
that sense—to the beauty itself, as it is understood

by Jonathan Edwards. Accordingly, the primary focus of
this study is Jonathan Edwards' concept of beauty, though
this cannot be treated entirely independently of the
corresponding sensibility or of Jonathan Edwards'
aesthetic/affectional model of the self."

Delattre makes many claims for the central importance of beauty in Edwards' thought: it is, Delattre
argues, "the decisive concept of his ontological philosophy of being, of his theology, and of his interpretation of the structure and dynamics of the moral and
spiritual life." For Edwards, beauty is the first
principle of being, the measure of goodness, the
objective foundation of goodness, and both the attrac-
tive and creative power of the apparent good. It is
Edwards' "primary model of order." Beauty is first
among the divine perfections, the formative principle
for the articulation of the divine being *ad intra* and
ad extra. Beauty, according to Delattre, provides
Edwards with "his model for the manner of the divine
governance; and beauty is itself both the goal and the
principal means of redemption."

Delattre, Roland Andre. *Beauty and Sensibility in the*
    Thought of Jonathan Edwards: An Essay in Aesthetics and
    Theological Ethics. New Haven, 1968.
    A revision of Delattre's doctoral dissertation.

    "The conviction upon which this book rests and the
validity of which it is designed to demonstrate is that
the aesthetic aspect of Jonathan Edwards' thought and
vision, which finds its definitive formulation in his
concepts of beauty and sensibility, provides a larger
purchase upon the distinctive features of his thought
than does any other aspect, such as the idealist,
empiricist, sensationalist, Platonist, scholastic,

Calvinist, or mystic."

Delattre provides a structural analysis of the twin concepts of beauty and sensibility. The volume does not make for easy reading; as one critic has observed, "It is a pity that a study likely to be of great interest to students of American literature should be so dense." Students of philosophy or theology will find it no less so.

Reviews

Davidson, Edward H. *American Literature*, 41 (1969), 282-283.

Holbrook, Clyde A. *New England Quarterly*, 42 (1969), 310-312.

Wilson, John F. *Union Seminary Quarterly Review*, 24 (1968), 107-109.

Delattre, Roland Andre. "Beauty and Theology: A Reappraisal of Jonathan Edwards." *Soundings*, 51 (1968), 60-79.

Delattre rehearses the central insights of his *Beauty and Sensibility*.

DeNormandie, James. "Jonathan Edwards at Portsmouth, New Hampshire." *Proceedings of the Massachusetts Historical Society*, series 2, 15 (1902), 16-20.

An account of Edwards' visit to Portsmouth in June, 1749, where he preached the sermon at the installation of the new minister, Job Strong. It was on this occasion that the Rev. Moody, flustered by having sung the praises of Edwards while unaware of his presence, remarked: "I didn't intend to flatter you to your face; but there's one thing I'll tell you; they say your wife is going to heaven by a shorter road than yourself." Includes extracts from a letter from

Edwards to his daughter Mary.

DeProspo, Richard Chris. "Nature and Spirit in the Writings
of Jonathan Edwards." Doctoral dissertation, University
of Virginia, 1977. In *Dissertation Abstracts
International*, 39 (1979), 4255A.
This study "examines Edwards' theories of Creation,
Providence, and Grace in an attempt to show the consistency with which he reconciled a complex, and increasingly secular historical experience with a conservative
theology according to which nature and spirit were
analogous, but distantly related."

DeProspo, Richard Chris. "The 'New Simple Idea' of
Edwards' *Personal Narrative*." *Early American
Literature*, 14 (1979), 193-204.
"The desultory structure and unspecific style of the
Personal Narrative signify both his harmonizing of
Locke's psychology with Puritan piety, and his
attempting in a deliberate and highly literate way to
make spiritual autobiography reflect his deepest
religious beliefs. Edwards' theoretical understanding
of the 'new simple idea' of Grace and his personal
descriptions of it, I will try to show, are perfectly
consistent."

Dewey, Edward Hooker. "Jonathan Edwards." In *American
Writers on American Literature*, ed. John Macy. New
York, 1931, pp. 13-24.
A verbose and somewhat vague consideration of Edwards
as a literary artist.
"Artistic justice must give to Edwards the earlier
palm, for, loathing evil as he worshipped sanctity, he
clothed his hatred in memorable words. Although the

sentiment and doctrine are repellent, the phrasing is
admirable."

DeWitt, John. "Historical Sketch of Princeton University."
   In *Memorial Book of the Sesquicentennial Celebration
   of the Founding of the College of New Jersey and of the
   Ceremonies Inaugurating Princeton University.* New York,
   1898, pp. 315-453.
   Includes a brief account of the administration of
   President Edwards.

DeWitt, John. "Jonathan Edwards: A Study." In *Jonathan
   Edwards. Union Meeting of the Berkshire North and South
   Conferences, Stockbridge, Massachusetts. October 5,
   1903.* Stockbridge, 1903. Reprinted in *Princeton
   Theological Review,* 2 (1904), 88-109; and in *Biblical
   and Theological Studies, by Members of the Faculty of
   Princeton Theological Seminary.* New York, 1912,
   pp. 109-136.
   A study of the spirituality of Edwards, seen as a key
   factor in understanding his life and thought. Still
   worth consulting.
      "We shall agree," observes DeWitt, "that the inward
   career of Edwards was singularly self-consistent; that
   from its beginning to its close it is exceptionally free
   from incongruities and contradictions; that in him
   Wordsworth's line, 'The child is father to the man,'
   finds signal illustration." When one finds a life so
   unified, DeWitt continues, "whose development along its
   own lines has not been hindered or distorted by external
   disturbances," one naturally looks for its principle of
   unity, some "master key" which will open to us the heart
   of his life and thought. DeWitt finds this master key
   in Edwards' spirituality and attempts to demonstrate how

it manifested itself "in the work to which he gave
himself, in the subjects on which he labored, in his
method of treatment, in the conclusions he reached...."

Dexter, Franklin Bowditch. *Biographical Sketches of the
    Graduates of Yale College, 1701-1745.* New York, 1885.

Dexter, Franklin Bowditch, ed. *Documentary History of Yale
    University.* New Haven, 1916.
    Includes three letters from Edwards, and other allusions
    to him.

Dexter, Franklin Bowditch. "The Manuscripts of Jonathan
    Edwards." *Proceedings of the Massachusetts Historical
    Society,* series 2, 15 (1902), 2-16. Reprinted in
    Dexter, *A Selection from the Miscellaneous Papers of
    Fifty Years.* New Haven, 1918, pp. 235-246.
    A brief account of the history of the Edwards
    manuscripts and the contents of the collection at New
    Haven.

Dexter, Franklin Bowditch. *A Sketch of the History of Yale
    University.* New York, 1887.

[Dod, William Armstrong]. *History of the College of New
    Jersey, from its Commencement, A.D. 1746, to 1783.*
    Princeton, 1844.

Dodds, Elisabeth D. *Marriage to a Difficult Man: The
    Uncommon Union of Jonathan and Sarah Edwards.*
    Philadelphia, 1971.
    A popularized biographical study.

Downes, R. P. "Jonathan Edwards." *Great Thoughts,* series 4,
6 (1900), 296-298.
A popularized sketch of Edwards' life and thought:
"With merciless logic he welded Christianity into a
system as hard as iron, and as cold. This is very
probably the reason why he is now well-nigh forgotten
—his name has died out, despite his splendid
intellect, with the unlovely doctrine which he
preached."

Duff, William Boyd. *Jonathan Edwards, Then and Now: A
Satirical Study of Predestination.* Pittsburgh, 1959.
The title of this volume is somewhat misleading, but a
glance at its contents quickly reveals the difficulties
under which Duff must have labored to find an appropriate designation. One chapter, for example, is
written as a modern day press interview with a resur-
rected Edwards.
Oddly enough, it is not Edwards himself who bears
the brunt of Duff's satire, but those moderns who have
rejected Edwards' vision as antiquated or irrelevant.
Essentially Duff attempts to read Edwards' conclusions
in the light of continuing philosophical discussion and
the discoveries of modern science, asking, "Would our
present light dissipate his primitive notions? Or is
it possible that current thought might be jarred by the
impact of Edwards' genius?" It is the latter question
which Duff answers in the affirmative. Particular
attention is paid to Edwards' notions of causality,
continuous creation, and predestination.

Dunning, Albert Elijah. *Congregationalists in America; A
Popular History of their Origin, Belief, Polity, Growth
and Work.* New York, 1894.

Dwight, Benjamin W. *The History of the Descendants of John
Dwight, of Dedham, Massachusetts.* 2 vols. New York,
1874.
Includes (II, pp. 1036-1043) a brief article on the
Edwards family, with extracts from the inventory of
Jonathan Edwards' estate.

Dwight, Sereno Edwards. *The Life of President Edwards.*
New York, 1830.
The first volume of Dwight's ten volume edition of
Edwards' *Works* (1829-30). Less a biographical essay
than a compilation, this volume remains invaluable for
its wealth of biographical detail and included documents
otherwise unavailable.

Dwight, Timothy. *Travels in New England and New York.*
4 vols. New Haven, 1882.
Includes (IV, pp. 312-316) brief remarks on Edwards as
a man of letters.

*The Edwardean. A Quarterly, Devoted to the History of
Thought in America,* ed. William Harder Squires.
Clinton, New York, 1903-04.
Only four issues of *The Edwardean* appeared. All of the
articles are about Edwards, all were written by
Squires, and all conform to Squires' fundamental
program: "it is his philosophy we commend and seek to
disseminate."
    In the closing pages of this short-lived journal
Squires explains his editorial policy: "the chief
purpose has steadily been to bring to the notice of
those who study Edwards the fact that Edwards was a
philosopher, with a philosophy founded on the most
defensible principles and up to date not only in this

country but in Europe. The great author of
voluntarism was not Schopenhauer, not Wundt, but
Jonathan Edwards.... Edwards will hold his position
and importance in the world's thought by means of his
philosophical contributions. His writings are not
formal, systematic treatises on abstract philosophy;
but his works cannot be comprehended without understanding what is ever dominant in his mind, that the
will of God is the essence of the universe and everything else finds its origin and reality in divine
volition."

Individual articles found in this journal are
listed under Squires.

Edwards, Andrew J. *Short Sketches of the Life and Service
of Jonathan Edwards*. Fort Worth, Texas, 1922.

Edwards, George Perry. "The Edwards Manuscripts." *Journal
of the Presbyterian Historical Society*, 2 (1903),
169-170.
See George Perry Morris.

Edwards, Jonathan, Jr. *A Dissertation Concerning Liberty
and Necessity; Containing Remarks on the Essays of Dr.
Samuel West, and on the Writings of several other
authors, on these subjects*. Worcester, 1797.
A lengthy defense of President Edwards' *Freedom of the
Will*. Edwards Amasa Park considered this work the best
exposition of President Edwards' theory of the will,
while other scholars (such as A. T. Bledsoe) have been
less than satisfied with Dr. Edwards' analysis.

Edwards, Jonathan, Jr. "Remarks on the Improvements Made in
Theology by his Father, President Edwards." In *The*

Works of Jonathan Edwards, D.D., Late President of Union College, ed. Tryon Edwards. Andover, 1842. Vol. I, pp. 481-492.
This essay is significant as an indication of what the Edwardseans had come to consider Edwards' major contributions to theology. It also provides a valuable index to how certain basic features of Edwards' thought had come to be interpreted.

Edwards, Maurice Dwight. *Richard Edwards and his Wife Catherine Pond May: Their Ancestors, Lives and Descendants*. St. Paul, 1931.
Includes brief remarks on the life and influence of Jonathan Edwards.

Edwards, Tryon. "Memoir [of Jonathan Edwards, the Younger]." In *The Works of Jonathan Edwards, D.D., Late President of Union College*, ed. Tryon Edwards. Andover, 1842. Vol. I, pp. ix-xl.
Information concerning the family life of the elder Edwards.

Edwards, Tryon. Quoted in *The Evangelist*, 22 July 1880.
Tryon Edwards responds to the call for the publication of Edwards' suppressed tract on the Trinity:
"Personally I know of no suppression of any opinions of Edwards, much less of any omission or change of expression that would modify, in the least, his well known doctrinal and theological views." See, however, the article by Richard C. Pierce below.

Edwards, William H. *Timothy and Rhoda Ogden Edwards of Stockbridge, Massachusetts, and their Descendants*. Cincinnati, 1903.

Includes (pp. 6-15) a brief account of Jonathan Edwards.

"The Edwards Bicentennial." *Journal of the Presbyterian Historical Society*, 2 (1903), 166-169.
Summary of various services held, papers delivered, and articles published, in recognition of the two hundredth anniversary of Edwards' birth.

"The Edwards Commemoration." *Outlook*, 65 (1900), 476-477.

"Edwards Number." See *The Congregationalist and Christian World*.

"Edwards Number." Editorial. *Hartford Seminary Record*, 14 (1903), 1.
Notes the dedication of the November issue of the *Record* to papers on Edwards. The editor comments on the late interest in Edwards "aroused all over the country," a "striking testimony to the hold that Edwards has on the imagination of... the present generation." This issue includes the papers by Samuel Simpson and Henry C. King noted below.

"Edwards's Habits and Tastes, as Portrayed by a Contemporary." *Congregationalist and Christian World*, 88 (1903), 471.
Brief excerpt from Hopkins' *Life* of Edwards.

Ellis, Charles Grant. "Ethics of Jonathan Edwards." Doctoral dissertation, New York University, 1910.

Elsbree, O. W. "Samuel Hopkins and his Doctrine of Benevolence." *New England Quarterly*, 8 (1935), 534-550.

Briefly compares Hopkins' doctrine of benevolence with
that of Edwards.

Elwood, Douglas J. *The Philosophical Theology of Jonathan
    Edwards.* New York, 1960.
    In an avowed attempt to reconcile Edwards the philoso-
    pher with Edwards the theologian, Elwood locates the
    principle of correlation in Edwards' doctrine of divine
    immediacy. Edwards, Elwood argues, was essentially a
    panentheist.
        "When he was not absorbed in some controversy or
    other, his reconstruction of Calvinism often took the
    form of an attempt at synthesis of the main lines of
    thought in traditional theism and classical pantheism.
    ...Much of his thought makes sense as a coherent—
    however unfinished—system only as it is seen in the
    context of the discussion of a theology of the 'third
    way.'"
        Elwood is concerned to demonstrate the essential
    modernity of Edwards, suggesting that it is at points
    where Edwards appears to deviate from the main line of
    Puritan thought "that the present day student has most
    to learn from America's most neglected theologian."
    Reviews and Criticisms
    Schafer, Thomas A. *American Literature,* 33 (1961),
        379-380.
    Whittemore, Robert C. "Jonathan Edwards and the
        Theology of the Sixth Way." *Church History,* 35
        (1966), 60-75.
    Winslow, Ola E. *New England Quarterly,* 34 (1961),
        255-257.

Emerson, Everett H. "Jonathan Edwards." In *Fifteen
    American Authors before 1900: Bibliographic Essays on*

Research and Criticism, ed. Robert A. Rees and Earl N.
Harbert. Madison, Wisconsin, 1971, pp. 169-184.
A fairly comprehensive and critical bibliographical
essay on twentieth century Edwards scholarship.

Erdt, Terrence. "The Calvinist Psychology of the Heart and
the 'Sense' of Jonathan Edwards." *Early American
Literature,* 13 (1978), 165-180.
Erdt examines the Calvinist psychology of the heart "so
that it and the subsequent Puritan version of it might
be seen as available to Edwards, informing his view of
regeneration as an aesthetic experience."

Erdt, Terrence. "Jonathan Edwards on Art and the Sense of
the Heart." Doctoral dissertation, University of
California, Santa Barbara, 1977.

Evans, W. Glyn. "Jonathan Edwards: Puritan Paradox."
Bibliotheca Sacra, 124 (1967), 51-65.
"As far as his stature as a theologian and philosopher
is concerned, opinion seems solidified. He was a
greatly gifted mind who squandered his talents on
theological trifles."
A vague and inconclusive attempt to explain Edwards'
effectiveness as a preacher.

*Exercises Commemorating the Two-Hundredth Anniversary of the
Birth of Jonathan Edwards, Held at Andover Theological
Seminary, October 4 and 5, 1903.* Andover, 1904.
Contents
Commemorative Sermon, by William Rogers Richards,
pp. 13-28.
Introductory Address, Religious Conditions in New
England in the Time of Edwards, by John W. Platner,

pp. 29-45.

The Philosophy of Edwards, by Frederick J. E.
    Woodbridge, pp. 47-72.

The Theology of Edwards, by Egbert C. Smyth, pp. 73-93.

A Witness to the Truth, by Samuel V. Cole, pp. 95-103.

The Influence of Edwards, by James Orr, pp. 105-126.

Appendix I: Extracts from the *Miscellanies* originally
    transcribed by Sereno E. Dwight and supplied here
    by Egbert C. Smyth (pp. 1-60).

Appendix II: Loan Exhibition. Partial list of the
    Edwards memorabilia on exhibit (pp. 61-65).

Fairbairn, A. M. "Prophets of the Christian Faith: VIII.
    Jonathan Edwards." *Outlook,* 53 (1896), 930-932.
    Reprinted in *The Prophets of the Christian Faith* by
    Fairbairn *et al.* New York, 1896, pp. 145-166.
    Edwards' "grim and terrible sermons," Fairbairn
    suggests, do not reveal the essence of his mind; they
    "were not the creations of his reason, which was
    Edwards's master faculty, but the work of his imagi-
    nation in a peculiar mood—as it were epic pictures
    thrown out while it was intoxicated with a spiritual
    passion or drenched by the wave of religious enthusiasm
    then rolling over New England." In truth, Fairbairn
    suggests, "the distinctive theology of Edwards was of
    quite another order, the creation of a reason all alive
    with speculative passion, and moved as if by an
    infinite hunger for the divine."
        Fairbairn attempts a brief exposition of the
    "heart" of Edwards' thought, drawing primarily upon his
    early idealistic conclusions, his speculations on God's
    end in creation, and his conception of the nature of
    virtue. Superficial.

Faust, Clarence H. "The Decline of Puritanism." In
Transitions in American Literary History, ed. Harry H.
Clark. Durham, 1953, pp. 3-47.
Faust examines Edwards' efforts to arrest the decline
of Puritanism "by reinterpreting Calvinistic theology
in the terms current in late seventeenth and early
eighteenth century philosophy."

Faust, Clarence H. *Ideological Conflicts in Early American
Books.* Syracuse, New York, 1958.

Faust, Clarence H. "Jonathan Edwards as a Scientist."
American Literature, 1 (1930), 393-404.
In response to a growing body of literature that views
the young Edwards as a scientific genius somehow lost
to the world of theology, Faust attempts a more
realistic estimate of Edwards' scientific abilities and
achievements, and seeks to place Edwards' scientific
interests in proper perspective.

Faust, Clarence H. "Jonathan Edwards' View of Human
Nature." Doctoral dissertation, University of Chicago,
1935.

Faust, Clarence H., and Johnson, Thomas H., eds. *Jonathan
Edwards: Representative Selections, With Introduction,
Bibliography and Notes.* New York, 1935; rev. ed. New
York, 1962.
"Edwards's whole thought life... was centered about the
deep conviction of the all-sufficient, all-encompassing
power of God which had mastered him as a young man.
This power he delighted to contemplate and made it his
chief purpose in life to proclaim. The conception of
it is basic in all his theorizing, much as that

theorizing was influenced by the psychological and
philosophical beliefs current in his day."

Faust's introductory essay on "Jonathan Edwards as
a Thinker" (pp. xiv-xcviii) remains the best general
introduction to Edwards' thought. Johnson contributes
an excellent, if brief, analysis of "Edwards as a Man
of Letters" (pp. xcviii-cxv) in which he discusses
Edwards' literary models and his literary style.

Major divisions of the annotated bibliography are
texts, biography and criticism, and background material
for the study of Edwards. The original bibliography
was updated for the 1962 edition by Stephen S. Webb.
All items cited by Webb under biography and criticism
can be found in this bibliography.

Reviews

Carpenter, Frederic I. *New England Quarterly,* 9 (1936),
    174-175.

Schneider, Herbert W. *Journal of Philosophy,* 33 (1936),
    327.

Fay, Jay Wharton. *American Psychology before William James.*
    New Brunswick, New Jersey, 1939.
    Includes a somewhat superficial discussion of Edwards'
    psychological theories and his studies of the "varieties
    of religious experience."

    "His influence was great along theological lines,
    and his reputation as a metaphysician reached across the
    Atlantic. In psychology he illustrates the conclusions
    a rigorous logic can reach from data supplied by
    imperfect observation and inadequate analysis."

Feaver, John Clayton. "Jonathan Edwards' Concept of God as
    Redeemer." Doctoral dissertation, Yale University,
    1949.

Ferm, Robert L. *Jonathan Edwards the Younger: 1745-1801.*
   Grand Rapids, 1976.
   Ferm analyzes the theology of the younger Edwards in
   relation to the thought of President Edwards: "The
   strain of New England theology represented by Edwards
   the Younger, Joseph Bellamy, and Samuel Hopkins took its
   departure from the theological labors of Jonathan
   Edwards, Sr. ...but these men departed swiftly from the
   central thrust of their teacher's thought. All of them
   honed their dialectical skills on specific issues raised
   by Edwards, Sr. ...But they were first of all defenders
   of Edwardsean theology, not original thinkers themselves, and in defending his thought they gave it a new
   and legalistic character."

Ferm, Vergilius. "Jonathan Edwards—Puritan Sage."
   Christian Century, 70 (1953), 1104-1106.
   A popularized account of the life and influence of
   Jonathan Edwards.
      "Edwards defended a lost cause—lost because men
   find that, however convincingly conclusions follow
   from premises the premises must sooner or later conform
   to rough experience. The God of Jonathan Edwards was
   too aristocratic for the expanding frontier life of
   America."

Fiering, Norman S. "Will and Intellect in the New England
   Mind." *William and Mary Quarterly,* series 3,
   29 (1972), 515-558.
   An important study. Fiering challenges Miller's appraisal of the influence of Newton and Locke on Edwards.

Fisher, George Park. *A Discourse Commemorative of the*
   History of the Church of Christ in Yale College, during

the First Century of its Existence. New Haven, 1858.
Reviewing the religious history of Yale College and
"what the College has done for theological science,"
Fisher briefly recounts the role of its graduates in the
rise and development of the New England Theology. "The
fathers of the New England theology—Edwards, Bellamy,
Hopkins, West, Smalley, Emmons, and Dwight—went forth
from Yale. The younger Jonathan Edwards is the only one
of the leading expounders of the New Divinity who was
educated elsewhere.... These men, and especially the
foremost one among them, who gave impulse to all the
rest, have strongly influenced the thinking of the age."

Fisher, George Park. *History of Christian Doctrine.* New
   York, 1896; rpt. 1923.
   Includes (pp. 395-410) a concise and reliable outline of
   the substance of Edwards' major works with particular
   attention to his doctrine of virtue.

Fisher, George Park. "The Philosophy of Jonathan Edwards."
   North American Review, 128 (1879), 284-303. Reprinted
   in Fisher, *Discussions in History and Theology.* New
   York, 1880, pp. 227-252.
   An excellent critical analysis of Edwards' thought,
   still worth consulting. At the time this article was
   written Fisher was of the opinion that "Edwards was a
   Berkeleian," though he was later less inclined to think
   so. See Fisher's *An Unpublished Essay of Edwards on the
   Trinity.*
      "If it be true that, in the last century, Berkeley,
   Hume, and Kant, are the three great names in philosophy,
   there might have been added to the brief catalogue, had
   he chosen to devote himself exclusively to metaphysics,
   the name of Jonathan Edwards."

Fisher, George Park. "Professor Allen's Life of Jonathan
Edwards." *New Englander and Yale Review,* 52 (1890),
85-88.
Review of A. V. G. Allen's *Life and Writings of
Jonathan Edwards* (Boston, 1889).

Fisher, George Park, ed. *An Unpublished Essay of Edwards
on the Trinity, With Remarks on Edwards and his
Theology.* New York, 1903.
Fisher provides (pp. 1-74) a perceptive analysis of
Edwards as a theologian, still worth consulting.
Reviews
W[alker], W[illiston]. "Edwards's Recovered Treatise."
Yale Alumni Weekly, 13 (4 November 1903), 106-107.
Nation, 77 (1903), 384.

Fisher, George Park. "The Value of Edwards for Today."
Congregationalist and Christian World, 88 (1903),
469-471.
"I thought of beginning by styling him 'The Saint and
Theologian of New England.' But this would perhaps be
considered an extravagant encomium. Nevertheless, I
believe it to be at least true that no other comes so
near deserving this title, if genius as a theological
thinker and holiness as a Christian believer are the
qualifications for this distinction."
Fisher briefly comments on those aspects of Edwards'
thought of potential significance for modern thinkers,
and his historical significance in the development of
the New England Theology. Superficial.

Fiske, Daniel T. "New England Theology." *Bibliotheca
Sacra,* 22 (1865), 467-512; 568-588.
A systematic study of "some of the peculiar and more

important doctrines" of the New England theologians,
namely their views of the nature of sin, of holiness,
original sin, natural ability, regeneration, the atonement, and divine decrees. Fiske is careful to detail
the important differences of opinion among the New
England theologians themselves on various doctrines,
and notes at what points the New England Theology in
general appears to diverge from the theology of Edwards.
Edwards, Fiske argues, "only laid the foundation of the
system, contributing little to the form of the super-
structure, while he retained some views inconsistent
with the fundamental principles of the system which he
founded."

Flower, Elizabeth, and Murphey, Murray G. "Jonathan
    Edwards." In their *History of Philosophy in America*.
    New York, 1977. Vol. I, pp. 137-199.
    "In his defense of Calvinism, Edwards formulated a
    theology, and a philosophy, which entitle him to
    the rank of the greatest American philosopher before
    the Civil War."
        An extensive, critical discussion of Edwards'
    theology and philosophy. The analysis provided of
    Edwards' early speculations is particularly valuable
    and in many respects the best available.

Flynt, William T. "Jonathan Edwards and his Preaching."
    Doctoral dissertation, Southern Baptist Theological
    Seminary, 1954.

Foster, Frank Hugh. "The Eschatology of the New England
    Divines." *Bibliotheca Sacra*, 43 (1886), 1-32.
    The first in a series of five articles in which Foster
    traces the development of eschatological thinking and

the doctrine of the atonement in New England Theology, with particular reference to the Universalist controversy. Only the initial article discusses Edwards at length, focusing on his thoughts concerning the future punishment of the wicked and the happiness of the saints; however, in the remaining articles developing ideas in the New England schools are frequently analyzed in relation to Edwards. Subsequent articles in this series: 43 (1886), 287-303; 710-727; 45 (1888), 669-694; 46 (1889), 95-123. See also chapter eight of Foster's *Genetic History*.

Foster, Frank Hugh. *A Genetic History of the New England Theology*. Chicago, 1907.
The only comprehensive history of the New England Theology. An extensive critical analysis of Edwards' theology is provided, focusing on what Edwards contributed to the improvement of the system which he had received from his teachers, and what ideas of Edwards were seminal for later divines of the New England schools. Foster pays particular attention to Edwards' theory of the will which in his reading proves to be of central significance in the subsequent development of the New England Theology.

"[Edwards] was profoundly attached to the Calvinistic system, and his first instinct was to restore it to its high place of influence. This was so far well, and he was hereby preserved from the first great danger of a leader at such a time, that of disloyalty to the past. But, though he may have had no thought of doctrinal change, his mind was too original and his studies too exact to let him remain where his fathers had been."

Reviews and Criticisms
Nation, 84 (1907), 459.
Outlook, 86 (1907), 120.
Haroutunian, Joseph G. *Piety Versus Moralism: The Passing of the New England Theology*. New York, 1932.

Foster, Frank Hugh. "Jonathan Edwards." In *New Schaff-Herzog Encyclopedia of Religious Knowledge*. New York, 1909. Vol. IV, pp. 80-82.
Biographical sketch with list of Edwards' major publications.

Foster, Frank Hugh. "New England Theology." In *New Schaff-Herzog Encyclopedia of Religious Knowledge*. New York, 1910. Vol. VIII, pp. 130-140.
A condensed, and condensed again, version of Foster's *Genetic History*.

Foster, J. Review of Jonathan Edwards' *Faithful Narrative*. *The Eclectic Review*, 4 (1808), 548-550.

Foster, Mary Catherine. "Hampshire County, Massachusetts, 1729-1754: A Covenant Society in Transition." Doctoral dissertation, University of Michigan, 1967. In *Dissertation Abstracts*, 28 (1968), 2620A.

Foster, W. E. "The Speculative Philosophy of Jonathan Edwards." *Monthly Reference Lists*, 3 (1883), 42.
A bibliography of biography and criticism of Edwards. All items cited by Foster can be found in this bibliography.

Frankena, William K., ed. *The Nature of True Virtue*. Ann
    Arbor, Michigan, 1960.
    In the Foreword to this edition Frankena provides a
    widely quoted but somewhat superficial and often
    misleading analysis of Edwards' doctrine of virtue.
    Frankena contends that "Edwards' essay was the beginning
    of a tradition of teleological and utilitarian thinking
    which strongly opposed the deontological intuitionism
    prevailing in American ethics in the nineteenth
    century." In view of the strong anti-utilitarian thrust
    of *The Nature of True Virtue* it is, as Delattre has
    observed, a "curious assertion" for Frankena to make.

Fraser, Alexander Campbell. *The Life and Letters of George
    Berkeley*. Oxford, 1871, pp. 182, 190.
    Fraser is the first to suggest that Edwards "adopted"
    and was "an able defender of Berkeley's great philosoph-
    ical principle." See, however, Fraser's second edition
    of Berkeley's *Works* (1901), Vol. III, p. 393.

Frothingham, W. "The Edwards Family." *Continental Monthly*,
    1 (1862), 11-16.
    Frothingham incidentally refers to Jonathan Edwards in
    this brief review of events in the life of Judge Ogden
    Edwards, a man "of an ancient and noble stock, being
    grandson of the author of the treatise on the *Freedom
    of the Will*." Ogden was the son of Pierrepont Edwards.

Frothingham, W. "Jonathan Edwards and the Old Clergy."
    Continental Monthly, 1 (1862), 265-272.
    "This man [Edwards] has but two pursuits, study and
    prayer. Of the other world he has ever remained in
    blissful ignorance, and even of his own parish he only
    knows what he has learned of his wife.... The secret of

this is, that he breathes an atmosphere of his own; his
soul is like a star and dwells apart."
    Frothingham briefly surveys a number of the early
New England clergy, describing them as men of "studious
and prayerful habits," and noting their permanent
influence on the New England character. Discussion of
Edwards is brief and superficial.

Fye, Kenneth Paul. "Jonathan Edwards on Freedom of the
    Will." Doctoral dissertation, Boston University
    Graduate School, 1977. In *Dissertation Abstracts
    International*, 37 (1977), 7789A-7790A.

Gabler, Ulrich. "Die Anfange der Erwectungsbewegung in Neu-
    England und Jonathan Edwards." *Theologische Zeitschrift*,
    34 (1978), 95-104.

Gardiner, Harry Norman. "The Early Idealism of Jonathan
    Edwards." *Philosophical Review*, 9 (1900), 573-596.
    Reprinted with variant title in *Jonathan Edwards: A
    Retrospect*, ed. Harry Norman Gardiner. Boston, 1901,
    pp. 113-160.
    An influential article. Gardiner investigates the
    sources of Edwards' idealism and estimates the signifi-
    cance of this philosophy for Edwards' subsequent
    thought. It can be shown, Gardiner contends, "both that
    the conception was with him an original expression of
    personal insight, and that there is no reason to suppose
    that he ever abandoned it; that in short, it was no
    mere accidental product of youthful fancy, or echo of
    another's teaching, but was intimately connected with
    the deepest and most permanent elements of his specula-
    tion."

Gardiner, Harry Norman, ed. *Jonathan Edwards: A Retrospect. Being the Addresses Delivered in Connection with the Unveiling of a Memorial in the First Church of Christ in Northampton, Massachusetts, on the One Hundred and Fiftieth Anniversary of his Dismissal from the Pastorate of that Church.* Boston, 1901.

These essays are published, Gardiner notes in his Introduction, "not merely as a memorial of an interesting event in the history of a local church, but as a contribution to the understanding of an event of wider historical significance, and of a great but only too often misjudged character." In this volume, Gardiner observes, most of Edwards' appreciative students and admirers choose to represent him "less as a theologian than as a prophet of the Christian faith, an interpreter of human life, a force in religious experience, and profess to see in him less affinity with Calvin than with Dante...."

Contents

Introduction, by Harry Norman Gardiner, pp. v-xvi.

The Place of Edwards in History, by A. V. G. Allen, pp. 1-31.

The Influence of Edwards on the Spiritual Life of New England, by Egbert C. Smyth, pp. 33-48.

The Significance of Edwards To-Day, by George A. Gordon, pp. 49-74.

Greetings

From Yale University, by George P. Fisher, pp. 75-79.

From Princeton University, by Alexander T. Ormond, pp. 80-86.

Edwards in Northampton, by Henry T. Rose, pp. 87-111.

The Early Idealism of Edwards, by Harry Norman Gardiner, pp. 113-160.

Appendix: Record of the Dedication, Prayer by Rev.
   Peter McMillan, Address of Welcome by Henry T. Rose,
   pp. 161-168.

Gardiner, Harry Norman, and Webster, Richard.   "Jonathan
   Edwards." *Encyclopedia Britannica*. 11th edition.
   Vol. IX, pp. 3-6.
   Summary sketch of Edwards' life and thought, and an
   evaluation of Edwards as a thinker. In outlining "The
   Edwardean System," Webster and Gardiner suggest that
   "the best criticism of Edwards' philosophy as a whole
   is that, instead of being elaborated on purely rational
   principles, it is mixed up with a system of theological
   conceptions with which it is never thoroughly combined,
   and that it is exposed to all the disturbing effects of
   theological controversy." This defect notwithstanding,
   Edwards is claimed as "the most able metaphysician and
   most influential religious thinker in America."

Gaustad, Edwin Scott. *The Great Awakening in New England*.
   New York, 1957.
   Now a standard work on the Great Awakening, Gaustad
   focuses on its "religious effects, institutional and
   theological." The chapter devoted to the Edwards-
   Chauncy debate is particularly valuable.

Gay, Peter. "Jonathan Edwards: An American Tragedy." In
   his *A Loss of Mastery: Puritan Historians in Colonial
   America*. Berkeley, 1966, pp. 88-117.
   Gay challenges Perry Miller's claims for Edwards as a
   modern "historian" through an examination of his *History
   of the Work of Redemption*. Contrasting this work with
   contemporary developments in modern historiography, Gay
   finds Edwards' *History* "reactionary" and "fundamental-

ist." It is "Calvinistic doctrine exemplified in a distinct succession of transcendent moments." Gay concludes that,"Far from being the first modern American ... he was the last medieval American—at least among the intellectuals." Includes a brief bibliographical essay on Edwards, pp. 153-157.

George, E. A. "Jonathan Edwards." *Yale Literary Magazine,* 50 (1884), 7-11.

Gerstner, John H. "American Calvinism until the Twentieth Century." In *American Calvinism: A Survey,* ed. Jacob T. Hoogstra. Grand Rapids, 1957, pp. 13-39. Within the context of a wider discussion of American Calvinism, Gerstner attempts a brief, concise statement of Edwards' position within the Calvinistic tradition.

Gerstner, John H. "Outline of the Apologetics of Jonathan Edwards." *Bibliotheca Sacra,* 133 (1976), 3-10; 99-107.

Gerstner, John H. *Steps to Salvation: The Evangelistic Message of Jonathan Edwards.* Philadelphia, 1959. A systematic study of Edwards' theory of evangelism. Drawing upon both published and unpublished sermons, Gerstner details Edwards' conception of the "steps" to salvation, from the Word of God, through the various workings of the Holy Spirit, from conviction to conversion. Edwards, Gerstner argues, was from first to last a predestinarian evangelist: he preached with equal vigor and insistence the responsibility of men and the ultimate and absolute sovereignty of God in the work of salvation.
Reviews
Braden, Charles S. *Christian Century,* 77 (1960), 696.

Heimert, Alan. *American Literature,* 32 (1960), 470-473.

Gillett, E. H. "The Clerical Members of the Council that
    Dismissed Jonathan Edwards from Northampton."
    Historical Magazine, series 2, 2 (1867), 183.
    Gillett attempts to determine the composition of the
    council and the particular line taken by its individual
    members. This study is concluded by Gillett in the same
    journal, series 2, 3 (1868), 53.

Gillett, E. H. "Jonathan Edwards, and the Occasion and
    Result of his Dismission from Northampton." *Historical
    Magazine,* series 2, 1 (1867), 333-338.
    Gillett details the events surrounding Edwards'
    dismissal from Northampton.

Gillette, Gerald. "A Checklist of Doctoral Dissertations
    on American Presbyterian and Reformed Subjects, 1912-
    1965." *Journal of Presbyterian History,* 45 (1967),
    203-221.
    Includes a comprehensive list of dissertations on
    Edwards, all of which can be found in this bibliography.

Godwin, William. *Enquiry concerning Political Justice.* 3rd
    rev. ed. London, 1798.
    In a brief marginal note, Godwin acknowledges that
    Edwards' treatise on *The Nature of True Virtue* suggested
    the line of thought developed in his discussion of
    gratitude. Godwin's ackowledgement of this treatise and
    his implicit interpretation of Edwards' doctrine of
    virtue were important factors in the nineteenth century
    controversy over *The Nature of True Virtue.*

Godwin, William. *Thoughts Occasioned by the Perusal of Dr. Parr's Spital Sermon, Preached at Christ Church, April 15, 1800.* London, 1801.
Godwin responds to Parr's strictures concerning his interpretation of Edwards.
"I affixed his name to the page, merely from a spirit of frankness, because in reality it was Jonathan Edwards's Essay there referred to, which first led me into the train of thinking on that point exhibited in Political Justice; and I believed it would be unmanly to suppress the name of my benefactor. If any person is either amused or instructed by Dr. Parr's distinction between virtue and true virtue, in order to prove that, though Jonathan Edwards denied gratitude to be true virtue, he admitted it to be virtue simply taken, I confess I have too much humanity to be willing to disturb his enjoyments."

Goen, C. C., ed. *The Great Awakening.* Volume IV of *The Works of Jonathan Edwards.* New Haven, 1972.
In his critical Introduction to this volume (pp. 1-94), Goen recounts the basic theological questions at issue in the criticisms and defense of the revival, provides an exposition of the various texts included in this volume largely in relation to the historical context in which they were written, and provides a particularly valuable account of their often confusing publication history. His notes on the texts should not be ignored. While Goen attempts little in the way of interpretation, his study is basic to any future analysis of "what Edwards was up to during the Great Awakening, and why."
Reviews
Cherry, C. Conrad. "Promoting the Cause and Testing the Spirits: Jonathan Edwards on Revivals of

Religion." *Journal of Presbyterian History,*
51 (1973), 327-337.
Hall, David C. *New England Quarterly,* 45 (1972),
455-457.

Goen, C. C. "Jonathan Edwards: A New Departure in
Eschatology." *Church History,* 28 (1959), 25-40.
"Edwards' doctrine of the last things, so far as it
describes the final End beyond history, is but a full
and realistic elucidation of concepts generally accepted
in the orthodox Calvinistic tradition. When he undertakes to construct the historical events preceding the
final consummation, however, he introduces a radical
innovation which had decisive consequences for the
future." Edwards' innovation, Goen argues, is his
belief in "a golden age for the church on earth, within
history, and achieved through the ordinary processes of
propagating the gospel in the power of the Holy Spirit."
Goen suggests that Edwards' conception of an imminent
millenium within ordinary history was "a definitive
factor in the religious background of the idea of
progress."

Gohdes, Clarence. "Aspects of Idealism in Early New
England." *Philosophical Review,* 39 (1930), 537-555.
Tracing the influence of the Cambridge Platonists in
America, Gohdes suggests Theophilus Gale as a possible
source of Edwards' early idealism.

Goodwin, Gerald J. "The Myth of 'Arminian-Calvinism' in
Eighteenth-Century New England." *New England Quarterly,*
41 (1968), 213-237.
Goodwin challenges the traditional reading of the
religious situation of Edwards' day which finds a

gradual "transformation of Calvinism into an
intellectual convention which hid the reality of
Arminianism." Goodwin argues that such interpreters
"have created a myth because Arminian-Calvinism never
existed." New England Congregationalists, Goodwin
contends, "self-consciously clung to Calvinist theological doctrines throughout the early eighteenth century
up to and through the Great Awakening." Thus Edwards,
Goodwin insists, cannot properly be painted as
"America's first authentic Calvinist because he... over-
leaped New England's doctrinal heritage to restate pure
Calvinism in modern terms," nor is the Great Awakening
properly seen as a struggle to uproot Arminian-
Calvinism and the spiritual lethargy that accompanied
it.

Gordon, George A. "The Significance of Edwards To-Day."
In *Jonathan Edwards: A Retrospect*, ed. Harry Norman
Gardiner. Boston, 1901, pp. 49-74.
"The purpose of this address is simply to emphasize the
importance of the attitude of critical homage to
Edwards."
A generalized but critical discussion of Edwards'
theology and the now inevitable evaluation of Edwards
as a thinker. "The greatest distinction of Edwards,"
suggests Gordon, "is as a theologian. The one supreme
thing in him that insures his permanence as a teacher
is his thought of God." What must also be acknowledged,
however, is Edwards' "failure to understand man."
According to Gordon, Edwards' "theology discredits his
anthropology; his idea of God, his conception of man;
his views of divine perfection, his scheme for human
salvation." In Edwards "as in no other great writer, a
glorious theology is brought into contradiction with a

doctrine of man which at best is inadequate, and which
at worst is incredible."

Grabo, Norman S. "Jonathan Edwards' *Personal Narrative:*
Dynamic Stasis." *Literatur in Wissenschaft und*
Unterricht, 2 (1969), 141-148.

Grant, Leonard T. "A Preface to Jonathan Edwards' Financial
Difficulties." *Journal of Presbyterian History,*
45 (1967), 27-32.
Grant produces a cash receipt written by Edwards in May
of 1742, indicating that he was forced to borrow money
against his overdue salary to provide for his family.
The receipt was found in an Edinburgh bookstall, pasted
to the inside front cover of a first edition of Hopkins'
Life of Edwards.

Grazier, James Lewis. "The Preaching of Jonathan Edwards:
A Study of his Published Sermons with Special Reference
to the Great Awakening." Doctoral dissertation, Temple
University, 1958.

Green, Ashbel. *Discourses Delivered in the College of New-*
Jersey; Addressed Chiefly to Candidates for the First
Degree in the Arts: With Notes and Illustrations,
Including an Historical Sketch of the College from its
Origin to the Accession of President Witherspoon.
Philadelphia, 1822.
In his historical sketch of the college Green (pp. 313-
326) reviews the brief administration of President
Edwards, and transcribes minutes of the Princeton
trustee meetings pertaining to Edwards' election to
the presidency. Also includes a brief biographical
sketch of Edwards admittedly drawn from a number of

previously published accounts.

Greene, W[illiam] B[atchelder]. *Remarks in Refutation of the Treatise of Jonathan Edwards, on the Freedom of the Will.* West Brookfield, Mass., 1848.

Griffin, Edward M. *Jonathan Edwards.* University of Minnesota Pamphlets on American Writers. No. 97. Minneapolis, 1971.

Griffith, John. "Jonathan Edwards as a Literary Artist." *Criticism,* 15 (1973), 156-173.
Griffith contends that Edwards' ideas are "dead, old-fashioned, quaint," that "the twentieth century reader cannot believe what Edwards asks him to believe." Griffith suggests, however, that as an artist Edwards remains accessible, and he contends that eventually Edwards' writings will be read "as literary through and through."

Griswold, Rufus W. "Jonathan Edwards." In his *Prose Writers of America, 1706-1870.* Rev. ed., Philadelphia, 1847, pp. 53-56.
"In whatever light he is regarded he commands our admiration. He was unequalled in intellect and unsurpassed in virtue."
A brief biographical sketch with even briefer comments concerning Edwards' prose style, his creative imagination, and his preaching ability.

Grosart, Alexander B. "The Handwriting of Famous Divines: Jonathan Edwards, M.A." *The Sunday at Home,* 31 (1897), 458-460.

Gustafson, James Walter. "Causality and Freedom in Jonathan Edwards, Samuel Alexander, and Brand Blanshard." Doctoral dissertation, Boston University Graduate School, 1967. In *Dissertation Abstracts*, 28 (1967), 1848A.

Hageman, John F. *History of Princeton and its Institutions.* 2 vols. Philadelphia, 1879. Includes (II, pp. 249-253) an account of Edwards' administration.

Hall, Robert. *Modern Infidelity Considered.* London, 1799. Included in Hall's collected *Works,* ed. Olinthus Gregory. London, 1866. In a lengthy footnote to this sermon Hall criticizes Edwards' notion of true virtue, said to "perfectly coincide" with that of the "modern infidels."

Hamilton, James E. and Madden, Edward H. "Edwards, Finney, and Mahon on the Derivation of Duties." *Journal of the History of Philosophy,* 13 (1975), 347-360. Edwards is found in odd company. Hamilton and Madden rehearse a complex argument intended to evaluate conflicting judgments as to whether Charles Grandison Finney was a utilitarian, and to demonstrate that Asa Mahon's critique of Finney was successful. Edwards' ethical theory is not considered in any depth; rather, Edwards is introduced as a background figure on the questionable premise that "Finney wholly accepted the general tenets of Edwards' moral philosophy."

Hand, James Albert. "Teleological Aspects of Creation: A Comparison of the Concepts of Being and Meaning in the Theologies of Jonathan Edwards and Paul Tillich." Doctoral dissertation, Vanderbilt University, 1969. In

Dissertation Abstracts International, 30 (1969), 796A.

Hankamer, Ernst W. "Das politische Denken von Jonathan
    Edwards." Doctoral dissertation, University of Munich,
    1972.

Haroutunian, Joseph G. "Jonathan Edwards: A Study in
    Godliness." *Journal of Religion,* 11 (1931), 400-419.
    "He was primarily neither a philosopher nor a theologian
    nor a 'hell-fire preacher.'"
        An unusually able statement of "the essentials of
    Edwards' character and thought." The key to Edwards'
    life and thought, suggests Haroutunian, is to be found in
    Edwards' vision of Godliness. "A survey of his works,"
    Haroutunian argues, "must soon convince a reader that
    his interest centered around investigations into the
    essentials of piety rather than around the particular
    doctrines which were its intellectual symbols."

Haroutunian, Joseph G. "Jonathan Edwards: Theologian of
    the Great Commandment." *Theology Today,* 1 (1944),
    361-377.
    A valuable essay which Haroutunian describes as a
    "prolegomenon to the theology of Edwards." Haroutunian
    elaborates Edwards' radically theocentric vision as an
    alternative to modern theology's profound indifference to
    the glory of God. "The Christian moralist will discover
    in Edwards a love of God which is the essence of all
    true virtue and the condition of justice, peace,
    dignity, and joy among men. But above all, Edwards will
    show us 'God the best Portion of the Christian.'"

Haroutunian, Joseph G. *Piety Versus Moralism: The Passing
    of the New England Theology.* New York, 1932. (Doctoral

dissertation, Columbia University, 1932.)
"As seen from the perspective of the theology of
Edwards, the history of the New England Theology is the
history of a degradation. It declined because its
theocentric character, its supreme regard for the glory
of God and his sovereignty over man, made it ill-fitted
to give expression to the ideals of the eighteenth-
century New England and to meet its immediate social
needs."

Haroutunian provides an excellent analysis of the
theology of Edwards, and details the gradual dissolution
of Edwards' vision as his successors unconsciously
adopted the humanitarian ideals of their rivals and
appropriated their philosophy and social moralism.
Includes an excellent bibliography for the period.

Harper, William Hudson. "Edwards: Devotee, Theologian,
Preacher." *Interior*, 34 (1903), 1272-1274.
A brief tribute to Edwards.

"We in this latter day can but faintly imagine the
compelling power of the words of a man of Edwards'
systematic and precise mental habits, speaking on the
most vital of themes with authority fiercely assertive
and almost superhuman."

Harpole, Ralph Orin. "The Development of the Doctrine of
Atonement in American Thought from Jonathan Edwards to
Horace Bushnell." Doctoral dissertation, Yale
University, 1924. In *Dissertation Abstracts*, 27 (1967),
4253A-4254A.

Harson, Alan G. "The Consistent Preacher: A Preliminary
Investigation of Jonathan Edwards." S.T.M. thesis,
Union Theological Seminary, 1954.

Hart, J. D., ed. "Jonathan Edwards." In *Oxford Companion
to American Literature*. New York, 1917, pp. 217-219.
Brief biographical sketch.

Hart, William S. *Remarks on President Edwards's Dissertation
concerning the Nature of True Virtue: Shewing that he
has given a Wrong Idea and Definition of Virtue, and is
Inconsistent with himself. To which is added an Attempt
to Shew wherein True Virtue does consist*. New Haven,
1771.
The first and the most elaborate criticism of *The Nature
of True Virtue*. Edwards' scheme, Hart argues, "tends to
destroy true virtue and real religion. It represents
virtue as an unnatural thing, places it upon a false and
indefensible foundation, and pours contempt upon it, by
representing its true beauty, and moral excellencies as
of the 'very same sort with the beauty of material
things.' If it is once believed that these are the
doctrines of the bible, christianity will be rejected
with great scorn; but they are not to be found there."

Hawksley, John. *Memoirs of the Reverend Jonathan Edwards*.
London, 1815.
A revised version of Hopkins' *Life* of Edwards, "with
numerous verbal emendations."

Hayes, Samuel Perkins. "An Historical Study of the
Edwardean Revivals." *American Journal of Psychology*,
13 (1902), 550-574.
Concerned with the larger question of the relation of
the Great Awakening to the rise and development of the
New England Theology, Hayes reviews the revival activities of Edwards and the "New Lights," the criticisms of
the revival movement by Chauncy and the "Old Lights,"

and the defense of the revival by Edwards.

"Called upon to meet a situation [Edwards] used the tools at his hands—he preached the Calvinism that was his by birthright and by training—but all the time his mind was intent upon the needs of the times and he used his theology as a means toward the ends of higher morality and a purer personal religion. Out of his attempt to explain the facts of his own religious experience and that of many of his hearers in terms of Calvinism, grew up the New England Theology; out of his experience in revival work grew up the working principle of the 'New Light' party—'Press unto the Kingdom.'"

In this analysis Hayes' primary focus is on two theological questions that were at issue in the criticism and defense of the revival: What is the nature of conversion, and, What must we do to be saved.

Hazard, Rowland Gibson. *Freedom of the Mind in Willing; Or, Every Being that Wills, a Creative Cause.* New York, 1866.
Includes (pp. 173-455) an extensive critique of *Freedom of the Will.*

Heam, Rosemary. "Stylistic Analysis of the Sermons of Jonathan Edwards." Doctoral dissertation, Indiana University, 1973. In *Dissertation Abstracts International*, 34 (1973), 1858A.

Heimert, Alan. "American Oratory: From the Great Awakening to the Election of Jefferson." Doctoral dissertation, Harvard University, 1960.

Heimert, Alan. *Religion and the American Mind: From the Great Awakening to the American Revolution.* Cambridge,

Mass., 1966.

A revisionist interpretation of the role of evangelical religion, and Edwards, in the formation of revolutionary ideals in eighteenth century America. Heimert argues that "Calvinism, and Edwards, provided pre-revolutionary America with a radical, even democratic, social and political ideology, and evangelical religion embodied, and inspired, a thrust toward American nationalism." Edwards' eschatology, Heimert contends, articulates the belief in a dawning New Age in which America would play a primary role. Edwards "made not God but men... the noblest object of Christian regard;" and "in substance, the God of Jonathan Edwards was a supremely excellent Christian commonwealth." The real content of Edwards' thought, suggests Heimert, is directed toward a "union of Americans."

As befits the work of a student of Perry Miller, Heimert's study is nothing if not controversial.

Reviews and Criticisms

Bryant, Marcus Darrol. "History and Eschatology in Jonathan Edwards: A Critique of the Heimert Thesis." Doctoral dissertation, Institute of Christian Thought, University of St. Michael's College, 1976.

Handy, Robert T. *Union Seminary Quarterly Review,* 22 (1967), 267-269.

McLoughlin, William S. "The American Revolution as a Religious Revival: 'The Millenium in One Country.'" *New England Quarterly,* 40 (1967), 99-110.

Mead, Sidney E. "Through and Beyond the Lines." *Journal of Religion,* 48 (1968), 274-288.

Middlekauff, Robert. *American Historical Review,* 72 (1967), 1482-1483.

Morgan, Edmund S. *William and Mary Quarterly,* series 3,

    24 (1967), 454-459.
Winslow, Ola E. *American Literature,* 39 (1967),
    402-405.

Helm, Paul. "John Locke and Jonathan Edwards: A
  Reconsideration." *Journal of the History of Philosophy,*
  7 (1969), 51-61.
  Helm challenges Perry Miller's conclusions concerning
  the influence of Locke on Edwards. Helm argues on
  philosophical grounds that Edwards "was not an
  empiricist, and it is too much to say that his
  philosophy was Locke-inspired; he draws on arguments
  from 'the new way of ideas' only when these serve his
  wider aims." An important study.

Henderson, G. D. "Jonathan Edwards and Scotland."
  Evangelical Quarterly, 16 (1944), 41-52.
  An introductory survey of Edwards' "connections" with
  Scottish theologians. Edwards was "not uninfluenced by
  Scottish friends and Scottish books, while on the other
  hand he certainly by his patient letter-writing gave
  encouragement and stimulus, and by the theological
  genius displayed in his numerous works he undoubtedly
  left a permanent impression upon Scottish thought." No
  attempt is made to delineate the nature and extent of
  Edwards' influence.

Henderson, Thomas F. "Jonathan Edwards." *Encyclopedia
  Britannica.* 9th edition. Vol. VII, pp. 688-691.
  "It was his overwhelming conviction of duty which gave
  to his system, theological, moral, and metaphysical,
  what unity it possesses. That unity, however, is nothing
  more than seeming...."
      Henderson provides a brief biographical sketch, a

summary outline and criticism of Edwards' theological "system," and a critical evaluation of Edwards as a thinker. Edwards' writings, Henderson suggests, "present a very remarkable conjunction of apparently contradictory qualities... attributable partly to a peculiar combination of natural mental characteristics [i.e., his "mysticism" and his "passion for ratiocination"], and partly to a habit of solitariness which rendered him almost completely ignorant of the dominant tendencies of contemporary thought, and placed him almost beyond the reach of any external influences fitted to aid him in freeing himself from the shackles of past systems." Edwards, argues Henderson, was "scarcely conscious of the presence of the new influence which was then stirring the stagnant waters of speculation; but it certainly influenced him unconsciously, and compelled him to check his vague unrest by more stedfastly [sic] clinging to his old convictions."

The later "rehabilitation" of Edwards as a thinker and his relation to Enlightenment thinking can readily be seen by comparing subsequent *Britannica* articles on Edwards by Brown, Gardiner and Webster, and most recently by Thomas A. Schafer.

Hendrix, E. R. "Jonathan Edwards and John Wesley." *The Methodist Review*, 62 (1913), 28-38.

Hendry, George S. "The Glory of God and the Future of Man." *Reformed World*, 34 (1977), 147-157.
A theological analysis of Edwards' conception of the glory of God as articulated in his late *Dissertation concerning the End for which God Created the World*.

Henry, Carl F. H.   "Jonathan Edwards' Still Angry God."
    Christianity Today, 2 no. 7 (1958), 20-22.
    An editorial recalling to Christian theologians the
    message of Jonathan Edwards: that God is angry.

Hitchcock, Orville A.   "A Critical Study of the Oratorical
    Technique of Jonathan Edwards." Doctoral dissertation,
    University of Iowa, 1937.

Hitchcock, Orville A.   "Jonathan Edwards." In *A History and
    Criticism of American Public Address*, ed. William N.
    Brigance. New York, 1943. Vol. I, pp. 213-237.
    "...Edwards was a speaker first and a writer afterward.
    Most of his time was employed in the preparation and
    delivery of sermons. These religious addresses were the
    most important things in his life, and toward them he
    directed most of his energy."
        Hitchcock presents a detailed, critical analysis of
    Edwards as a speaker. While acknowledging Edwards'
    obvious and effective appeal to the emotions in his
    sermons, Hitchcock stresses the fact that Edwards
    depended primarily upon appealing to the understanding
    of his listeners.

Hobby, William, *et al.*   *The Result of a Council of Nine
    Churches Met at Northampton, June 22, 1750. With a
    Protest against the same, by a Number of the said
    Council.*   Boston, 1750.
    Contains a brief, "authorized" account of the composi-
    tion and proceedings of the council, with a protest
    against its decision to dismiss Edwards from Northampton.
    The writers argue, among other things, that Edwards'
    position on qualifications for communion was "perfectly
    harmonious with the Mind" of the Lord Jesus Christ, and

that there was no proportion between the nature of the controversy and Edwards' dismissal.

Hobby, William. *A Vindication of the Protest Against the Result of the Northampton-Council.* Boston, 1751.
Hobby replies to Breck and his co-writers. Hobby defends the propriety of publishing the *Protest* and attempts to place the controversy and the decision of the council in historical perspective, arguing that Edwards had sought to reinstate the traditional requirements for full church membership against the "improvements" of Solomon Stoddard.

Hodge, Charles. "Professor Park and the Princeton Review." *Biblical Repertory and Princeton Review,* 23 (1851), 674-695. Reprinted in Hodge, *Essays and Reviews.* New York, 1879, pp. 613-633.
Hodge claims Edwards as an Old Calvinist whose theology is at odds with the fundamental principles of the New England schools.

Hoffman, Gerhard. "Seinsharmonie und Heilsgeschichte bei Jonathan Edwards." Doctoral dissertation, University of Göttingen, 1957.

Holbrook, Clyde Amos. "Edwards and the Ethical Question." *Harvard Theological Review,* 60 (1967), 163-175.
Holbrook examines Edwards' theocentric vision of the nature of virtue, which is offered as an alternative to the views of those modern moral philosophers who would argue that "man's moral autonomy is such that reference to deity in any decisive way is either irrelevant or at best an optional addendum to the moral life."

Holbrook, Clyde Amos. "Edwards Re-examined." *Review of*
    Metaphysics, 13 (1960), 632-641.
    A critical review of Paul Ramsey's edition of *Freedom*
    of the Will (New Haven, 1957) and John E. Smith's
    edition of *Religious Affections* (New Haven, 1959).

Holbrook, Clyde Amos. "The Ethics of Jonathan Edwards: A
    Critical Exposition and Analysis of the Relation of
    Morality and Religious Conviction in Edwardean Thought."
    Doctoral dissertation, Yale University, 1945. In
    Dissertation Abstracts, 26 (1965), 2892-2893.
    "This study is a critical exposition and analysis of the
    relation between Edwards' profound conviction of the
    supreme reality and moral excellence of God, and moral
    conduct and theory. It shows that the determining
    factor in Edwards' life and thought was an almost over-
    powering God-consciousness, which expressed itself in
    Calvinistic and Neoplatonic terms without being
    completely bound to either. This factor, in distinction
    from Calvinistic and Neoplatonic doctrines, is treated
    as vital personal experience and is designated as
    'theological objectivism.'"

Holbrook, Clyde Amos. *The Ethics of Jonathan Edwards:*
    Morality and Esthetics. Ann Arbor, Michigan, 1973.
    A revision of Holbrook's doctoral dissertation.
    Holbrook analyzes Edwards' ethical theory using
    "theological objectivism" as his primary interpre-
    tative tool.
    Reviews
    Delattre, Roland A. *New England Quarterly,* 47 (1974),
        155-158.
    Mead, Sidney E. *American Historical Review,* 79 (1974),
        844-845.

Holbrook, Clyde Amos. "Jonathan Edwards and his
    Detractors." *Theology Today,* 10 (1953), 384-396.
    An excellent review of two major lines of interpretation
    which have a long and continuing history in Edwards
    scholarship. The first is entirely negative, viewing
    Edwards as an evil force or a catastrophe in American
    cultural history. The second line, somewhat more
    sympathetic, views Edwards as a tragic figure who failed
    to realize his true potential, or whose time made him
    irrelevant. Such criticisms, Holbrook points out,
    reveal more about the critics themselves than they
    reveal about Edwards.

Holbrook, Clyde Amos, ed. *Original Sin.* Volume III of *The
    Works of Jonathan Edwards.* New Haven, 1970.
    In his critical Introduction to this volume (pp. 1-101),
    Holbrook reviews the New England controversy over
    original sin, documents Edwards' increasing interest in
    the doctrine in the period prior to the composition and
    publication of his treatise, and provides an excellent
    exposition of the principal arguments of *Original Sin*
    in relation to the "arguings" of John Taylor. Includes
    notes on the manuscripts and texts, biographical notes
    on authors cited by Edwards, and a brief review of
    the reception of Edwards' treatise.
    Reviews
    Grabo, Norman S. *American Literature,* 43 (1971),
        286-287.
    Watkins, H. K. *Encounter,* 33 (1972), 203-205.

Holmes, Clement Elton. "Jonathan Edwards and Northampton."
    Manuscript in Forbes Library, Northampton.

Holmes, Clement Elton. "The Philosophy of Jonathan Edwards
    and its Relation to his Theology." Doctoral disserta-
    tion, Boston University, 1904.

Holmes, Oliver Wendell. "Jonathan Edwards." *International
    Review*, 9 (1880), 1-28. Reprinted in Holmes, *Pages from
    an Old Volume of Life: A Collection of Essays*. Boston,
    1891, pp. 361-401.
Holmes' long, rambling essay is more instructive in the
attitude toward Edwards which it displays than in its
lively and amusing, if somewhat misleading, exposition of
Edwards' thought. Like many scholars who were to follow,
Holmes was torn between his appreciation of Edwards as a
man and thinker, and his aversion to most of the conclusions that Edwards reached. Holmes' response to this
dilemma was to attempt to excuse Edwards for some of
his conclusions.

Edwards, Holmes argues, was engaged in theological
controversy throughout his life: "This may have given
extravagance to some of his expressions, and at times
have blinded him to the real meaning as well as the
practical effect of the doctrines he taught...." Holmes
also suggests that much that was "morbid" in Edwards
was the result of ill health, a melancholic temperament,
and his habit of constant introspection amounting almost
to a "spiritual hypochondriasis." Holmes even sought to
put some distance between Edwards and the Enfield
sermon, suggesting that a large part of the language and
imagery of this infamous piece is actually the property
of Thomas Boston of Scotland. Edwards, Holmes argues,
"can be partially excused for doing violence to human
feelings. It is better, perhaps, to confess that he
was an imitator and a generous borrower than to allow
him the credit of originality at the expense of his

better human attributes."

Finally, suggesting that there was reason to fear that Edwards "has not been fairly dealt with" by his literary executors, Holmes calls for the publication of a supposedly heterodox tract on the Trinity that was rumored to exist among the Edwards manuscripts. Holmes trusted that this manuscript would evidence the eventual triumph of Edwards' "better human attributes" over the "worse than heathen conceptions which had so long chained his powerful, but crippled understanding."

Holmes, Oliver Wendell. "Jonathan Edwards." In *Sketches and Reminiscences of the Radical Club of Chestnut Street, Boston,* ed. Mrs. John T. Sargent. Boston, 1880, pp. 362-375.
A preview of Holmes' essay in *International Review,* followed by remarks by various members of the club— among them, James Freeman Clarke: "I cannot see that Jonathan Edwards is likely to exercise a permanent influence, either as a metaphysician, theologian, or mystic. His metaphysics have long since been outgrown; his theology is too superficial to endure; and his mysticism is not in accordance with the atmosphere of New England thought. He will be chiefly remembered as a powerful thinker, whose thoughts produced no lasting results."

Holmes, Oliver Wendell. "The Pulpit and the Pew." In his *Pages from an Old Volume of Life: A Collection of Essays.* Boston, 1891, pp. 402-433.
"...[I]f one of our ancestors built on an unsafe or an unwholesome foundation, the best thing we can do is to leave it and persuade others to leave it if we can. And if we refer to him as a precedent, it must be as a

warning and not as a guide."

Holmes again discusses Edwards' suppressed tract on the Trinity and explains his concern in having it published.

Holtrop, Elton. "Edwards' Conception of the Will in the Light of Calvinistic Philosophy." Doctoral dissertation, Case Western Reserve University, 1948.

Hopkins, Mark. "Life of Edwards at Stockbridge." In *Memorial Volume of the Edwards Family Meeting,* ed. Jonathan E. Woodbridge. Boston, 1871, pp. 131-138. Brief, superficial remarks.

Hopkins, Samuel. *An Inquiry into the Nature of True Holiness, With an Appendix containing an Answer to the Reverend Mr. William Hart's Remarks on President Edwards's Dissertation on "The Nature of True Virtue".* Newport, 1773.
Despite some avowed "improvements" Hopkins claims, in his *Inquiry,* to be at one with Edwards on the question of the nature of holiness or true virtue: "President Edwards, in his dissertation on the nature of virtue, has given the same account of holiness for substance, though under a different name, which the reader will find in the following inquiry." In an Appendix which is nearly double the length of the *Inquiry* itself, Hopkins offers a detailed examination and defense of Edwards' treatise against the criticisms of William Hart. Both the *Inquiry* and the Appendix are important pieces in the history of interpretation of Edwards' notion of the nature of true virtue.

Hopkins, Samuel. *The Life and Character of the Late Reverend Mr. Jonathan Edwards, President of the College of New-Jersey. Together with a Number of his Sermons on Various Important Subjects.* Boston, 1765.

"...[T]he design of the following memoirs, is not merely to publish these things, and tell the world how eminently great, wise, holy and useful President *Edwards* was; but rather to inform in what way, and by what means he attained to such an uncommon stock of knowledge and holiness; and how, in the improvement of this he did so much good to mankind; that others may hereby be directed and excited to go and do likewise." The reader is desired "not to look on the following composure so much an act of friendship to the *dead,* as of kindness to the *living;* it being only an attempt to render a life that has been greatly useful, yet more so."

The influence of this particular life of Edwards by his student, friend, associate, and later interpreter cannot be overestimated. The volume remains invaluable for its inclusion of Edwards' *Personal Narrative,* since lost. Hopkins' *Life* has recently been reprinted by David Levin in *Jonathan Edwards: A Profile* (New York, 1969).

Hornberger, Theodore. "The Effect of the New Science upon the Thought of Jonathan Edwards." *American Literature,* 9 (1937), 196-207.

Hornberger attempts to demonstrate that "Edwards's metaphysics, and hence his theology, were markedly influenced by the new science, however subordinate science may have been in the mind of the theologian." The new science, Hornberger suggests, "appears to be the thread that unravels much that is difficult to understand in Edwards's intellectual outlook."

Horne, R. A. "The Atomic Theory of Jonathan Edwards."
    Crane Review, 3 (1961), 65-72.
    Another chapter in the continuing saga of a brilliant
    mind, ill-used.
        Investigating the atomic theory of the young
    Edwards, Horne finds him anticipating "with marvelous
    clarity, the theories of modern chemistry, the idea of
    COLLISION EFFECTIVENESS and the idea of STERIC
    HINDRANCE." Horne notes with regret that Edwards'
    "scientific aspiration was truncated, his considerable
    literary ability made the servant of sterile doctrine."

Howard, Leon. "The Creative Imagination of a College Rebel:
    Jonathan Edwards' Undergraduate Writings." *Early
    American Literature*, 5 (Winter, 1970-71), 50-56.
    Howard sketches the "rebellious" character of the young
    Edwards, apparently bolstered by his experience of the
    politically rebellious environment at Wethersfield, and
    revealing itself in his early philosophical notes which
    are said to attack the whole intellectual system at
    Yale.

Howard, Leon. *"The Mind" of Jonathan Edwards: A
    Reconstructed Text*. Berkeley, 1963.
    "...[T]he lost manuscript of the Notes on *The Mind* is
    one of the most tantalizing documents in American
    intellectual history."
        This important contribution to Edwards scholarship
    has not received adequate recognition. Drawing upon the
    known sources (Dwight's description of the manuscript,
    the Dwight text, and the Index to *The Mind*), Howard
    attempts to reconstruct the order of composition of
    Edwards' notes. In the Introduction to this study
    ("Young Edwards and the Problems of his Notes on *The*

Mind," pp. 1-24), Howard re-examines the early biography of Edwards insofar as it relates to the dating and circumstances of composition of *The Mind*. Howard contends that the two works Edwards had at his side while writing *The Mind* were Locke's *Essay concerning Human Understanding* and *The Art of Thinking* by Arnauld and Nicolet, though Howard admits that evidence of the latter's influence is "rather subtle."

In the reconstructed text itself Howard attempts to indicate the train of thought that connects Edwards' notes with his sources; and in the conclusion of his study ("The Mind of Jonathan Edwards," pp. 120-135) Howard summarizes the insights into Edwards' early intellectual development provided by the new arrangement of notes.

Hoyt, Arthur S. "Jonathan Edwards." In his *The Pulpit and American Life*. New York, 1921, pp. 19-39.

Hughes, Philip E. "Jonathan Edwards on Revival."
Christianity Today, 2 no. 24 (1958), 3-4.
An appeal to modern evangelists to look to Edwards for "the true meaning of revival."

Humphrey, Griffith H. *Jonathan Edwards: An Address Delivered in Utica, N.Y., on the 200th Anniversary of his Birth, Oct. 5th, 1903.* n.p., n.d.
"Doubtless, he was born regenerated."
Humphrey remarks briefly and superficially on Edwards' career, his physical appearance, his illustrious descendants, his wife (the "world is under everlasting obligation to her"), his piety, his convictions, his expulsion from Northampton ("he himself was forced out of the house and the door

slammed and bolted at his back. ...The church had been
transformed into a mob"), and his later reputation.
Little attention is given to the particulars of Edwards'
life and thought. It is a popularized tribute to
Edwards.

Hutch, Richard A. "Jonathan Edwards' Analysis of Religious
    Experience." *Journal of Psychology and Theology*,
    6 (1978), 123-131.
    "Jonathan Edwards' appraisal of religious experience is
    analyzed from three perspectives: (a) the cultural and
    historical setting in which he lived; (b) his psycho-
    logical understanding of human nature; and (c) his
    theological analysis of religious experience. The
    conclusion is that for Edwards such experience is not
    a product of an 'either/or' choice between reason and
    emotion. Rather, it is an integrated experience of
    seizure of the whole man expressed thereafter in the
    inclination of love."

"The Injustice to Jonathan Edwards." *Hartford Courier*,
    23 June 1880.
    A call for the publication of Edwards' supposedly
    heterodox manuscript on the Trinity.

"Interesting Conversions. President Edwards." *The Religious
    Monitor and Evangelical Repository*, 6 (1830), 414-416.

Iverach, James. *The Evangelical Succession*. Edinburgh,
    1882-84.
    A course of lectures delivered at St. George's Free
    Church, Edinburgh. Includes a brief biography of
    Edwards.

James, William. *The Varieties of Religious Experience: A Study in Human Nature*. New York, 1902.
Includes occasional references to Edwards' *Religious Affections* and *Personal Narrative*. The work is not significant as criticism or interpretation of Edwards but as evidence of the continuing vitality of his thought.

Jeanes, W. P. "Jonathan Edwards' Conception of Freedom of the Will." *Scottish Journal of Theology*, 14 (1961), 1-14.
Jeanes outlines Edwards' arguments in support of the position that the acts of men may be rendered inevitably certain without destroying their liberty, and offers some vague responses to possible objections to Edwards' theory of the will. Superficial.

Johnson, Thomas H. "Jonathan Edwards." In *Literary History of the United States*, ed. R. E. Spiller *et al*. New York, 1949. Vol. I, pp. 71-81.
"To read the world in terms of love was Edwards' unique contribution to the philosophic system of Calvin."
A rather diffuse discussion of Edwards' thought in which Johnson repeatedly stresses the importance of *The Mind* for understanding the mature Edwards.

Johnson, Thomas H. "Jonathan Edwards." *Princeton University Library Chronicle*, 12 (1951), 159-160.
Reports the library's acquisition of a sermon by Edwards and a 1738 German translation of the *Faithful Narrative*.

Johnson, Thomas H. "Jonathan Edwards and the 'Young Folks' Bible.'" *New England Quarterly*, 5 (1932), 37-54.
A dispute over church discipline, which began when

Edwards discovered that certain young people of the town
had been reading "immoral books," was an important
factor in the decline of harmony between Edwards and his
congregation. Johnson provides an account of this
episode and identifies the hitherto unknown book.

From Edwards' unpublished papers Johnson presents,
among other items, a lengthy transcription of the notes
which Edwards made at various meetings, as he sat
listening to the testimony of the accusers and the
defendants. The testimony makes clear, notes Johnson,
"that the reading had been going on for some time; that
it was from a volume of midwifery put to pornographic
uses .... Quite evidently the book was the *Works* of the
pseudonymous Aristotle ...."

Edwards, Johnson concludes, "does not seem to have
been unduly meddlesome in the literary divertisements of
his parishoners. We may indeed conclude that Edwards,
both as a moralist and literary judge, was keener and
wiser than has been hitherto supposed."

Johnson, Thomas H. "Jonathan Edwards as a Man of Letters."
Doctoral dissertation, Harvard University, 1932.

Johnson, Thomas H. "Jonathan Edwards' Background of
Reading." *Publications of the Colonial Society of
Massachusetts,* 28 (1931), 193-222.
An investigation into Edwards' background of reading
from evidence provided in his published treatises,
private correspondence, and private notebooks. Johnson
concludes that Edwards' "wide literary acquaintance
would have been unusual for any colonial minister; it
was phenomenal for a provincial one."

Impressed by Edwards' obvious intellectual and
scholarly abilities, Johnson laments the use to which

Edwards chose to put them. "One of the greatest of the
many tragedies in Edwards' life is strikingly illus-
trated in his refusal to use with any breadth of application the full power of a mind that had the rarely
coupled talent for keen observation and philosophical
analysis. Of all the Americans of his day... none had
more notable endowments for pure scholarship or a more
original metaphysical mind, yet none has left monuments
so crumbled and overgrown. One cannot refrain, in
conclusion, from pondering what this intellectual arm
might have accomplished of permanent value in other
feats had it not been so tightly bound by theological
dogma."

"Jonathan Edwards." *American Journal of Education*,
27 (1877), 721-723.
A note on Edwards as a student and educator, with
extracts from Dwight's *Life* and from Edwards' letter
to the Princeton trustees indicating his habits of
study and his "view of his activity as chief officer of
the college."

"Jonathan Edwards." Editorial. *Journal of the
Presbyterian Historical Society*, 2 (1903), 157-160.

"Jonathan Edwards." *Nation*, 49 (1889), 314-315.
Review of A. V. G. Allen's *Life and Writings of Jonathan
Edwards* (Boston, 1889).

"Jonathan Edwards." *Outlook*, 75 (1903), 248-251.
Edwards is praised on the two hundredth anniversary of
his birth, and a summary of his theological system is
provided "for the sake of readers who have neither the
inclination nor the ability to study Edwards or his

interpreters."

"Jonathan Edwards." *The Spectator,* 64 (1890), 58-59.
Review of A. V. G. Allen's *Life and Writings of Jonathan Edwards* (Edinburgh, 1889).

"The Jonathan Edwards Bicentennial." New York *Tribune,* 4 October 1903, pt. 2, p. 7.

"The Jonathan Edwards Memorial [at Northampton]." *Harper's Weekly,* 23 June 1900, p. 574.

Jonathan Edwards. Union Meeting of the Berkshire North and South Conferences. Stockbridge, Massachusetts, October 5, 1903. Stockbridge, 1903.
Addresses delivered at Stockbridge in commemoration of the two hundredth anniversary of Edwards' birth.
Contents
Introduction, by Henry Hopkins
Address of Welcome, by E. S. Porter
The Edwards Family, by G. W. Andrews
The Modern Note in Edwards, by I. C. Smart
The Other Side of Edwards, by L. S. Rowland
Jonathan Edwards: A Study, by John DeWitt
Edwards at Stockbridge, by W. E. Park

"Jonathan Edwards's Last Will, and the Inventory of his Estate." *Bibliotheca Sacra,* 33 (1876), 438-447.
Documents.

"Jonathan Edwards. Yale's Commemoration of his Two Hundredth Anniversary." *Yale Alumni Weekly,* 13 (7 October 1903), 1.

Jones, Adam Leroy. *Early American Philosophers*. New York, 1898.
Three of the six chapters in this slim volume are devoted to Edwards. Jones presents a summary statement of Edwards' early idealism, the psychological theories developed in his early notes, his concept of the nature of virtue, and his theory of the will. Little is provided in the way of interpretation and no attention is given to the historical context of Edwards' thought.

Jones, Charles Edwin. "The Impolitic Mr. Edwards: The Personal Dimension of the Robert Breck Affair." *New England Quarterly*, 51 (1978), 64-79.
An historical account of the Breck case. Focus is on Breck not Edwards.

Jones, Electa F. *Stockbridge, Past and Present; or Records of an Old Mission Station*. Springfield, 1854.
Includes a brief section on "President Edwards and his Wife."

Jones, James W. "Reflections on the Problem of Religious Experience." *Journal of the American Academy of Religion*, 40 (1972), 445-453.
Jones suggests that the "new sense" described by Edwards "not only provokes new insights into the nature of religious experience but may also enable us to live in a world of plural experiences without all loss of intellectual and psychological unity."

Keating, Jerome Francis. "Personal Identity in Jonathan Edwards, Ralph Waldo Emerson, and Alfred North Whitehead." Doctoral dissertation, Syracuse University, 1972. In *Dissertation Abstracts International*,

33 (1973), 5682A.

Kimnach, Wilson Henry. "The Brazen Trumpet: Jonathan
    Edwards' Conception of the Sermon." In *Jonathan
    Edwards: His Life and Influence*, ed. Charles Angoff.
    Rutherford, New Jersey, 1975, pp. 29-44.
    Kimnach examines the Edwardsean sermon as a literary
    form, what the form was and what Edwards did with it
    over the course of the years. Kimnach notes a dual
    "development" in Edwards' use of the sermon. In the
    first decade of his career as a preacher, Edwards
    gradually differentiated the hortatory from the philo-
    sophical. "More and more the hortatory sermon became
    an instrument for manipulation," culminating in the
    Enfield sermon which marks the "climax of Edwards'
    efforts in the genre of the sermon." The hortatory
    sermon was supplemented by instructional or philoso-
    phical sermons; but, Kimnach argues, Edwards gradually
    became dissatisfied with the limitations of the form
    and eventually drifted away from it, as if "he felt
    his profoundest thoughts were unsuitable to it."

Kimnach, Wilson Henry. "Jonathan Edwards' Early Sermons:
    New York, 1722-1723." *Journal of Presbyterian History,*
    55 (1977), 255-266.
    Edwards' initial efforts in this genre are evaluated and
    further light is shed on a critical phase in Edwards'
    life through a study of the sermons, as yet unpublished,
    preached during his first pastorate. If Edwards'
    mastery of the sermon form was at this stage incomplete,
    concludes Kimnach, he had at least "established himself
    in it and, in the process, had managed to exploit its
    potential as a means of inquiry into the processes of
    his own religious experience."

Kimnach, Wilson Henry.   "Jonathan Edwards' Sermon Mill."
   Early American Literature, 10 (1975), 167-178.
   Drawing upon the mine of Edwards' sermon material as yet
   unpublished, Kimnach discusses Edwards' techniques of
   revising and recasting sermons, and the means by which
   Edwards strove "to make his sermon file a carefully
   inventoried warehouse of parts and wholes to be visited
   whenever the demands of the pulpit strained his creative
   energies or (especially in later years) threatened other
   projects dear to his heart." Kimnach suggests, however,
   that the sermon file was more than a warehouse but
   "seems to have become a generator of sermons, since the
   re-examination of old sermons inevitably facilitated and
   shaped the production of new sermons."

Kimnach, Wilson Henry.   "The Literary Techniques of Jonathan
   Edwards." Doctoral dissertation, University of
   Pennsylvania, 1971.   In *Dissertation Abstracts Inter-*
   national, 32 (1971), 2093A.
   "This study attempts a comprehensive investigation of
   the means by which Jonathan Edwards produced his
   writings. The routine of the study, preparation for
   publication, technical strategies of style, and the
   theories or plans behind all of these procedures
   constitute the subject of investigation."

King, Henry Churchill.   "Jonathan Edwards as Philosopher and
   Theologian." *Hartford Seminary Record,* 14 (1903),
   23-57.
   A critical estimate of Edwards as a philosopher and
   theologian, his influence upon his own and later times,
   and his present significance.
   Though Edwards is counted "the severest logician of
   American writers, I think it must be straightly said,"

notes King, "that Edwards is great because of his
inconsistencies." He is greater than any of his more
consistent successors, "and great enough to be the
source of several tendencies. His personality was too
large, his reason too enkindling, his mind too eager and
open for all truth, to be confined within the logically
consistent limits of the theological system which he
seems to himself to have adopted."

Knoepp, Walther T. "Jonathan Edwards: The Way of
   Sanctification." Doctoral dissertation, Hartford
   Seminary Foundation, 1937.

Knox, Ronald A. *Enthusiasm: A Chapter in the History of
   Religion, with Special Reference to the XVII and XVIII
   Centuries.* New York, 1950.
   An historical study of religious enthusiasm, providing a
   useful background for the study of the Great Awakening.
   Knox makes only a few, general references to the Great
   Awakening in America and that "flinty-minded Calvinist,"
   Jonathan Edwards; however, he includes lengthy
   discussions of Whitefield's revival activities in
   Europe and those of Edwards' great contemporary, John
   Wesley.

Kolodny, Annette. "Imagery in the Sermons of Jonathan
   Edwards." *Early American Literature,* 7 (1972),
   172-182.
   Insisting that one must treat Edwards not merely as a
   theologian but as a literary artist, Kolodny examines
   Edwards' techniques of employing imagery for the purpose
   of emotional persuasion. The primary text examined is
   the Enfield sermon; however, Kolodny insists that "this
   conscious artistic manipulation of figurative language

is characteristic of *all* Edwards' sermons—not just
the infamous *Sinners in the Hands of an Angry God.*"
"What we have typically, in each of Edwards' sermons,
is an aggregate of images, contrasting to, adding to,
or alluding to one another in such a way as to *force* the
listener to go through very specific and analyzable
emotional responses."

Lanty, Chesley S. "A Comparative Study of Certain Aspects
of the Theology of Jonathan Edwards and Aurelius
Augustine." S.T.M. thesis, Union Theological Seminary,
1939.

Larson, David Mitchell. "The Man of Feeling in America:
A Study of Major Early American Writers' Attitudes
toward Benevolent Ethics and Behavior." Doctoral
dissertation, University of Minnesota, 1973. In
Dissertation Abstracts International, 34 (1974), 2568A.
Includes an analysis of Edwards' ethical theory.

Larson, Robert F. "Jonathan Edwards' Arguments for Divine
Sovereignty." Th.M. thesis, Pittsburgh Theological
Seminary, 1960.

Laskowsky, Henry J. "Jonathan Edwards: A Puritan
Philosopher of Science." *Connecticut Review,* 4 (1970),
33-41.

Laurence, David Ernst. "The Foolishness of Edwards."
Worldview, 18 (1975), 49-51.
Review of Harold P. Simonson's *Jonathan Edwards* (Grand
Rapids, 1974).

Laurence, David Ernst. "Jonathan Edwards, Solomon Stoddard, and the Preparationist Model of Conversion." *Harvard Theological Review*, 72 (1979), 267-283.
Laurence argues that the "marked discrepancy" that Edwards found between his own experience of conversion and what theorists such as Stoddard said he ought to experience provided the basis for an inquiry that "eventually led him to reject the step-by-step model of conversion that had provided the framework for New England's discussion of the knotty problem... of how to formulate a reliable procedure for determining who were the visible saints."

Laurence, David Ernst. "Religious Experience in the Biblical World of Jonathan Edwards: A Study in Eighteenth Century Supernaturalism." Doctoral dissertation, Yale University, 1976. In *Dissertation Abstracts International*, 37 (1977), 4432A.

Lawrence, E[dward] A. "New England Theology: The Edwardean Period." *American Theological Review*, 3 (1861), 36-69. Reprinted in *British and Foreign Evangelical Review*, 11 (1862), 1-26.
Lawrence provides a detailed exposition of the basic theological doctrines of the four treatises from Edwards' Stockbridge period, contending that "The *genuine* Edwardean theology lies in these treatises." Lawrence is not suggesting that Edwards' other writings reflect less than genuine convictions; rather, he is concerned to make clear that he is detailing those doctrines which Edwards himself taught, and not those which are, "by a metaphor," called "Edwardean." Lawrence examines a number of the "misinterpretations" of these treatises that had emerged.

Lawrence, Frank A. "The Decline of Calvinism in New England before Jonathan Edwards." Th.M. thesis, Pittsburgh-Xenia Theological Seminary, 1951.

Lawrence, Mrs. M. W. "Old Time Minister and Parish." *Putnam's Magazine*, new series, 4 (1869), 166-168.

Lee, Marc Frank. "A Literary Approach to Selected Writings of Jonathan Edwards." Doctoral dissertation, University of Wisconsin-Milwaukee, 1973. In *Dissertation Abstracts International*, 34 (1974), 7710A-7711A.

Lee, Sang Hyun. "The Concept of Habit in the Thought of Jonathan Edwards." Doctoral dissertation, Harvard University, 1972.

Lee, Sang Hyun. "Jonathan Edwards' Theory of the Imagination." *Michigan Academician*, 5 (1972), 233-241. A reconstruction of Edwards' psychology of mental activity. The "imagination" is here broadly defined as that creative power of the mind which actively contributes to experience in the ordering of ideas passively received by the senses.

Lee, Sang Hyun. "Mental Activity and the Perception of Beauty in Jonathan Edwards." *Harvard Theological Review*, 69 (1976), 369-396.

Lensing, George. "Robert Lowell and Jonathan Edwards: Poetry in the Hands of an Angry God." *South Carolina Review*, 6 (1974), 7-17.

Leroux, Emmanuel. "Le Développement de la Pensée Philosophique aux États-Unis." *Revue de Synthèse*

Historique, 29 (1919), 125-149.

"Let There Be Light." Editorial. *Boston Transcript,*
    25 June 1880.
    A call for the publication of Edwards' supposedly
    heterodox manuscript on the Trinity.
        "It is an open secret that the MSS of Edwards has
    [sic] been more or less 'edited', and edited with
    reference not to elucidating his own meaning always, but
    to make them consistently conform to a certain doctrinal
    standard...."

Levin, David, ed. *Jonathan Edwards: A Profile.* New York,
    1969.
    A collection of previously published interpretations of
    Edwards, attempting to profile him as a man of "both
    rigorous thought and uncompromising piety." The most
    valuable part of the collection is a reprint of Hopkins'
    Life of Edwards, a work that had not been reprinted for
    more than a century, and never without editorial
    improvements which made substantive changes in both
    Edwards' and Hopkins' texts. (See Shea, *Spiritual Auto-
    biography in Early America*).
        The remainder of this volume is composed of excerpts
    from studies by Perry Miller, Henry B. Parkes, Ola E.
    Winslow, Williston Walker, Peter Gay, and John E. Smith.
    Also includes poems by Robert Lowell.

Lewis, R. W. B. "The Drama of Jonathan Edwards." *Hudson
    Review,* 3 (1950), 135-140.
    A review of Perry Miller's *Jonathan Edwards* (New York,
    1949).

"The Life and Character of Rev. Jonathan Edwards, President
of Nassau-Hall College, New Jersey." *Connecticut
Evangelical Magazine,* 1 (1808), 161-178; 201-212.
A biographical study derived almost entirely from
Hopkins' *Life* of Edwards. Includes the text of the
Personal Narrative.

"The Life and Experience of the Reverend Jonathan Edwards."
In Jonathan Edwards' *History of the Work of Redemption.*
New York, 1793, pp. 3-34.

The Life of President Edwards. Written for the American
Sunday School Union, and Revised by the Committee of
Publication. Philadelphia, 1832.

*Life of the Rev. Jonathan Edwards, President of Princetown
College, New Jersey.* Religious Tract Society. London,
n.d.
Composed of selections from the biographies of Edwards
written by Samuel Hopkins and Sereno E. Dwight.

Lips, Roger Cameron. "The Spirit's Holy Errand: A Study
of Continuities of Thought from Jonathan Edwards to
Ralph Waldo Emerson." Doctoral dissertation,
University of Wisconsin-Madison, 1976. In *Dissertation
Abstracts International,* 37 (1976), 310A.

"A List of Printed Materials on Jonathan Edwards, 1703-
1758." Manuscript in the Library of Congress Reading
Room, Washington, D.C.
Lists printed materials "to be found in the Library of
Congress [Reading Room]; including biographies, appre-
ciations, criticisms, and fugitive references. With
Supplementary Lists of material not in the Library, and

with Notes on his Manuscripts and Works. Compiled in
the Office of the Superintendent of the Reading Room,
November, 1934." (29 pp.)
     With the exception of "fugitive references," all
entries identifying biographies or criticisms of Edwards
can be found in this bibliography.

Loewinsohn, Ron. "Jonathan Edwards' Opticks: Images and
     Metaphors of Light in Some of his Major Works." *Early
     American Literature*, 8 (1973), 21-32.
     Loewinsohn suggests that Edwards' conventional and often
     quite unconventional use of light metaphors reveals a
     coherence in his thought, largely the result of his
     early acquaintance with the new science. The scientific
     ground of his thought, Loewinsohn contends, "allowed
     Edwards to make two crucial reconciliations or
     syntheses." The first, "stemming from his early reading
     of Locke, was the reunification of man's head and
     heart." The second was "nothing less than the reconcil-
     iation of God with nature, and the concurrent reconcil-
     iation of man with the world he inhabits."

Long, G. W. "Jonathan Edwards, 1703-1758: His Theory and
     Practice of Evangelism." Doctoral dissertation,
     University of Edinburgh, 1958.

Long, Gary Dale. "The Doctrine of Original Sin in New
     England Theology: From Jonathan Edwards to Edwards
     Amasa Park." Doctoral dissertation, Dallas Theological
     Seminary, 1972.

Lossing, Benson J. "Jonathan Edwards." In his *Eminent
     Americans: Comprising Brief Biographies of 330
     Distinguished Persons.* New York, 1857, pp. 177-179.

Brief biographical sketch of Edwards, the "most acute
metaphysician and sound theologian which our country has
yet produced." Of Edwards' writings Lossing offers but
a single comment: "The published theological writings
of President Edwards are voluminous, and are ranked
among the most valuable uninspired contributions to
religious literature, of any age." It was a compliment.

Lowance, Mason I. "From Edwards to Emerson to Thoreau: A
Revaluation." *American Transcendental Quarterly,*
18 (1973), 3-12.

Lowance, Mason I. "Images and Shadows of Divine Things:
Puritan Typology in New England from 1660 to 1750."
Doctoral dissertation, Emory University, 1967.

Lowance, Mason I. "Images or Shadows of Divine Things:
The Typology of Jonathan Edwards." *Early American
Literature,* 5 (1970), 141-181.
An important study. "Edwards' typology of nature,"
Lowance suggests, "represented a new departure in the
epistemology of divine revelation. That he provided a
conservative force against liberalism in Covenant
theology, and particularly against the excesses of
Stoddardeanism, does not alter his influence in typology
toward a broadening of the avenues by which man might
perceive the will of God."

Lowell, D. O. S. "The Descendants of Jonathan Edwards."
Munsey's Magazine, 35 (1906), 263-273.
"...[T]he writer does not remember to have seen in any
work on heredity that the tendency to be a college
president may run in the blood. That this is a fact,
however, the following sketch goes far to prove, or else

we have a set of unexampled coincidences." Lowell
enumerates the college presidents found among Edwards'
descendants through the seventh generation.

Luisi, Miriam P. "The Community of Consent in Jonathan
    Edwards." Doctoral dissertation, Fordham University,
    1976. In *Dissertation Abstracts International*,
    37 (1976), 1026A-1027A.

Lynen, John F. "The Choice of a Single Point of View:
    Edwards and Franklin." In his *The Design of the
    Present: Essays on Time and Form in American
    Literature*. New Haven, 1969, pp. 87-152.
    It is essential, Lynen contends, "to make Edwards the
    literary artist a central consideration in any study of
    Edwards as a thinker."
        Lynen suggests that the essential difference between
    Edwards and Franklin is that between the two sides of
    the Puritan consciousness: where Franklin speaks from
    the perspective of the particular individual, Edwards
    speaks from the "eternal" point of view. "Edwards is a
    theologian, not a philosopher, and, as I shall undertake
    to show, his mere system cannot stand alone. It is
    incomplete; indeed, it does not make sense unless it is
    considered with reference to a vision or experience
    which transcends the rational scheme. The latter is, as
    it were, a kind of notation or way of speaking by which
    Edwards would indicate something beyond the reasonable-
    ness of his arguments."

Lyon, Georges. *L'Idéalisme en Angleterre au XVIIIe Siècle.*
    Paris, 1888.
    "There are few names in the eighteenth century which
    have obtained such celebrity as that of Jonathan

Edwards. Critics and historians down to our own day
have praised in dithyrambic terms the logical vigor and
the constructive powers of a writer whom they hold...
to be the greatest metaphysician America has yet
produced. Who knows, they have asked themselves, to
what heights this original genius might have risen, if,
instead of being born in a half-savage country, far from
the traditions of philosophy and science, he had
appeared rather in our old world, and there received the
direct impulse of the modern mind. Perhaps he would
have taken a place between Leibniz and Kant among the
founders of immortal systems, instead of the work he has
left, reducing itself to a sublime and barbarous
theology, which astonishes our reason and outrages our
heart, the object at once of our horror and admiration."
  If the claims made for Edwards be true, Lyon
observes, then Edwards becomes equal to many Pascals, a
genius whose intellectual gifts surpass those of Newton
and Galileo combined; and, by a double miracle, the
prodigy disappears all of a sudden. Finding it difficult to accept such an estimate, Lyon questions the
early dating of Edwards' philosophical writings, questions the originality of some of Edwards' collegiate
and pre-collegiate compositions, and attempts to demonstrate in detail Edwards' dependence on Berkeley in the
development of his philosophical idealism.
  Lyon's arguments and suggestions did not gain
general acceptance, but he succeeded in delineating an
area of discussion that would dominate the next years
of Edwards scholarship.

Lyttle, David J. "Jonathan Edwards on Personal Identity."
Early American Literature, 7 (1972), 163-171.
Lyttle examines the theory of personal identity found

in *The Mind* and later employed by Edwards to explain the
unity of the race in the sin of Adam. Lyttle argues
that Edwards "utilized Lockean terminology in defining
how men are punished for a crime of which they are not
aware, but his use of this terminology, like his use of
it in his definition of the Supernatural Light, is a
mere facade in front of a medieval structure."

Lyttle, David J. "Jonathan Edwards' Symbolic Structure of
   Experience." Doctoral dissertation, Pennsylvania State
   University, 1965. In *Dissertation Abstracts,* 26 (1966),
   4665-4666.

Lyttle, David J. "The Sixth Sense of Jonathan Edwards."
   Church Quarterly Review, 167 (1966), 50-59.
   Lyttle analyzes Edwards' concept of grace, or the divine
   and supernatural light, arguing that Edwards "used
   empirical terminology to describe what is fundamentally
   a Calvinistic concept."

M., E. "President Edwards's View of Original Sin." *The
   Quarterly Christian Spectator,* series 2, 1 (1827),
   625-629.
   The writer challenges T. R.'s interpretation of
   Edwards' doctrine of original sin, while conceding
   T. R.'s basic contention: that Edwards "does not hold
   to the doctrine of physical depravity." See T. R.,
   "Edwards's Views of Original Sin."

MacClelland, George. *Predestination and Election
   vindicated from dependence on Moral Necessity, and
   reconciled with Free Will and a Universal Atonement:
   preceded by an answer to the system of Edwards.*
   Edinburgh, 1848.

McCook, Henry C. "Jonathan Edwards as a Naturalist."
Presbyterian and Reformed Review, 1 (1890), 393-402.
Following Silliman's evaluation of Edwards' essay on the
flying spider, McCook proposes to examine the essay
"from the standpoint of a specialist" on North American
spiders. Edwards' observations and conclusions are
painstakingly compared with the facts as known in
McCook's day, generally to the credit of the young
Edwards. "It is true," McCook notes, "that the boy fell
into some mistakes, and it would have been marvelous had
this not been so; but it is noticeable that his mistakes are more in matters of speculation than observation." McCook concludes that Silliman's estimation of
Edwards as a potential peer of Newton in the world of
natural science was more than justified.

The only area in which McCook takes the young
Edwards to task concerns Edwards' all too common notion
of the "corrupting nauseousness" of spiders. Actually,
McCook explains, spiders are "the greatest philanthro-
pists of the world of invertebrate animals."

MacCormac, Earl R. "Jonathan Edwards and Missions."
Journal of the Presbyterian Historical Society,
39 (1961), 219-229.

MacCracken, Henry Mitchell, ed. Ferdinand Piper's *Lives of
Church Leaders... with Added Lives by American Writers.*
Cleveland, 1900.
Includes a biographical sketch of Edwards.

MacCracken, John H. *Jonathan Edwards Idealismus.* Halle,
1899. (Doctoral dissertation, University of Halle,
1899.)
MacCracken disputes the hypothesis that Edwards may have

been acquainted with the writings of Berkeley, admits
the significance of Newton and Locke in the development
of Edwards' youthful idealism, but suggests that the
work which first turned Edwards' thoughts in the
direction of idealism was Arthur Collier's *Clavis
Universalis* (1713).

MacCracken, John H. "The Sources of Jonathan Edwards's
Idealism." *Philosophical Review*, 11 (1902), 26-42.
"To search the intellectual history of Edwards is to
ask, not merely for the antecedents of a great thinker,
but for the genealogy of a new race."
MacCracken rehearses the arguments of his major
study of Edwards, suggesting that Arthur Collier is
"the key to the mystery" concerning the source of
Edwards' early idealism.

McCreary, Edward Daniel, Jr. "Representative Views of the
Atonement in American Theology: A Study of Jonathan
Edwards, Horace Bushnell, and Reinhold Niebuhr,
Including the Major Trends in 18th, 19th, and 20th
Century American Theology." Doctoral dissertation,
Union Theological Seminary (Virginia), 1951.

McGiffert, Arthur Cushman. *Jonathan Edwards*. New Yoṛk,
1932.
An excellent, critical analysis of Edwards' thought,
written in a biographical mode. Described by Herbert
W. Schneider as an "exceptionally keen portrayal of a
keen mind."
Reviews
Brown, E. Francis. "Jonathan Edwards, Theologian and
Philosopher," *New York Times*, 24 April 1932, p. 2.

Carpenter, Frederic I. *New England Quarterly*,
    5 (1932), 395-397.
Schneider, Herbert W. *Journal of Religion*,
    10 (1932), 400-401.
Warren, Austin. *American Literature*,
    4 (1932-33), 314-318.

McGiffert, Arthur Cushman. *Protestant Thought before Kant*.
   London, 1911.
   Includes a perceptive analysis of Edwards' ethical
   theory; McGiffert later incorporated the body of this
   discussion in his *Jonathan Edwards* (1932).
      "His practical interest throughout was to humble
   man, to convince him of his total depravity and absolute
   bondage to sin, and so startle him out of his easy
   indifference and complacent self-confidence.... It was
   not the greatness of God, but the nothingness of man
   that he was primarily interested to enforce, and all his
   theology was dominated by this aim."

McGinley, Phyllis. "The Theology of Jonathan Edwards." In
   her *Times Three*. New York, 1961, p. 19.
   A poem, reading in part:

      "And if they had been taught aright
         Small children carried bedwards,
      Would shudder lest they meet that night
         The God of Mr. Edwards.

      Abraham's God, the Wrathful One,
         Intolerant of error—
      Not God the Father or the Son
         But God the Holy Terror."

McKenzie, [Alexander?]. Remarks. *Proceedings of the
Massachusetts Historical Society*, series 2, 15 (1902),
23-24.
At the meeting of the Society in March, 1901, McKenzie
offered an interesting explanation for the great antipathy toward Edwards' sermon, *Sinners in the Hands of
an Angry God*. It was a problem of spiders.

"The opinion of Edwards upon the matter under
discussion did not differ from those of other men of his
time, and would have passed without special comment if
he had not, by way of enforcing it, made a most unhappy
reference to the spider. It is not an uncommon experience for even a thoughtful man to be ruined by an
illustration." Why did Edwards use such an illustration?
McKenzie suggests that this choice of illustration
should be ascribed to Edwards' "early and persistent
interest in the spider itself, rather than to an utter
lack of sensibility and good taste."

Mackintosh, Sir James. *Dissertation on the Progress of
Ethical Philosophy*. Philadelphia, 1834.
Mackintosh offers a brief and largely unsympathetic
critique of Edwards' late treatise on *The Nature of True
Virtue*, suggesting that Edwards had not always maintained the ideas expressed in that work. His criticisms
notwithstanding, Mackintosh speaks of Edwards' power of
subtle argument as "perhaps unmatched, certainly
unsurpassed among men."

Maclean, John. *History of the College of New Jersey*.
2 vols. Philadelphia, 1877.
Includes a brief chapter on the election and administration of President Edwards (I, pp. 169-177), and a
biographical sketch of Edwards (I, pp. 178-191).

Macphail, Andrew. *Essays in Puritanism*. London, 1905.
"The old name for a revival was an awakening and
Jonathan Edwards awakened the people thoroughly. Once
awake they could be trusted to find out a way for themselves. The path they followed has not been precisely
the one marked out for them by the great divine, but it
led in a new and right direction. To turn the people
anew and aright is the greatest work any man can
accomplish, and it is for that supreme reason the name
of Jonathan Edwards is held in remembrance."

Macphail's lengthy and very readable essay on
Edwards is essentially an examination of Edwards as a
thinker. Macphail is out of sympathy with so many
things that his general antipathy toward Edwards' theological convictions does not detract from his argument.
His observations are often untrustworthy; but, behind
the irony, they are equally as often enlightening and
insightful. Little detailed attention is given to the
particulars of Edwards' thought.

Magoun, George F. "President Edwards as a Reformer."
Congregational Quarterly, new series, 1 (1869),
259-274.
"One such man as Jonathan Edwards is sufficient alone to
redeem the nation, the Church, the age to which he
belonged."

Essentially a character study, attempting to highlight Edwards as an eminent theological and practical
reformer. Superficial.

Magoun, George F. "Unpublished Writings of President
Edwards." *Congregational Review*, 10 (1870), 19-27.

Mahan, Asa. *The Doctrine of the Will*. New York, 1845.
    Includes a critique of Edwards' *Freedom of the Will*.
    Edwards, observes Mahan, "confused the Will with the
    Sensibility .... His whole work is constructed without
    an appeal to Consciousness, the only proper and
    authoritative tribunal of appeal in the case."

Martin, J. Alfred. "The Empirical, the Esthetic, and the
    Religious." *Union Seminary Quarterly Review*, 30 (1975),
    110-120.
    "...Edwards and others see the beautiful as the category
    most naturally linked with the divine, and the esthetic
    as the most useful notion to employ in further charac-
    terization of the religious as such."
        Concerned with the larger question of developing a
    general theory of religion, Martin examines the
    "fundamental affinity of the religious with the
    esthetic" in the thought of Edwards and John Dewey, and
    notes complementary expressions in modern process
    thought. In his treatment of Edwards, Martin relies
    heavily on Delattre's analysis of the role of beauty in
    Edwards' thought.

Martin, James P. *The Last Judgment in Protestant Theology
    from Orthodoxy to Ritschl*. Grand Rapids, 1963.
    Martin employs the Last Judgment as the focus for this
    history of interpretation of the New Testament within
    Protestantism. Edwards is a figure who appears often in
    this study, and Martin provides relatively brief but
    valuable discussions of Edwards' eschatology, his
    thoughts on the millenium, and his view of history.
    Martin takes Perry Miller to task on a number of points
    of interpretation and in general attempts to underscore
    the biblical character of Edwards' thought that modern

interpreters have tended to overlook or ignore.

"Edwards' early biographer Hopkins mentions that Edwards studied the bible more than all other books. This source of much of Edwards' theology is not given sufficient recognition. Too many modern interpretations of Edwards discuss him as a philosopher and are quite apologetic about the biblical character of much of his theology. Everything original is attributed to Locke or Newton." Martin suggests that "Edwards' use of Locke's sensationalism as a means of communicating truth and his recognition of the new concepts of causality inherent in Newtonianism do not alter the fact that the content of Edwards' theology was essentially biblical in character."

Martin, Jean-Pierre. "Edwards' Epistemology and the New Science." *Early American Literature*, 7 (1973), 247-255.
Suggesting that previous efforts to link Edwards to the science of his age have not been "wholely satisfactory," Martin attempts to "outline the points at which philosophy and science meet—and fail to meet—in the mind of Edwards." The focus is on Edwards' epistemology: "Does the science of the time lie behind it—and within it?" Martin argues that "As in theological matters, Edwards was in the area of science embarassingly conservative."

Maurice, Frederick D. *Moral and Metaphysical Philosophy.* London, 1872.
Includes a brief and somewhat superficial discussion of Edwards as a philosopher.

"In his own country Edwards remains, and must always remain, a great power. We should imagine all American theology and philosophy, whatever change it may undergo,

and with whatever foreign elements it may be associated,
must be cast in his mould. New Englanders who try to
substitute Berkeley, or Butler, or Malebranche, or
Condillac, or Kant, or Hegel, for Edwards, and to form
their minds upon any of them, must be forcing themselves
into an unnatural position, and must suffer from the
effort."

Mayhew, George N. "The Relation of the Theology of Jonathan
    Edwards to Contemporary Penological Theory and
    Practice." Doctoral dissertation, University of
    Chicago, 1935.

Middleton, Erasmus. "Jonathan Edwards." In his
    Evangelical Biography. Rev. ed., London, 1816. Vol IV,
    pp. 294-317.
    A biographical sketch. Little attention is given to the
    particulars of Edwards' thought.

Millar, Albert Edward. "Spiritual Autobiography in Selected
    Writings of Sewall, Edwards, Byrd, Woolman, and Franklin:
    A Comparison of Technique and Content." Doctoral
    dissertation, University of Delaware, 1968. In
    Dissertation Abstracts, 29 (1968), 1873A-1874A.

Miller, Edward Waite. "The Great Awakening and its Relation
    to American Christianity." *Princeton Theological
    Review*, 2 (1904), 545-562.
    Following a brief survey of the course of the Great
    Awakening in the colonies, Miller outlines the long term
    affects of the revival—positive, negative, and
    ambiguous—on American Christianity.
        "In view of the various and far-reaching results of
    the revival of 1740, we may acknowledge that Edwards

displayed singular insight in estimating it as a crisis in the kingdom of God."

Miller, Glenn Thomas. "The Rise of Evangelical Calvinism: A Study in Jonathan Edwards and the Puritan Tradition." Doctoral dissertation, Union Theological Seminary, 1971. In *Dissertation Abstracts International,* 32 (1971), 1614A.
"The thesis of this dissertation is that the Evangelical Calvinism of Jonathan Edwards was a development of the preparationist-Stoddardean tradition and that Edwards' theology, consequently, can be best understood from that perspective."

Miller, Perry. "Edwards, Locke, and the Rhetoric of Sensation." In *Perspectives of Criticism*, ed. Harry Levin. Cambridge, 1950, pp. 103-123. Reprinted with new title in Miller's *Errand into the Wilderness*. Cambridge, 1956, pp. 167-183.
A study of Locke and Edwards on the nature of language, described by Buranelli as "the best article ever written on Edwards."
Miller contends that "Edwards' great discovery, his dramatic refashioning of sensational rhetoric, was his assertion that an idea in the mind is not only a form of perception but is also a determination of love or hate. To apprehend things only by their signs or words is not to apprehend them at all; but to apprehend them by their ideas is to comprehend them not only intellectually but passionately. For Edwards, in short, an idea became not merely a concept but an emotion.... For Edwards it was the most important achievement of his life and the key to his doctrine and practice."

Miller, Perry. *Errand into the Wilderness.* Cambridge, 1956.

A collection of previously published essays by Miller which he describes as "a rank of spotlights on the massive narrative of the movement of European culture into the vacant wilderness of America." The essays appear with new introductions and some modifications. ("A few of my more egregious lapses I have silently expunged for this edition. However, some of my *gaffes* are so much a part of the record that, assuming the record be worth preserving, I let them stand, with prefatory warning that readers may fully profit by my mistakes.")

The contents list below includes only those essays of direct significance to students of Edwards.

Contents

The Marrow of Puritan Divinity, pp. 48-98.
Jonathan Edwards and the Great Awakening, pp. 153-166.
The Rhetoric of Sensation, pp. 167-183.
From Edwards to Emerson, pp. 184-203.

Miller, Perry, ed. *Images and Shadows of Divine Things by Jonathan Edwards.* New Haven, 1948.

"Although he is customarily represented as an arch-reactionary Calvinist, Edwards is properly to be described as the first American empiricist ...."

In his provocative Introduction to *Images* (pp. 1-41), Miller suggests that to appreciate "what Edwards was attempting in this manuscript, we must read it in full awareness that behind it loom the figures of Newton and Locke." Miller argues that Edwards developed a new extension of typology reinterpreted by the new science and psychology. Edwards' *Images,* Miller suggests, "was what the *Prelude* was to Wordsworth, a

secret and sustained effort to work out a new sense of
the divinity of nature and the naturalness of divinity."
Reviews
Niebuhr, Reinhold. *Nation,* 168 (1949), 79.
Richards, I. A. *New England Quarterly,* 22 (1949),
409-411.
Schneider, Herbert W. *Journal of Philosophy,* 46 (1949),
569-571.
Smith, H. Shelton. *American Literature,* 22 (1950),
192-194.
Townsend, Harvey G. *Philosophical Review,* 57 (1948),
622-623.

Miller, Perry. *Jonathan Edwards.* New York, 1949.
This intellectual biography of Edwards is the single
most important volume in modern Edwards scholarship and
now the inevitable starting point for any consideration
of Edwards as a thinker. Miller incorporates in this
study many of the themes of previous scholarship: that
there was a difference between what Edwards himself
believed and what he taught to others (or rather, what
he appeared to teach to others); that Edwards' writings
are an immense "cryptogram"—"a hoax, not to be read but
to be seen through;" and that the key to the "real
meaning" of Edwards' writings is to be found in the
philosophical and scientific speculations of his youth.
In no sense, however, can Miller's *Edwards* be read as a
simple recasting of the conclusions of earlier scholars.
Indeed, Miller proposes so many distinctive and
provocative theses concerning Edwards and the meaning of
Edwards for America that they cannot be suggested in
this brief space. One must be content with noting
Miller's central thesis.
Edwards' early reading of Locke, Miller suggests,

was "the central and decisive event in his intellectual
life." Locke made Edwards an "empiricist" in the sense
that Edwards "scorned the doctrinaire," and insisted
that "history, observation, and experience are the
things which must determine the question." Miller also
emphasizes the decisive influence of Newton on Edwards'
thought, and argues that Edwards' absorption in
Newtonian science, reinforced by his Lockean "empiricism," combined to make Edwards a "naturalist." This,
Miller suggests, was Edwards' great secret: "His supernaturalism was naturalized, or if you will, he supernat-
uralized nature."

It is easy, popular, and often necessary to find
fault with Miller's interpretation; and Peter Gay is
one scholar who has suggested that Miller's *Edwards* is,
in a word, "perverse." Yet few would question the
judgment of James H. Nichols: that "For the first time
America's first great theologian has been interpreted
with passion and brilliance measurably adequate to his
own."

Reviews and Criticisms

This listing is extremely selective. The works that
have either built upon Miller's insights or attempted to
correct his conclusions are too numerous to mention. As
one writer has observed, Miller's work "has been praised
and damned, but it has left no one indifferent."

Gay, Peter. "Jonathan Edwards: An American Tragedy."
    In his *A Loss of Mastery: Puritan Historians in
    Colonial America*. Berkeley, 1966, pp. 88-117.
Haroutunian, Joseph G. *Theology Today*, 7 (1951),
    554-556.
Johnson, Thomas H. *Saturday Review of Literature*,
    7 January 1950, p. 17.

Larrabee, Harold A. *New England Quarterly,*
    23 (1950), 106-109.
Lewis, R. W. B. "The Drama of Jonathan Edwards."
    Hudson Review, 3 (1950), 135-140.
Nichols, James H. *Church History,* 20 (1951), 75-82.
Niebuhr, Reinhold. *Nation,* 169 (1949), 648-649.
Roberts, Preston. *Journal of Religion,* 30 (1950),
    267-270.
Tomas, Vincent. "The Modernity of Jonathan Edwards."
    New England Quarterly, 25 (1952), 60-84.

Miller, Perry. "Jonathan Edwards and the Great Awakening."
In *America in Crisis,* ed. Daniel Aaron. New York, 1950,
pp. 3-19. Reprinted in Miller's *Errand into the
Wilderness.* Cambridge, 1956, pp. 153-166.
Miller discusses what the "Great Awakening did to the
conception of the relation of the ruler—political or
ecclesiastical—to the body politic." Miller suggests
that, from one perspective, what the "hysterical
agonies" of the Great Awakening meant was "the end of
the reign over the New England and American mind of a
European and scholastic conception of an authority put
over men because men were incapable of recognizing their
own welfare." Edwards is not put forth as a prophet of
democracy; rather, Miller contends that the "greatness
of Jonathan Edwards is that he understood what had
happened."

Miller, Perry. "Jonathan Edwards—Speculative Genius."
Saturday Review of Literature, 30 March 1940, pp. 6-7.
Review of Ola E. Winslow's *Jonathan Edwards* (New York,
1940).

Miller, Perry. "Jonathan Edwards to Emerson." *New England Quarterly*, 13 (1940), 589-617. Reprinted with new title in Miller's *Errand into the Wilderness*. Cambridge, 1956, pp. 184-203.
A study in continuities of thought from Edwards to Emerson. In the new introduction to this essay in *Errand* Miller notes that the argument of this essay "has been unhappily construed by many readers" since its first appearance in 1940. Miller insists that he is not suggesting a "direct line of intellectual descent, as though Edwards were a Holinshed to Emerson's Shakespeare." "On the crudest of levels, I am arguing that certain basic continuities persist in a culture... which underlie the successive articulation of 'ideas.'" What is persistent, Miller suggests, "from the covenant theology (and from the heretics against the covenant) to Edwards and to Emerson is the Puritan's effort to confront, face to face, the image of a blinding divinity in the physical universe, and to look upon that universe without the intermediacy of ritual, of ceremony, of the Mass and the confessional."

Miller, Perry. "The Marrow of Puritan Divinity." *Publications of the Colonial Society of Massachusetts*, 32 (1935), 247-300. Reprinted in Miller's *Errand into the Wilderness*. Cambridge, 1956, pp. 48-98.
Miller analyzes the development of the Puritan covenant theology, reading its basic thematic as a response to the task "of bringing God to time and to reason, of justifying His ways to man in conceptions meaningful to the intellect, of caging and confining the transcendent force, the inexpressible and unfathomable Being, by the laws of ethics, and of doing this somehow without losing the sense of the hidden God, without reducing the

Divinity to a mechanism, and without depriving Him of unpredictability, absolute power, fearfulness, and mystery."

Miller mentions Edwards only at the close of his analysis where he makes the provocative statement: "It is... not surprising to find that when Jonathan Edwards came to feel that rationalism and ethics had stifled the doctrine of God's sovereignty and dethroned the doctrine of grace, he threw over the whole covenant scheme, repudiated the conception of transmission of sin by judicial imputation, declared God unfettered by any agreement or obligation, made grace irresistible, and annihilated the natural ability of man." Edwards, Miller contends, became "the first consistent and authentic Calvinist in New England." See, however, Miller's new introduction to this essay in *Errand*.

Miller, Raymond Clinton. "Jonathan Edwards and his Influence upon Some of the New England Theologians." Doctoral dissertation, Temple University, 1945.

Miller, Samuel. *The Life of Jonathan Edwards, President of the College of New Jersey.* In *Library of American Biography*, ed. Jared Sparks. New York, 1837. Vol. VIII, pp. 1-256.
"The writer of these pages... considered himself as called upon, not to be the apologist of a party, but faithfully to exhibit one of the greatest of men just as he was, and to endeavor to render his history and character useful to the great cause to which he consecrated his life."

Miller provides a readable narrative of Edwards' life that includes lengthy extracts from Edwards' autobiographical writings and generous quotations from

European philosophers and theologians attesting to
Edwards' greatness. The content and context of Edwards'
major writings are briefly reviewed, but there is little
in the way of critical analysis. Despite Miller's
avowed concern "not to be the apologist of a party," his
Princeton affiliation is more than apparent in his
attempt to claim Edwards as an "Old Calvinist;" to
dissociate Edwards from his so-called followers ("not a
few of his professed admirers are, insidiously,
attempting to turn his heavy artillery against that very
citadel which it was his honor to have long and successfully defended"); and to caution against Edwards'
problematic treatise on *The Nature of True Virtue*—the
one treatise at which "the sound theologian should
hesitate."

Minton, Henry Collin. "President Jonathan Edwards."
    Presbyterian Quarterly, 13 (1899), 68-94.
    "...[W]e may be well assured of this, that with all
    our boasting greatness, in all that makes a great
    thinker, a great preacher, a great, good, godly man,
    either in brain or in heart, there hath not arisen among
    us a greater than Jonathan Edwards, the Elder."
        A critical sketch of Edwards as a philosophical
    theologian, with particular reference to his
    "eccentric" theory of the nature of virtue. Still
    worth reading.

Mitchell, Donald G. "Dr. Jonathan Edwards." In his
    American Lands and Letters. New York, 1897-99. Vol. I,
    pp. 58-67.

More, Paul Elmer. "Edwards." In *Cambridge History of
    American Literature*. New York, 1917. Vol. I,

pp. 57-71. Reprinted with minor revisions in More's *A New England Group and Others*. Boston, 1921, pp. 35-65. Once described as a "brilliant essay but not very informative." Essentially, More presents Edwards as a man who devoted his life to the service of one particular dogma: the doctrine of original sin. Again, however, the suggestion is made that what Edwards preached to others could not be taken as a sure guide to the real Edwards.

"It is a misfortune," More suggests, "but one for which he is himself responsible, that his memory in the popular mind today is almost exclusively associated with certain brimstone sermons and their terrible effect." Edwards, More contends, "not only suppressed his personal ecstasy in his works for the press, but waived it largely in his more direct intercourse with men. He who himself, like an earlier and perhaps greater Emerson, was enjoying the sweetness of walking with God in the garden of earth, was much addicted to holding up before his people the 'pleasant, bright, and sweet' doctrine of damnation."

Morris, George Perry. "The Human Side of Edwards." *Congregationalist and Christian World*, 88 (1903), 461-462.
"A great man awaits a great biographer."
Morris argues the need for a biography which sets forth "the man Edwards and not Edwards the theologian," suggesting the resources upon which such a biographer might draw. Morris suggests that "when this more human, normal, earthly side of the man is described, and he is brought down among men, we perhaps will have an end of such misrepresentations of him as O. W. Holmes displayed during his life...." Includes a brief note on the

Edwards manuscripts which was later reprinted (but
incorrectly attributed to George Perry Edwards) as "The
Edwards Manuscripts," *Journal of the Presbyterian
Historical Society*, 2 (1903), 169-170.

Morris, William S. "The Genius of Jonathan Edwards." In
   Reinterpretation in American Church History, ed. Gerald
   C. Brauer. Chicago, 1968, pp. 29-65.
   Edwards' genius, Morris suggests, lay in a combination
   of both Lockean empiricism and scholastic logic.
   Edwards "mediated between a philosophical and theological heritage which he treasured and a contemporary
   mentality which, critically, he shared."
       Morris attempts to demonstrate in detail the influ-
   ence of the concepts and methods of both Locke and
   Burgersdijck in the development of Edwards' thought,
   focusing primarily on Edwards' early philosophical
   notes.

Morris, William S. "The Reappraisal of Edwards." *New
   England Quarterly*, 30 (1957), 515-525.
   "...[W]hat preeminently distinguishes Edwards is not his
   character nor his career but his thought. What his
   philosophy and theology need is analysis rather than
   translation into the terms of biography, drama, or
   tragedy."
       An essay review of Paul Ramsey's *Freedom of the Will*
   (New Haven, 1957). In a generally favorable review of
   Ramsey's editorial accomplishments and his interpretive
   Introduction to the text, Morris challenges Ramsey's
   analysis of the philosophical argument of Edwards'
   treatise. In particular, Morris rejects Ramsey's "novel
   but ambiguous thesis" that Edwards' account of volition
   does not preclude it from being self-moved. Morris'

essay includes a brief but instructive review of the
history of Edwards scholarship.

Morris, William S. "The Young Jonathan Edwards: A
    Reconstruction." Doctoral dissertation, University of
    Chicago, 1956.
    The most extensive, critical analysis of Edwards' early
    thought available. Morris stresses the importance of
    Heereboord and Burgersdijck as major sources of Edwards'
    early metaphysical conclusions: "It is an essential
    part of my contention... that not only were they, along
    with Newton and Locke, the major contributing factors in
    the formation of his own metaphysics, but also that in
    Heereboord, and to a lesser extent in Burgersdicius,
    Edwards found the principles whereby he was able to
    relate his philosophy to theology."

Mothersill, Mary. "Professor Prior and Jonathan Edwards."
    Review of Metaphysics, 16 (1962), 366-373.
    A critique of A. N. Prior's response to Edwards on
    limited indeterminism.

Moulton, Charles W., ed. "Jonathan Edwards." In *Library of*
    Literary Criticism. Buffalo, 1902. Vol. III,
    pp. 380-398.
    An extensive collection of remarks on Edwards from
    previous publications. Includes quotations from many
    works in the general area of American literature that
    have not been included in this bibliography.

Murphy, Arthur E. "Jonathan Edwards on Free Will and Moral
    Agency." *Philosophical Review,* 68 (1959), 181-202.
    Edwards was "a theologian first and last and a philoso-
    pher only in between and where such 'inquiry' served a

higher purpose. Unless we keep this in mind as firmly
as Edwards himself did, we shall fail to appreciate the
power or the limitations of his thinking."

Murphy provides a critical analysis of Edwards'
philosophical argument in *Freedom of the Will*, and
evaluates the interpretation of this treatise proposed
by Paul Ramsey. Murphy challenges Ramsey's conclusion
that "there is nothing in Edwards' account of an act of
free, responsible volition which precludes it from being
independent and self-moved." To speak of an act of
volition as being self-moved, insists Murphy, "is, on
Edwards' own repeated showing, an absurdity."

Nagy, Paul J. "The Beloved Community of Jonathan Edwards."
Transactions of the Charles S. Peirce Society, 7 (1971),
93-104.

Nagy, Paul J. "The Doctrine of Experience in the
Philosophy of Jonathan Edwards." Doctoral dissertation,
Fordham University, 1968. In *Dissertation Abstracts*,
29 (1968), 639A.
"A number of basic themes suggest themselves as focal
points for a study of the thought of Jonathan Edwards.
The dissertation is an attempt to argue that experience
is one of them, and that an attentive eye to the
doctrine of experience will reveal it as the unifying
theme of his philosophy. Specifically, at the center
of Edwards' aesthetic and religious vision there lies a
rich and profound sense of experience, and of the
relation of all things to some form of perception."

Nagy, Paul J. "Jonathan Edwards and the Metaphysics of
Consent." *The Personalist*, 51 (1970), 434-446.
"I suggest that Edwards did not merely bring an older

Calvinism up to date by modifying it to the demands of
Locke's empiricism and Newton's physics, but that he
embarked from these two points upon an exploration of
uncharted regions of the mind and thereby added some
highly original thoughts to common understanding."

Nagy finds the key to Edwards' philosophy in his
"highly original notion" of consent to being, and
unpacks the meaning of this concept under three
headings: consent as relation, as response to value,
and as communication.

Naples, Diane Clark. "The Sensible Order: An Interpretation and Critical Edition of Jonathan Edwards' *Personal
Narrative.*" Doctoral dissertation, University of
California, Los Angeles, 1973. In *Dissertation
Abstracts International,* 34 (1973), 3421A.
This study "is chiefly concerned with the personal
motivations and philosophical assumptions that shaped
the *Personal Narrative.* Edwards' spiritual autobiography is examined in the light of his theory of
spiritual epistemology and of theories of developmental
psychology implicit in his writings."

Nelson, Roscoe. "Jonathan Edwards." In *Founders and
Leaders of Connecticut, 1633-1783,* ed. Charles Edward
Perry. Boston, 1934, pp. 147-150.

Newlin, Claude M. *Philosophy and Religion in Colonial
America.* New York, 1962.
Three major sections of this work are devoted to
Edwards: "Jonathan Edwards Vs. Arminianism," "Jonathan
Edwards, the New Divinity, and the Moral Sense," and
"Jonathan Edwards on the Emotions." Of these the first
two are the most valuable, dealing with Edwards'

Freedom of the Will and the companion treatises
Concerning the End for which God Created the World and
The Nature of True Virtue. Newlin details the central
arguments of these works, the occasion of their publication, and outlines subsequent responses by both
critics and followers of Edwards.

Newtoun, Beach. *A Preservative against the Doctrine of
Fate: Occasioned by reading Mr. Jonathan Edwards
against Free Will... Proposed to the Consideration of
Young Students in Divinity*. Boston, 1770.
One of the least formidable of the responses to Edwards'
Freedom of the Will. "The sum of all the controversy,"
observes Newtoun, "between Mr. *Edwards* and those he
calls *Arminians*, is this, whether man has truly any free
will at all, which is not moved as necessarily as any
natural motions are caused?" "Whether man is not an
engine moved by God and other causes, no less necessarily than a clock or a watch, but only by more invisible
causes, and to us unknown?" If this is the case,
Newtoun argues, then "we are no more subjects of virtue
and vice than an ax, sword, or gun: nor are we any more
capable of being called to account, or judged for things
done in the body, than the winds and clouds are account-
able for their motions." To accept Edwards' scheme,
Newtoun contends, is "to exempt men and devils from all
guilt and blame, and to cast the whole load on God
blessed forever;" to "contradict common sense, and to
overthrow morality and religion, and to encourage an
atheistical course of life under the pretence of
philosophy."

Nichol, John. "Jonathan Edwards." In his *American
Literature*. Edinburgh, 1882, pp. 52-55.

Niebuhr, H. Richard. *The Kingdom of God in America.*
Chicago, 1937.
This work is primarily important not as criticism or
interpretation of Edwards, but because it reveals
Edwards as a major influence on Niebuhr's thought. For
discussions of Niebuhr's relation to Edwards, see the
article by Leo Sandon below; see also Sandon,
"H. Richard Niebuhr's Interpretation of the American
Theological Tradition," Doctoral dissertation (Boston
University, 1971); Sydney E. Ahlstrom, *A Religious
History of the American People* (New Haven, 1972); and
Libertus A. Hoedemaker, *The Theology of H. Richard
Niebuhr* (Boston, 1970).

Nordell, Philip G. "Jonathan Edwards and Hell Fire,"
Forum, 75 (1926), 860-869.
Essentially a biographical sketch of Edwards. Despite
the appropriation of Edwards by the eugenists, Nordell
makes bold to suggest that "there was more in him than
the seeds of a famous family." Along with his
undisputed powers of intellect, Nordell finds hell fire
in great abundance: "One finds in a survey of his
religious writings that they simply reek and seethe with
implacable arguments proving the horrible reality of
God's wrath upon the wicked."
Nordell indicts Edwards not because of his
imprecatory sermons as such ("he was an extreme product
of his environment"), but because "with all his endowments of intellect he never summoned the courage or the
will to question his most fundamental premises."
Edwards, Nordell concludes, "presents the pitiful consequences, carried to their logical extremity of
conforming oneself without compromise to a false, harsh,
and artificial standard of morality, —in itself a

negation of the best in life."

Oldmixon, Felix. [pseud.] "Old Colonial Characters. I.
Jonathan Edwards." *Connecticut Quarterly*, 1 (1895),
33-38.

Oldmixon, Felix. [pseud.] "Old Colonial Characters. II.
Edwards and Burr: A Series of Sorrows." *Connecticut
Quarterly*, 1 (1895), 155-159.

Olsen, Wesley A. "The Philosophy of Jonathan Edwards and
its Significance for Educational Thinking." Doctoral
dissertation, Rutgers University, 1973.

O'Malley, J. Steven. "Edwards and the Problem of Knowledge
in the Protestant Tradition." *Drew Gateway*, 40 (1970),
54-79.
"Although the Protestant Reformers denied that reason
is the basis for theology, they did not examine reason
critically. With the rise of scientific thinking,
reason challenged theology more than ever. Jonathan
Edwards responded by saying, 'There is no other way
which any means of grace whatsoever can be of any
benefit, but by knowledge.' Edwards stripped reason of
its metaphysical meaning and it came to be understood
in its public meaning, as the reason why we do the
things we do. He thus provided a cognitive basis for
theology that was at once philosophically sublime and
corporately meaningful; the everyday world provided the
model for our knowledge of God" through the Word.

Opie, John, Jr. "Conversion and Revivalism: An Internal
History from Jonathan Edwards through Charles Grandison
Finney." Doctoral dissertation, University of

Chicago, 1964.

Opie, John, Jr., ed. *Jonathan Edwards and the Enlightenment.*
Lexington, Mass., 1969.
Opie provides selections from Edwards' writings and
lengthy extracts from previously published studies of
Edwards, attempting to illumine Edwards' relationship to
Enlightenment thinking. Included are the contrasting
judgments of Perry Miller and Vincent Tomas concerning
the modernity of Edwards' thought, of Hornberger and
Faust on Edwards as a scientist, and of Parrington, Gay,
Winslow, and Cherry on the continuing significance of
Edwards. Includes a brief bibliographical essay.

Ormond, Alexander T. "Jonathan Edwards as Thinker and
Philosopher." *Princeton University Bulletin,*
15 (1904), 62-74. An abstract of this paper can be
found under the title, "Jonathan Edwards as a Thinker."
Philosophical Review, 13 (1904), 183-184.
A suggestive study that has generally been overlooked by
Edwards scholars. Edwards, Ormond observes, "is such a
master of speculation, and his works are so rich in
speculative elements, that the presumption becomes
strong that his thought follows some system, if only the
key to that system could be found." Ormond discovers
that key in Edwards' doctrine of decrees and election.

Orr, James. "The Influence of Edwards." In *Exercises
Commemorating the 200th Anniversary of the Birth of
Jonathan Edwards.* Andover, 1904, pp. 105-126.
A superficial, generalized review of Edwards' theology
and philosophy. Orr cites European thinkers who
acknowledge their indebtedness to Edwards or attest to
his metaphysical genius.

"The admiration I have expressed for the genius
and character of Edwards is not to be construed as if I
were insensible of the limitations that inhere in the
piety and thought of this truly great and saintly man."
Orr observes that the "intensity of his nature on the
side of religion—absorbing, dwarfing all other interests—was not without an effect in limiting the range
of his human sympathies. There is a lack of the humanist element in him.... There is a lack also of full
sympathy with human nature in the individual."

Orr, James. "Jonathan Edwards: His Influence in Scotland."
Congregationalist and Christian World, 88 (1903),
467-468.
"When it comes to honoring Edwards, Scotland will not
be wanting with her wreath!"
    When Orr finally gets to the supposed point of his
paper, he provides a brief, superficial discussion of
the influence of Edwards' doctrine of the Atonement on
the work of John McLeod Campbell.

Osgood, Samuel. "Jonathan Edwards." *Christian Examiner*,
44 (1848), 367-386.
A discussion of Edwards as a revivalist, a summary
outline of his theology, and an evaluation of Edwards
as a thinker.
    "Theocrat in heart, his system was, after all, the
creature of his intellect, working at the bidding of his
emotions. It is not difficult to imagine him, under the
influence of other associations, giving his mind to the
defence [sic] of far other doctrines."

Osgood, Samuel. "Jonathan Edwards and the New Calvinism."
In his *Studies in Christian Biography*. New York,

1850, pp. 348-377.

Otto, M. C. "A Lesson from Jonathan Edwards." *The Humanist*, 1 (1941), 37-40.
Edwards is presented as a religious conservative *par excellence*, whose "stubborn opposition" to any humanitarian and liberalizing forces of his day "was merely the negative side of an aggressive determination to perpetuate, with all of their earlier authority and power, the conceptions and institutions, the whole practice of life, based upon the control of affairs, secular and spiritual, by the 'few wisest and best.'" Waxing prophetic, Otto parallels Edwards' activities with more recent efforts "to bring all the desires and practices of men under universal church authority," most notably, the efforts of Roman Catholicism, "which may prove startling to the general public when its design and success are better known."

"*Outlines of Moral Science*, by Archibald Alexander." *Biblical Repertory and Princeton Review*, 25 (1853), 1-43.
What is purportedly a review of Alexander's volume becomes a vehicle for criticizing Edwards' treatise on *The Nature of True Virtue* and a general attack upon the New England Theology. Alexander's work was published after his death, but published at his direction and upon the responsibility of the author. This is not, the reviewers note, true of all posthumous publications. "We doubt whether it was true of President Edwards's posthumous work on one important branch of the subject, his *Dissertation on the Nature of Virtue*; a work which has 'astonished most of his admirers,' while it has, partly by a perversion, and partly by a fair use of its

leading principle, been employed to subvert doctrines
which that great divine gained his chief celebrity in
defending."

The reviewers contend that this late treatise stands
in conflict with Edwards' previous statements concerning
the nature of virtue, and suggest that the work reflects
occasional, tentative speculations, "outside of the main
fabric of his theology."

Park, Edwards Amasa. "Characteristics of Edwards." In *The
Memorial Volume of the Edwards Family Meeting,* ed.
Jonathan E. Woodbridge. Boston, 1871, pp. 104-121.
Park speaks *ex tempore* at the Edwards family meeting,
remarking on "the comprehensiveness" of Edwards'
character and writings. "They contain elements to which
different classes of partisans appeal, and from which
they seem to draw strength; yet they harmonize with
each other well enough to form a distinct system."
This theme is elaborated through a consideration of
Edwards' personal concerns, practical activities and
methods of discourse, his role as both advocate and
critic of the Great Awakening, and his relation to the
"old" and "new" divinity of the next generation.

Park, Edwards Amasa. "Dr. Alexander's *Moral Science.*"
Bibliotheca Sacra, 10 (1853), 390-414.
Under the guise of a review of Alexander's volume, Park
attempts an elaborate response to the criticisms and
"misconstructions" of *The Nature of True Virtue* by both
Alexander and the *Princeton Review* essayists (see
"Outlines"), and a general defense of the New England
Theology and its continuity with Edwards. The argument
of this article is continued in "President Edwards's
Dissertation on the Nature of True Virtue" in the same

volume of *Bibliotheca Sacra.*

Park, Edwards Amasa. "Jonathan Edwards." In *Cyclopaedia of Biblical, Theological and Ecclesiastical Literature,* ed. John McClintock and James Strong. New York, 1867-1887. Vol. III, pp. 63-67.

Park, Edwards Amasa. "Jonathan Edwards, the Elder." In *Schaff-Herzog Encyclopedia.* New York, 1882-1884. Vol. II, pp. 697-699.
Brief biographical sketch with list of Edwards' publications.

Park, Edwards Amasa. "New England Theology." *Bibliotheca Sacra,* 9 (1852), 170-219.
An elaborate explanation and defense of the New England Theology and its continuity with the theology of Edwards. The New England theologians, Park argues, did not harmonize on all issues, but in the main they agreed on "three radical principles" which distinguished their theology and entitled them to a generic name: namely, "that sin consists in choice, that our natural power equals, and that it also limits, our duty." These three principles, Park insists, were clearly maintained by the elder Edwards.

Park, Edwards Amasa. "Remarks of Jonathan Edwards on the Trinity." *Bibliotheca Sacra,* 38 (1881), 147-187; 333-369.
Park responds to the call for the publication of Edwards' supposedly heterodox tract on the Trinity, and enters into a lengthy discussion concerning the problems involved in the interpretation of those writings left unpublished at Edwards' death. Includes extracts from

Edwards' unpublished *Miscellanies*.

Park, Edwards Amasa. "The Rise of the Edwardean Theory of
    the Atonement: An Introductory Essay." Editor's
    Introduction to *The Atonement: Discourses and Treatises
    by Edwards, Smalley, Maxcy, Emmons, Griffin, Burge, and
    Weeks*. Boston, 1859, pp. i-lxxx.
    A fascinating study in which Park details the develop-
    ment of the Edwardsean theory of the Atonement from its
    genesis in the writings of President Edwards. Edwards
    himself, Park insists, did not hold the "Edwardean"
    theory: Edwards "adopted, in general, both the views
    and the phrases of the Older Calvinists with regard to
    the atonement, but like those Calvinists, he made vari-
    ous remarks, which have suggested the more modern
    theory." See Cooke for a devastating criticism of
    Park's essay.

Parker, Gail Thain. "Jonathan Edwards and Melancholy." *New
    England Quarterly*, 41 (1968), 193-212.
    Parker explores Edwards' personal experiences of
    melancholy and his attempts to deal with the "virulent
    form the disease had assumed" during the revival,
    suggesting that there was an intimate connection between
    Edwards' emphasis on the need for experimental religion
    and his familiarity with the disease of melancholy in
    himself and others. Underlying Edwards' conception of
    experimental religion, "with the mind neither in lock-
    step with objective reality nor locked within itself,
    was a profound suspicion that those experiences which
    'remain in the soul...; begin and are terminated there,
    without any immediate relation to anything done out-
    wardly,' could never provide truly reliable evidence of
    an individual's inclination."

Parker, William H. "Jonathan Edwards: Founder of the
Counter-Tradition of Transcendental Thought in America."
Georgia Review, 27 (1973), 543-549.
"In insisting on the reality and efficacy of religious
affections, in valuing them more highly than 'the
speculative faculty, or the understanding,' and in
holding them to be the essential springs of growth and
[c]hange, Edwards adumbrated the key tenets of the
transcendental tradition in American thought."

Parker, William H. "The Social Theory of Jonathan Edwards:
As Developed in his Works on Revivalism." Doctoral
dissertation, Syracuse University, 1968. In *Dissertation Abstracts*, 29 (1969), 4104A-4105A.
"The purpose of this study is to demonstrate that
Edwards' works on revivalism can be read as an attempt
to work out a theory for the realization of a
universal, Christian social order."

Parkes, Henry Bamford. *Jonathan Edwards: The Fiery
Puritan*. New York, 1930.
"He fastened upon the neck of his countrymen a
Puritanism such as we know today."
    A popularized biography of Edwards providing only
a superficial and often misleading treatment of Edwards'
thought. The title reveals Parkes' bias and the
perspective from which he writes. Parkes delights in
pointing out the "negative" aspects of Edwards as a
thinker and his role in the history of American culture.
Edwards' theology is presented from its bleakest side,
the Enfield sermon is cited as evidence of the
"sadistic" or "sinister" side of Edwards, and the Great
Awakening is discussed largely in terms of its more
unfortunate effects. While one is advised to look else-

where for a more trustworthy exposition of Edwards'
thought, Parkes' study offers valuable information
concerning the social context of the period. See also
Parkes, "New England in the Seventeen-Thirties." *New
England Quarterly*, 3 (1930), 397-419.

Reviews

Johnson, Thomas H. *New England Quarterly*, 4 (1931),
    354-356.

Schneider, Herbert W. *Nation*, 131 (1930), 584-585.

Van Doren, Carl. "The Metaphysical Messiah." New York
    Herald Tribune Books, 21 September 1930, p. 7.

Warren, Austin. *American Literature*, 4 (1932-33),
    314-318.

Parr, Samuel. *A Spital Sermon [on Gal. vi. 10] preached...
upon Easter Tuesday, April 15, 1800. To which are added
notes.* London, 1801.

In the course of this sermon Parr challenges William
Godwin's understanding of Edwards' doctrine of virtue.

    "Mr. Edwards is a writer who exercises our minds,
even where he does not satisfy them; who interests us,
where he does not persuade; who instructs and improves
us, where he does not ultimately convince; and as I
know his authority to be very great, among a numerous
and pious class of Christians, it is of some importance
that his real opinions should be clearly understood.
From his own words then, I will endeavor to show that,
in his estimation, gratitude is, in many respects, not
unconnected with justice; and that the virtue from
which he distinguishes it, is essentially different from
the virtue of which the author of Political Justice
pronounces it to be no part."

Parrington, Vernon L. "The Anachronism of Jonathan
Edwards." In his *Main Currents in American Thought*.
New York, 1927. Vol. I, pp. 149-163.
Parrington presents Edwards as a tragic figure, who
devoted his life to the thankless task of preaching an
already archaic theology, and a theology that was also
at odds with Edwards' own intellectual leanings.

Parrington suggests that the basic trend of Edwards'
thinking was toward some form of transcendentalism or
mysticism, but "the normal unfolding of his mind was
interrupted by his conversion," and Edwards turned from
philosophy to the theology of Calvinism. This theology,
Parrington suggests, "did unconscious violence to the
instincts of the mystic." Edwards had to choose between
that transcendentalism which marked his early career, or
the doctrine of total depravity: "Instead," Parrington
argues, "he sought refuge in compromise, endeavoring to
reconcile what was incompatible. Herein lay the tragedy
of Edwards's intellectual life; the theologian
triumphed over the philosopher, circumscribing his
powers to ignoble ends."

Parton, James. *The Life and Times of Aaron Burr*. 2 vols.
Boston and New York, 1892.
Includes (I, pp. 25-30) a chapter on Edwards, "the
father of Aaron Burr's mother."

Patterson, Robert Leet. *The Philosophy of William Ellery
Channing*. New York, 1952.
Patterson examines the influence of Edwards on the
thought of Channing, particularly Edwards' notion of a
spiritual or supernatural sense.

Patton, William Weston, ed. *Edwards on Revivals*. London,
1839.
Includes the texts of Edwards' *Faithful Narrative* and
Some Thoughts, with introduction and notes by Patton.
Frequently cited (e.g., by Coss) in bibliographies of
biography and criticism of Edwards.

Perry, Ralph Barton. *Puritanism and Democracy*. New York,
1944.
Includes brief but insightful comments on Edwards'
theology.
        "Edwards differs from other orthodox Christians, not
in a failure to relieve God of responsibility, but in
his rejection of the attempt. Semi-Pelagians,
Arminians, and even the covenant theologians do not
succeed in exculpating God; their attempt to do so only
betrays their unwillingness to love God as he is. It
signifies a conditional love of God, a judgment of God
by standards other than himself. For Edwards God needs
no justification."

Pfisterer, Karl Dieterich. "The Prism of Scripture:
Studies on History and Historicity in the Work of
Jonathan Edwards." Doctoral dissertation, Columbia
University, 1973. In *Dissertation Abstracts Inter-
national*, 35 (1974), 570A.

Phelps, William Lyon. "Makers of American Literature:
Edwards and Franklin—The Man of God and the Man of the
World: A Dramatic Contrast." *Ladies Home Journal*,
39 (November, 1922), 16ff. Reprinted in Phelps, *Some
Makers of American Literature*. Boston, 1923, pp. 1-33.
An insightful contrast of Edwards and Franklin by a man
sympathetic to both.

"If in the future some man should appear who should
combine the sincere piety, idealism, purity, and
uncompromising morality of Jonathan Edwards with the
profound wisdom, insight, humor, tact and kindliness of
Franklin, then we should have the ideal American. If
such men became numerous, we should have the millenium."

Phelps, William Lyon. "Two Colonial Americans [Edwards and
    Franklin]." In *Papers and Addresses of the Society of
    Colonial Wars in the State of Connecticut.* n.p., 1910.
    Vol. II, pp. 197-204.

Pierce, David Clarence. "Jonathan Edwards and the New Sense
    of Glory." Doctoral dissertation, Columbia University,
    1965. In *Dissertation Abstracts,* 27 (1967), 4333A.

Pierce, David Clarence. "Jonathan Edwards and the 'New
    Sense' of Glory." *New England Quarterly,* 41 (1968),
    82-95.
    Pierce suggests that the *Personal Narrative* "is more
than merely a testimony to the depth of Edwards' devotion to God and to the warmth of his piety; it
provides an interesting insight into that discontinuity
which has so often been noted in regard to the career of
this 'Puritan sage.'" In the light of the *Narrative,*
Pierce argues, "one is led to conclude that the discontinuity so frequently noted in Edwards' mind was one
that cut to the heart of his religious experience. The
account suggests, in fact, that Edwards was embracing
two forms of piety at one and the same time. On the one
hand, he declared his devotion to the God of absolute
sovereignty and, on the other hand, he voiced his
delight in the divine omnipresence in all creation.
Closely related as these forms were, they involved

fundamentally differing frames of reference."

Pierce, Howard Franklin. "Jonathan Edwards and his Relation
    to New England Theology." Doctoral dissertation, Temple
    University, 1912.

Pierce, Richard C. "A Suppressed Edwards Manuscript on the
    Trinity." *Crane Review*, 1 (1959), 66-80.
    Pierce relates the public controversy surrounding
    Edwards' supposedly heterodox manuscript on the Trinity,
    and details what was happening behind the scenes as evi-
    denced by the private correspondence among the custo-
    dians of the Edwards manuscripts.
        "The Nineteenth Century custodians of the Edwards
    manuscripts... in the interests of keeping Edwards in
    conformity with their own position saw fit to withhold
    his discussions of the trinity until suspicion rested so
    heavily upon them that they were forced to discuss and
    publish the controversial documents lest their ancestor
    be imputed with even greater heresies."

Piper, John. "Jonathan Edwards on the Problem of Faith and
    History." *Scottish Journal of Theology*, 31 (1978),
    217-228.

Platner, John W. "Religious Conditions in New England in
    the Time of Edwards." In *Exercises Commemorating the
    200th Anniversary of the Birth of Jonathan Edwards*.
    Andover, 1904, pp. 29-45.
    The introductory address at the Andover celebration. It
    is a popularized and somewhat superficial evaluation of
    Edwards' role in American religious history: Edwards
    found New England un-theological; he left it equipped
    with all the apparatus for an energetic theological life,

opening a new chapter in American religious thought.
Platner suggests, however, that "when we ask ourselves
what service Edwards rendered which appeals most
strongly to the religious sympathies of today, I think
we shall not find it in his theology. We must seek it
rather in his spiritual insight and his mysticism."

Plues, Robert. *The Reverend C. H. Spurgeon and his
Brethren, Drs. Payne and Wardlaw, President Edwards, and
others, in the Crucible; or, the peculiarities of
Calvinism tested.* North Shields, 1862.

Pond, Enoch. "Review of Edwards on the Will." *Literary and
Theological Review,* 1 (1834), 523-539.

Porter, Noah. "Philosophy in Great Britain and America."
An Appendix to Überweg's *A History of Philosophy,* trans.
George S. Morris. New York, 1893. Vol. II, pp. 348-460.
Porter includes in this essay a brief item on Edwards
("Jonathan Edwards," pp. 442-448) presenting a concise
statement of the content of Edwards' major treatises.
Particular attention is given to *Freedom of the Will,*
"the work on which Edwards' reputation chiefly rests."
Porter notes the modifications of Edwards' doctrine of
the will made by his followers, and provides valuable
bibliographical references concerning the early discussion and criticism of this treatise.
    Also included is a summary review of the Edwardseans
("The Disciples of Edwards," pp. 449-450) who are said to
have "deviated more or less pronouncedly from the doctrines of Edwards in respect to the Will, the Nature of
Holiness and of Sin, the Nature and Authority of the
Moral Government of God, and the Atonement and the Work
of Christ...."

Porter, Noah. "The Princeton Review on Dr. Taylor and the
    Edwardean Theology." *New Englander*, 18 (1860),
    726-773.
    The largest portion of this lengthy article is devoted to
    a defense of Taylor's theology against the criticisms of
    Lyman Atwater [see "Dr. Taylor's Lectures on the Moral
    Government of God," *Biblical Repertory and Princeton
    Review*, 31 (1859), 489-538]; but Porter also responds to
    Atwater's article on "Successive Forms of New Divinity."
        Porter is amazed at Atwater's suggestion that
    Edwards "was nothing more or less than a good old fash-
    ioned Calvinist, like Stapfer, excepting only that he
    held an eccentric theory on virtue." Porter contends
    that in his analysis of Edwards, Atwater had overlooked
    the "grand and distinguishing feature" of Edwards'
    thought. "The leading peculiarity which distinguished
    Edwards as a theologian," Porter argues, "was, that he
    was a philosopher as well as a divine. He not only
    dared to think, but he felt bound to think as a philo-
    sopher, in order that he might think as a theologian."
    Edwards "developed a new method in theology, uncon-
    sciously to himself. He asserted principles in respect
    to theology, which excited and directed the minds of his
    so-called successors, and which, by right, entitle them
    to the appellation of Edwardean—which made them what
    they were, bold, enterprising, logical, consistent
    thinkers."

Porter, Noah. *The Two-Hundredth Birthday of Bishop George
    Berkeley. A Discourse Given at Yale College on the
    12th of March, 1885.* New York, 1885.
    Brief remarks on whether Edwards' early philosophical
    conclusions suggest a dependence on Berkeley.

Potwin, L. S. "Freedom of the Will:—Edwards and Whedon."
    New Englander, 24 (1865), 285-302.

Powell, Lyman P. "Jonathan Edwards, 1703-1758." In his
    Heavenly Heretics. New York, 1909, pp. 1-29.
    "He was orthodox from first to last, according to the
    tenets of New England Puritanism. He had to be. He
    lacked the special gifts of the originating thinker. He
    had the logic of the mathematician and the imagination of
    the poet, but they were rarely found in combination with
    historic sense or common sense or sense of humour."
        A popularized, superficial biographical sketch and
    evaluation of Edwards as a thinker. Little attention is
    given to the particulars of Edwards' theology or
    philosophy, while a great deal of attention is given to
    the Enfield sermon: "Shocking doctrine to this age of
    ours it seems. Where did Edwards learn it? Not from
    personal experience."

Pratt, Glenn Ralph. "Jonathan Edwards as a Preacher of
    Doctrine." Doctoral dissertation, Temple University,
    1958.

"President Edwards and New England Theology." *The
    Panoplist; or, The Christian's Armory*, 1 (1850),
    386-397; 430-436.

"President Edwards on Charity and its Fruits." *New
    Englander*, 10 (1852), 222-236.
    A review of *Charity and its Fruits* (London, 1851),
    edited by Tryon Edwards. Apart from some general
    comments on the style and content of these sermons, and
    a brief discussion of the Edwards manuscripts, the
    review consists largely in a number of lengthy extracts

from this work.

"President Edwards on Revivals." *The Quarterly Christian
    Spectator*, series 2, 1 (1827), 295-308.
    The writer recalls to the attention of ministers
    Edwards' work, *Some Thoughts concerning the Present
    Revival of Religion in New England*. A "few particulars"
    of this work are discussed in the light of the problems
    of current evangelical religion. The article is signed,
    "A Friend to Revivals."
    .

"President Edwards's Dissertation on the Nature of True
    Virtue." *Bibliotheca Sacra*, 10 (1853), 705-738.
    This article is invaluable. Written by a group of New
    England Theologians ("it cannot with truth be ascribed to
    any one individual"), it attempts a definitive statement
    of the doctrine of this treatise, responds to every major
    criticism that had ever been leveled against it, and
    attempts to refute the claim that in writing this
    treatise Edwards had contradicted his normative position
    on the nature of virtue. Their defense of Edwards'
    treatise is made the more intriguing by their less than
    fragile grasp of its content.

Price, Rebecca R. "Jonathan Edwards as a Christian
    Educator." Doctoral dissertation, New York University,
    1938.

Price, William Winfield. "The Eschatology of Jonathan
    Edwards." Doctoral dissertation, University of
    Göttingen, 1966.

Prior, A. N. "Limited Indeterminism." *Review of
    Metaphysics*, 16 (1962), 55-61.

Prior attempts to refute one of Edwards' arguments in *Freedom of the Will*, where Edwards argues that one cannot admit a limited indeterminism, that if indeterminism is admitted anywhere, then one must allow that it may appear everywhere. Prior's colleagues have judged his argument less than convincing. See, in the same volume, Mary Mothersill, "Professor Prior and Jonathan Edwards," pp. 366-373; and J. B. Schneewind, "Comments on Prior's Paper," pp. 374-379.

"Questions of the Two Edwardses for their Pupils in Theology." *Bibliotheca Sacra*, 39 (1882), 367-381.
A list of study questions. No answers are provided.

R., T. "Edwards's View of Original Sin: Reply to E. M." *The Quarterly Christian Spectator*, series 2, 2 (1828), 16-18.
See next entry. T. R. responds to E. M.'s criticisms of his interpretation of Edwards by attempting to clarify Edwards' conception of the unity of the race in the sin of Adam. T. R. suggests that "imperfect and incorrect notions of Edwards's views of *our representation in Adam*, are the principal source of disagreement respecting his opinions."

R., T. "Edwards's Views of Original Sin." *The Quarterly Christian Spectator*, 6 (1824), 567-575.
The writer attempts to ascertain whether or not Edwards maintains the doctrine of physical depravity: i.e., "that there is con-created with man a substantial property or attribute of his nature, which is in itself sinful and deserving of punishment." Following a detailed examination of various arguments in Edwards' *Original Sin*, the writer concludes: "I will not say

that this is a scriptural, common-sense account of the
matter, nor that it is one which tells in the universal
consciousness of men, nor that men know as well why they
sin as why they eat and drink; but I cannot hesitate to
affirm that here there is not the remotest resemblance
of the doctrine of physical depravity."

Ramsey, Paul, ed. *Freedom of the Will*. Volume I of *The
Works of Jonathan Edwards*. New Haven, 1957.
Ramsey's critical Introduction to *Freedom of the Will*
(pp. 1-128) provides little discussion of the theological issues involved. Rather, it is focused primarily on
analyzing the philosophical argument of this treatise,
and examining the relation of Edwards' position to
Lockean psychology and the writings of Edwards' principal antagonists: Isaac Watts, Thomas Chubbs, and Daniel
Whitby.
   Ramsey's analysis of the influence of Locke on
Edwards is not to be ignored. His interpretation of the
philosophical argument of this treatise has been widely
criticized: that "there is nothing in Edwards' account
of an act of free, responsible volition which precludes
it from being independent and self-moved."
Reviews and Criticisms
Beach, Waldo. "The Recovery of Jonathan Edwards."
   Religion in Life, 27 (1958), 286-289.
Holbrook, Clyde A. "Edwards Re-examined." *Review of
   Metaphysics*, 13 (1960), 623-641.
Morris, William S. "The Reappraisal of Edwards." *New
   England Quarterly*, 30 (1957), 515-525.
Murphy, Arthur E. "Jonathan Edwards on Free Will and
   Moral Agency." *Philosophical Review*, 68 (1959),
   181-202.

Rand, Benjamin. *Bibliography of Philosophy, Psychology, and Cognate Subjects.* In *Dictionary of Philosophy and Psychology,* ed. James M. Baldwin. New York, 1901-1905. Includes (III, pp. 188-189) bibliography of Edwards' *Works* and biography and criticism of Edwards. All items cited by Rand can be found in this bibliography.

[Rand, William]. *The Late Religious Commotions in New-England considered. An Answer to the Reverend Mr. Jonathan Edwards's Sermon, Entitled, "The Distinguishing Marks of a Work of the Spirit of God."* ...*By a Lover of Peace and Truth.* Boston, 1743.
A brief critique of Edwards and the revival. Rand suggests that Edwards' "distinguishing" marks, "instead of arguing a Work to be a Work of the *Spirit* of God, do rather offer a *strong* presumption to the contrary."

Rankin, J. E. "The Jonathan Edwards Letters." *The Independent,* 47 (1895), 1603.
Supplementary note on the letters previously published by Rankin in the same journal, 47 (1895), 1121, 1185.

Reaske, Christopher R. "The Devil and Jonathan Edwards." *Journal of the History of Ideas,* 33 (1972), 123-138.
Edwards is found to have a second monomania (see Crooker). Reaske examines the devil as he appears in Edwards' writings, analyzing where in these writings he appears, what characteristics Edwards gives him, and what sources these characteristics suggest.
Reaske argues that the devil "does not simply emerge in the writing of Edwards at the time of the Great Awakening and then vanish. Rather, it seems that a mild preoccupation with the devil in the beginning of his life turned into a monomania with him during the Revival,

and a subdued awareness of him even in later life."
The revival, Reaske suggests, "served almost like a
catalyst, bringing to life a dark part of Edwards'
psyche where the devil resided."

Reaske, Christopher R. "An Unpublished Letter concerning
    Sanctification by Elisha Williams, Jonathan Edwards'
    Tutor." *New England Quarterly*, 45 (1972), 429-434.

Review of Jonathan Edwards' *Freedom of the Will*. *Monthly*
    Review, 27 (1762), 434-438.

Review of Jonathan Edwards' *The Great Christian Doctrine of*
    Original Sin Defended. *Monthly Review*, 36 (1767),
    17-21.

Review of Jonathan Edwards' *History of the Work of*
    Redemption. *Monthly Review*, 52 (1775), 117-120.

Review of Jonathan Edwards' *The Justice of God in the*
    Damnation of Sinners. *Monthly Review*, 51 (1774),
    246-247.

Review of Jonathan Edwards' *Treatise concerning Religious*
    Affections. *The Christian Disciple*, new series,
    4 (1822), 445-463.

Review of Jonathan Edwards the Younger's *The Injustice and*
    Impolicy of the Slave Trade. *The Quarterly Christian*
    Spectator, 5 (1823), 39-48.
    Compares the two Edwards as preachers.

Review of *The Works of Jonathan Edwards, D.D., Late*
    President of Union College, edited by Tryon Edwards

(Andover, 1842). *Biblical Repertory and Princeton
Review*, new series, 15 (1843), 42-65.
Examines the younger Edwards' theology in relation to
that of President Edwards.

Review of *The Works of President Edwards*, edited by Samuel
  Austin (Worcester, 1808). *The Quarterly Christian
  Spectator*, 3 (1821), 298-315; 357-365.
What is purportedly a review of the 1808 edition of
Edwards' *Works* is actually a vehicle for a lengthy
sketch of Edwards' "most prominent features as an author,
especially his character as a theologian, a controver-
sialist and a preacher."
  "If any are inclined to accuse us of partiality to
Edwards, and to remark that in this review of his
writings and character, we have given no place to
censure, we answer, that we have no desire to refute
the accusation. Who, that feels in his bosom *any*
admiration of excellence, or has any sympathy with the
great and good in their desires and efforts to glorify
God, and promote the happiness of his creatures, can
fail to be wrought into partiality by contemplating
the character of Edwards?"

Review of *The Works of President Edwards*, edited by Sereno
  E. Dwight (New York, 1829-30). *The Quarterly Christian
  Spectator*, series 3, 3 (1831), 337-357.
The reviewer focuses on Dwight's *Life* of Edwards which
makes up the whole of the first volume of the Dwight
edition. He was not concerned to evaluate Dwight the
biographer but chose rather to detail items of interest
culled from the narrative and to highlight the image of
Edwards that the narrative reveals: a man of both
extraordinary intellectual ability and moral excellence.

Review of *The Works of President Edwards*, edited by E.
   Hickman (London, 1834). *The Eclectic Review*, series 3,
   12 (1834), 181-198.

Rhoades, Donald H. "Jonathan Edwards: America's First
   Philosopher." *The Personalist*, 33 (1952), 137-147.
   Rhoades provides a rather uncritical, summary statement
   of Edwards' philosophy under five headings: his
   theories of being, causation, value, and knowledge, and
   his methodology.
       In assessing Edwards the philosopher, Rhoades
   attempts to correct the impression encouraged by many
   studies, that the concerns of Edwards' faith had little
   impact on the development of his thought. Rhoades
   argues that Edwards' "distinctive emphases had quite
   personal roots; they reached down into his own ideal
   of Christian piety. Precisely this piety, moving
   within the bounds of Calvinist orthodoxy, was the primary canon and determinant of all his thought. By this
   canon he developed his method, selected and modified his
   categories, acknowledged his premises, and more or less
   determined his conclusions."

Rhoades, Donald H. "Jonathan Edwards: Experimental
   Theologian." Doctoral dissertation, Yale University,
   1945.

Rice, Howard C., Jr. "Jonathan Edwards at Princeton: With
   a Survey of Edwards Material in the Princeton
   University Library." *Princeton University Library
   Chronicle*, 15 (1954), 69-89.

Richards, C. A. "An American Religious Leader." *Dial*,
   10 (1889), 166-167.

Review of A. V. G. Allen's *Life and Writings of Jonathan Edwards* (Boston, 1889).

Richards, William Rogers. "Commemorative Sermon." In *Exercises Commemorating the 200th Anniversary of the Birth of Jonathan Edwards*. Andover, 1904, pp. 13-28.

Richardson, Charles F. "Jonathan Edwards." In his *American Literature, 1607-1885*. New York, 1889. Vol. I, pp. 139-146.
"To reconcile Calvinistic theology with the laws of sound thought was the life-work which he set before himself."
Brief, superficial introduction to Edwards' thought, focusing primarily on his *Freedom of the Will*.

Richardson, Herbert Warren. "The Glory of God in the Theology of Jonathan Edwards: A Study in the Doctrine of the Trinity." Doctoral dissertation, Harvard University, 1962.
In Sandon's estimation, "as definitive a treatment of Edwards' theology as Perry Miller's work was for Edwards' position as a whole."
Richardson demonstrates that Edwards developed John Locke's epistemology in the same way that Newton developed Robert Boyle's physics. The chief problem posed both by Locke's theory of ideas and by Boyle's atomism was the status of relations. Newton's theory of gravity was a solution to the problem raised by Boyle's physics, namely, the relation of atoms. In Newton's gravitational theory, Richardson argues, Edwards found the leads that were to aid him in solving the problem raised by Locke's epistemology, namely, the relation of simple ideas. Edwards' solution was his theory of consent, or excel-

lency, which exhibits structural similarities to
Newton's theory of gravity. In the second part of this
study, Richardson demonstrates how Edwards employed his
new theory of relation to interpret the doctrine of the
Trinity, and the ideas of God and of Excellency.

Ridderbos, Jan. *De Theologie van Jonathan Edwards*. The
    Hague, 1907.
    Described by Warfield (1912) as "the most comprehensive
    survey of Edwards' theological teaching."

Riforgiato, Leonard R. "The Unified Thought of Jonathan
    Edwards." *Thought*, 47 (1972), 599-610.
    Riforgiato elaborates the "harmony" between Edwards'
    early speculations on the nature of being and his later
    theological formulations. This paper, Riforgiato
    insists, "makes no claim that the scientific-philosoph-
    ical conclusions served as models for his later works,
    for Edwards had already established a framework for his
    mature theology when he embarked on *Notes on the Mind*.
    Rather, it attempts to indicate that Edwards never aban-
    doned his ontology but blended it into his theology.
    The link between the two appears to be his trinitarian
    thought which served as the basic model for philosophy
    and theology alike."

Riley, Isaac Woodbridge. "Jonathan Edwards." In his
    American Philosophy, The Early Schools. New York,
    1907, pp. 126-187.
    Riley provides a valuable summary of the various
    interpretations of Edwards proposed from the publication
    of Allen's volume, and attempts to resolve these
    interpretations into one coherent picture of Edwards as
    philosopher and theologian. Riley concludes that

Edwards was essentially a mystic, whose mysticism was at
odds with his inherited theology. There was a difference, Riley suggests, between what Edwards himself
believed and what, "being called for by the exigencies
of his theological position, he was obliged to teach to
others." Includes an excellent account of the early
search for the sources of Edwards' idealism.

Riley, Isaac Woodbridge. "Jonathan Edwards, Mystic." In
his *American Thought from Puritanism to Pragmatism and
Beyond*. New York, 1915, pp. 28-36.
Riley attempts to identify in Edwards the marks of the
mystic, suggesting that it is not the logical side of
Edwards but "the poetical and mystical which give a
truer insight into his nature."

Riley, Isaac Woodbridge. "The Real Jonathan Edwards."
Open Court, 22 (1908), 705-715.
"In a variety of metaphors Jonathan Edwards has been
presented as an exponent of an odius Puritanism, the
very embodiment of the sulphurous side of Calvinism.
The greatest of American divines has been called the
fire-brand philosopher, the black-winged raven of the
North, the relentless logician who left the print of his
iron heel upon the New England conscience." These
images present the truth, Riley argues, but not the
whole of the truth. "...[W]hile tradition has
represented him as a sort of bloodless spectre, with
pale drawn face, recent scrutiny has found a mind more
congruous with the beaming eye and sensitive mouth of
his portrait. In a word," Riley continues, "when freed
from the dust of the past, the real Edwards shines out
as a poet, a mystic, and a philosopher of the feelings."
By way of lengthy extracts from Edwards' writings,

Riley presents the real Jonathan Edwards.

Rinehart, Keith. "A Comparison of the Writings of Jonathan
    Edwards concerning God's End in Creation as Found in his
    Early Unpublished *Miscellanies* and in a *Dissertation*
    Posthumously Published." M.A. thesis, University of
    Oregon, 1941.
    "Specifically the question to be answered is this: Does
    Jonathan Edwards' later thought, as represented by his
    Dissertation, contain any significant change from his
    early thought on this topic, as found in his earlier
    Miscellanies?" Rinehart concludes that in later life
    Edwards maintained "fundamentally the same doctrine"
    that is found in the early *Miscellanies*. Rinehart's
    thesis, written under the direction of H. G. Townsend,
    provides evidence for dating the earliest of Edwards'
    Miscellanies.

Roback, Abraham A. *A History of American Psychology*. New
    York, 1952.
    In a brief section entitled, "The Fiery Puritan Takes a
    Hand," Roback discusses Edwards' psychology of the will
    and the affections, and notes some of the responses to
    Edwards' *Freedom of the Will*. Very superficial.

Roberts, Cecil Albert, Jr. "The Apologetic Significance of
    Jonathan Edwards' Doctrine of Religious Experience."
    Doctoral dissertation, Southwestern Baptist Theological
    Seminary, 1960.

Robinson, Edward. "[Review of] The Works of President
    Edwards [New York, 1843]." In his *Bibliotheca Sacra:
    Or Tracts and Essays on Topics connected with Biblical
    Literature and Theology*. New York, 1843, pp. 391-392.

Rogers, Henry. "An Essay on the Genius and Writings of
    Jonathan Edwards." In *The Works of President Edwards,*
    ed. E. Hickman. London, 1834. Vol. I, pp. v-lii.
    An extensive, critical examination of Edwards' major
    publications. While generally in awe of Edwards'
    intellect and uncommon piety, Rogers is particularly
    critical of Edwards' treatise on *The Nature of True
    Virtue*: "one of the most profound," but "the least
    satisfactory, of all Edwards's pieces."

Rooy, Sidney. *The Theology of Missions in the Puritan
    Tradition; A Study of Representative Puritans:
    Richard Sibbes, Richard Baxter, John Eliot, Cotton
    Mather, and Jonathan Edwards.* Grand Rapids, 1965.

Rose, Henry T. "Edwards in Northampton." In *Jonathan
    Edwards: A Retrospect,* ed. Harry Norman Gardiner.
    Boston, 1901, pp. 87-111.
    A somewhat sketchy biographical and character study of
    Edwards, by the pastor of the First Church, Northampton.

Rowe, Henry Kalloch. "Jonathan Edwards." In his *Modern
    Pathfinders of Christianity.* New York, [1928],
    pp. 102-113.

Rudisill, Dorus P. "The Doctrine of the Atonement in
    Jonathan Edwards and his Successors." Doctoral disser-
    tation, Duke University, 1945.

Rudisill, Dorus P. *The Doctrine of the Atonement in
    Jonathan Edwards and his Successors.* New York, 1971.
    A comparative analysis of President Edwards, Samuel
    Hopkins, Joseph Bellamy, Stephen West, and the younger
    Edwards on the atonement.

Rupp, George. "The 'Idealism' of Jonathan Edwards."
     Harvard Theological Review, 62 (1969), 209-226.
     Rupp attempts to qualify the extent to which the young
     Edwards can properly be called a philosophical idealist
     by situating Edwards' early idealistic conclusions
     within the wider context of his theological, scientific,
     and epistemological thought. An important study.

Sanborn, F. B. "The Puritanic Philosophy and Jonathan
     Edwards." *Journal of Speculative Philosophy,*
     17 (1883), 402-421.
     A rather offhand discussion of Edwards as a represen-
     tative Puritan philosopher. Sanborn appreciates
     Edwards' powers of intellect while rejecting the "shock-
     ing and damnatory" conclusions that this great intellect
     reached. "It was indeed the noble error of Edwards...
     to approach philosophy too exclusively from the side of
     the received Christian theology."
          Sanborn cannot resist speculating about what Edwards
     might have been had he not been Edwards. In fact,
     Sanborn finds it "surprising" that, "with these remark-
     able powers of analysis and reasoning, which would have
     made Edwards a match for Hume on his own ground, and
     with this demand of his age to be fed on that sort of
     food, the Puritan minister stood preaching Christianity
     as he understood it to the poor Indians of Stockbridge,
     and the anxious saints and sinners of New England,
     wherever he encountered them."

Sandon, Leo, Jr. "Jonathan Edwards and H. Richard Niebuhr."
     Journal of Religious Studies, 12 (1976), 101-115.
     A discussion of "Niebuhr's appropriation of Edwardsean
     concepts in the development of a theology of 'radical
     monotheism.'" The essay, Sandon observes, is intended

to illuminate an aspect of Niebuhr's thought rather than
to add to the scholarship on Edwards. In his analysis
Sandon relies heavily on what he considers the
"definitive" treatment of Edwards' theology, that of
Herbert Richardson.

Savelle, Max. *Seeds of Liberty: The Genesis of the
American Mind*. New York, 1948.
Contains a brief discussion of Edwards as a
"reactionary."

Schafer, Charles H. "Jonathan Edwards and the Principle of
Self-Love." *Papers of the Michigan Academy of Science*,
35 (1951), 341-348.
A largely superficial discussion of Edwards' "preoccupation" with the notion of self-love. Schafer notes that
the idea of self-love "was among his earliest philosophical considerations; that it furnished material for
many of his sermons; that it lent impetus to his
running feud with Arminianism; and that it is scarcely
overstating the case to say his efforts to guard the
church from its effects cost him his parish."

Schafer, Thomas Anton. "The Concept of Being in the Thought
of Jonathan Edwards." Doctoral dissertation, Duke
University, 1951.

Schafer, Thomas Anton. "Jonathan Edwards." In
Encyclopedia Britannica. 15th edition. Vol. VI,
pp. 440-442.

Schafer, Thomas Anton. "Jonathan Edwards and Justification
by Faith." *Church History*, 20 (1951), 55-67.
Schafer examines the place of the doctrine of justifica-

tion by faith in Edwards' thought, suggesting that the
doctrine occupies "an ambiguous and somewhat precarious
place in his theology." While prominent in his first
publications, Schafer notes an "almost total lack of
emphasis on the doctrine in the great works of his last
twenty years." Schafer does not suggest that Edwards in
any way departed from his earlier convictions. Rather,
Edwards "went beyond the doctrine of justification,
which had agitated the reformers, to the 'real' acts and
regulations which underlie it. He thereby helped make
paramount for American theology during the next century
the anthropological questions of original sin, the
freedom of the will, and the relation of the natural to
the supernatural in the doctrines of grace and
conversion."

Schafer, Thomas Anton. "Jonathan Edwards' Conception of the
    Church." *Church History,* 24 (1955), 51-66.
    A preliminary investigation into Edwards' conception of
    the church in which Schafer attempts to correct in some
    measure "the general impression of his ecclesiology as a
    revivalist (in the latter connotations of the term) and
    perhaps thereby of contributing to an understanding of
    our own American church-tradition." Edwards, Schafer
    contends, "must be seen as a theologian who in
    intention (and to some extent in accomplishment)
    strengthened the classical Protestant conception of the
    Church." Schafer finds the roots of Edwards' conception
    of the Church in his metaphysics.

Schafer, Thomas Anton. "Manuscript Problems in the Yale
    Edition of Jonathan Edwards." *Early American
    Literature,* 3 (Winter, 1968-69), 159-171.
    Schafer briefly outlines the Edwards manuscript

collection, its history, the physical characteristics of the manuscripts which have "in great measure lengthened out the work," and the general editorial policies of the Yale editors. One reads with regret Schafer's observation that the Yale edition proposes to be "complete, at least relatively to previous editions," at the probable expense of a complete rendering of such important collections as the *Miscellanies* and sermons.

Schafer, Thomas Anton. "The Role of Jonathan Edwards in American Religious History." *Encounter,* 30 (1969), 212-222.
Schafer admits that the purpose of this paper is more modest than its title would indicate; his aim is to "discuss briefly Edwards' own conception of his task and to suggest some of the lines along which his influence was felt in his own day and in subsequent history. The present address is therefore intended, as Adlai Stevenson once said a fan dancer's fan should be, more to call attention to the subject than to cover it."

Scheick, William J. "Family, Conversion, and the Self in Jonathan Edwards' *A Faithful Narrative of the Surprising Work of God.*" *Tennessee Studies in Literature,* 19 (1974), 79-89.
An interesting discussion of the image of the family as the structural motif of the *Narrative.*

Scheick, William J. "The Grand Design: Jonathan Edwards' *History of the Work of Redemption.*" *Eighteenth Century Studies,* 8 (1975), 300-314.
Scheick argues that Edwards thought of his *History* as innovative "because in it he treats history as an allegory of the conversion experience. History, in his

view, merely manifests in large the experiences of the
individual soul undergoing the regenerative process....
It was the vision of merging the motions of nature, of
history, and of the saint's private self into one theological tract, 'shewing the admirable contexture and
harmony of the whole,' that Edwards considered the
original facet of his proposed treatise."

Scheick, William J. *The Writings of Jonathan Edwards:*
   Theme, Motif, and Style. College Station, Texas, 1975.
   "He was no precursor of modern thought. At best
   Edwards was a moderate with a distinct prejudice, which
   deepened over the years, for traditions of the Puritan
   past. For him real departures from established conventions, as distinct from merely clarifications of them,
   signified the failure of the New Israelites."
      Scheick enters the ongoing discussion concerning the
   modernity of Edwards, arguing that from his youth
   Edwards leaned toward "tradition and orthodoxy, a
   disposition which should be considered as much a conse-
   quential influence on his later thought as was his early
   interest in Locke and Newton"; that he was a "spokesman
   for the Puritan tradition"; that he accepted the new
   ideas of his age if they could be made to conform to
   "established Puritan dogma." This theme is elaborated
   through an examination of Edwards' writings. Scheick
   also examines the "relevance of the artistic qualities"
   of Edwards' writings to his doctrines, suggesting that
   "the language of many of his works provides stylistic
   or imagistic clues to certain deep-seated feelings which
   he may have been disinclined to express overtly or of
   which he was only partially aware."
   Review
   Akers, Charles W. *Eighteenth Century Studies,*

10 (1977), 527-528.

Schlaeger, Margaret Clare. "Jonathan Edwards' Theory of
Perception." Doctoral dissertation, University of
Illinois, 1964. In *Dissertation Abstracts*,
25 (1965), 4754.

Schneider, Herbert W. *A History of American Philosophy*.
New York, 1946.
Contains brief but valuable comments concerning
Edwards' "reworking of the Puritan tradition under the
stimulus of pietism," his indebtedness to Newton, Locke,
and the Cambridge Platonists, and the philosophical
significance of Edwards' *Freedom of the Will*.

Schneider, Herbert W. *The Puritan Mind*. New York, 1930.
Includes an extensive, critical treatment of Edwards'
thought, viewed in relation to traditional Puritanism
and the opposing forces of the eighteenth century.
"As for Jonathan Edwards himself, he was a
stumbling-block to his contemporaries, and a horrible
example to his posterity. Whatever the value of his
philosophy in its essential structure, the particular
application he gave to it was even in his own day
impractical, and today obviously absurd. Had his own
love for God been less sentimental and pathological...
his philosophy would have exercised more power. As
it was, however, his philosophical insight was buried
under the ruins of his religion. He failed to see the
futility of insisting on the Puritan principles."

Schultz, Joseph P. "The Religious Psychology of Jonathan
Edwards and the Hassidic Masters of Habad." *Journal of
Ecumenical Studies*, 10 (1973), 716-727.

"The eighteenth century religious polarization between
intellect and emotions, between thought and feeling, was
successfully bridged by Jonathan Edwards and by the
Habad branch of Hassidism. Both Edwards and the Habad
masters in their psychology of religious experience
aimed at clarifying the difference between authentic
religious fervor and sham enthusiasm, and at showing
that feelings have a legitimate place in the intellectual process."

Schultz outlines the similarities between the
religious psychology of Edwards and that of the Habad
masters.

Scott, Barbara Jean. "The Quest for Meaning in the Writings
of Jonathan Edwards and William James." Doctoral
dissertation, Syracuse University, 1979. In
Dissertation Abstracts International, 41 (1980),
298A-299A.

Scott, Lee Osborne. "The Concept of Love as Universal
Disinterested Benevolence in the Early Edwardeans."
Doctoral dissertation, Yale University, 1952.
The most extensive, critical analysis of Edwards'
doctrine of love available. Scott's thesis is that
"Jonathan Edwards' concept of Christian love is not
monolithic, but is composed of diverse elements which
come to light and disintegrate in the hands of his
successors. The metaphysical love of plenitude deflects
the evangelical love or 'mutual indwelling' between
beings. Read thus, we can account for the antimonies of
love, and grasp the inner reason for the deline of the
New England theology."

Four of the five chapters in this study are devoted
to analyzing and contrasting the metaphysical and

evangelical, or the impersonal and the personal strands
in Edwards' concept of love. In the final chapter,
through a study of Bellamy and Hopkins, Scott attempts
to illustrate the "full effects of the cleavage between
philosophical and evangelical strands in Edwards'
teaching."

Seitz, Don C. "Jonathan Edwards: Consistent Theologian."
    Outlook, 143 (1926), 315-316.
    Popularized, summary statement of Edwards' theology by
    one who admits to having read Edwards "rather
    casually."

Seldes, Gilbert. "Jonathan Edwards." *Dial*, 84 (1928),
    37-46.
    "Psychologists have yet to discover from the meagre
    biographical details, what it was that turned Edwards
    away from his critical philosophy to the dark theology
    he adopted...."
    A vague and inconclusive foray into the history of
    ideas. Seldes discusses certain aspects of Edwards'
    thought as are connected with "the revival system," and
    notes how these elements, largely "in Edwards' own
    despite," place him at the beginning of a long series of
    movements and cults of the nineteenth century.

Serio, John N. "From Edwards to Poe." *Connecticut Review*,
    6 (1972), 88-92.

Shea, Daniel B. "The Art and Instruction of Jonathan
    Edwards's *Personal Narrative*." *American Literature*,
    37 (1965), 17-32. Appears with minor revisions in Shea,
    Spiritual Autobiography in Early America. Princeton,
    1968; and in *The American Puritan Imagination*, ed.

Sacvan Bercovitch. New York, 1974.
"Once it is accepted, then, that Edwards set down his
spiritual autobiography with more than 'private
Advantage' in mind, the *Personal Narrative* can be seen
as governed by the purposes that informed most of his
work during the period of the Great Awakening. By
narrative example he will teach what is false and what
is true in religious experience, giving another form to
the argument he carried on elsewhere; and he hopes
actually to affect his readers by both the content and
the presentation of his exemplary experience."

Shea, Daniel B. "Jonathan Edwards: The First Two Hundred
    Years." *Journal of American Studies,* 14 (1980),
    181-198.
    An instructive review of Edwards scholarship, examining
    the history of the "use and misuse of Jonathan Edwards,
    or less moralistically, the observable process of
    advocacy, condemnation, adaptation, and creative
    redefinition focussed on his life and work...."

Shea, Daniel B. "Jonathan Edwards: Historian of
    Consciousness." In *Major Writers of Early American
    Literature,* ed. E. H. Emerson. Madison, Wisconsin,
    1972, pp. 179-204.
    Shea examines the essentials of Edwards' thought under
    the conviction that "it is appropriate to consider
    Edwards's thought, not as a system, but as the expres-
    sion of a profound experience of the interrelatedness
    of things or as the intellectual symbol of his pious
    passion for unity, especially since, for Edwards, to
    study history was to study the religious consciousness,
    among masses of people and in individuals."
        It is evident, Shea argues, that "while Edwards took

care to articulate consistent arguments, he devoted
himself utterly to maintaining their consistency with
the sovereign demands of his deity, an allegiance won
from him just as his intellectual development crested.
If equating Edwards's ideas with his personality makes
too simple a formula," Shea continues, "his ideas are
nevertheless inseparable from his piety, as Edwards
asserted they should be, and his piety arose from a
crystallization of personality which took place in him
before he ever preached a sermon."

Shea, Daniel B. "Spiritual Autobiography in Early America."
    Doctoral dissertation, Stanford University, 1966. In
    Dissertation Abstracts, 27 (1967), 2134A.
    Includes an analysis of Edwards' *Personal Narrative.*

Sherman, David. "Jonathan Edwards." In his *Sketches of New
    England Divines.* New York, 1860, pp. 138-182.
    A biographical study.

Silliman, Benjamin. "Juvenile Observations of President
    Edwards on Spiders." *American Journal of Science and
    Arts,* 21 (1832), 109-122.
    Silliman's article appears as an appendix to "On North
    American Spiders," by N. M. Hentz. Silliman reprints
    Edwards' essay on the flying spider from Dwight's *Life*
    and comments on the young Edwards' ability as a natural
    scientist.
        "The observations recorded by him," notes Silliman,
    "present a very curious and interesting proof of philo-
    sophic attention in a boy of twelve years, and evince
    that the rudiments of his great mind were even at that
    immature age more than beginning to be developed."
    Silliman concludes that "had he devoted himself to

physical science, he might have added another Newton to
the extraordinary age in which he commenced his career;
for his star was just rising, as Newton's was going
down."

Simonson, Harold P. "Jonathan Edwards and the Imagination."
   Andover Newton Quarterly, 16 (1975), 109-118.
   An excellent analysis of Edwards' notion of the natural
   and the sanctified imagination. Simonson suggests that
   to "come to grips with this subject may correct what has
   become a distorted emphasis upon Edwards as a literary
   artist. For it is Edwards' concept of the imagination
   that must first be understood before one can even
   tentatively call Edwards an imaginative artist, a
   designation he himself never claimed." Edwards,
   Simonson insists, "is first and last a Christian theologian, not a literary artist."

Simonson, Harold P. *Jonathan Edwards: Theologian of the
   Heart*. Grand Rapids, 1974.
   Suggesting that modern scholars, and notably Perry
   Miller, have failed to give sufficient note to "the
   heart-felt pietism that was the foundation of Edwards'
   life and thought," Simonson examines Edwards' "sense of
   the heart": that "capacity beyond Lockean sensationalism, beyond ratiocination, beyond speculation and
   'understanding,' beyond aesthetic vision—the capacity,
   through faith, finally to experience God's glory and to
   see it as the ultimate end and purpose of His creation."
   Simonson's study, though brief, is generally perceptive
   and worthy of greater attention than it has received.
   Review
   Laurence, David E. "The Foolishness of Edwards."
      Worldview, 18 (1975), 49-51.

Simpson, Samuel. "Jonathan Edwards—A Historical Review."
    Hartford Seminary Record, 14 (1903), 3-22.
    A biographical sketch.

Sizer, Theodore. "The Story of the Edwards Portraits."
    Yale University Library Gazette, 34 (1959), 82-88.
    A brief note on the Edwards family portraits and letters
    at Yale.

Sliwoski, Richard S. "Doctoral Dissertations on Jonathan
    Edwards." *Early American Literature,* 14 (1979-80),
    318-327.
    Should be consulted for recent dissertations not
    explicitly devoted to Edwards by title, but which
    "devote considerable attention to Jonathan Edwards as
    part of a study of a problem or a theme...."

Slosson, Edwin E. "Jonathan Edwards as a Freudian."
    Science, new series, 52 (1920), 609.
    On the heels of Cattell's note in the same journal,
    Slosson observes: "Since Jonathan Edwards has been
    brought forward as a precursor of Einstein, I wish to
    file a claim on his behalf as a pre-Freud Freudian."
    Citing entries from Edwards' *Diary* ("that very remark-
    able record of autoanalysis") Slosson finds Edwards
    using dream analysis for the discovery of his "secret"
    sins, and employing the Freudian therapeutics of
    "frank self-examination starting with random reverie and
    following the thread of association until he reached the
    complex that he desired to eradicate by confession and
    sublimation."

Smith, Chard Powers. *Yankees and God.* New York, 1954.
    Includes a somewhat superficial review of the "salient

features" of Edwards' thought. Smith suggests that "the
chief work of the controversial part of Edwards' life"
was his attempt to maintain the "Holy Ratio," the "fine
line between the opposing Errors of Emotion and
Reason ...."

"Accepting without a tremor the Materialism of
Newton and the Sensational Psychology of Locke, he was
America's first major modern mind, and his Creative
Aesthetic still speaks to our condition. If we were to
select America's contribution to the gallery of the
world's indispensable thinkers, we must mention James,
and we must mention Edwards, and after that we must
hesitate and weigh."

Smith, Claude A. "Jonathan Edwards and 'The Way of Ideas.'"
Harvard Theological Review, 59 (1966), 153-173.
Smith argues that Edwards "found it necessary to go
beyond Locke, because he regarded the latter's treatment of the sources of the materials of knowledge to be
inadequate in the area of man's knowledge of God. He
explicitly disagreed with Locke's analysis of the relation of reason and revelation. And underlying this disagreement is the conviction that Locke's empiricism is
based on a too-narrow understanding of experience and
man's means for apprehending it." Smith suggests that
for Edwards, "it is through man's 'aesthetic sensi-
tivity' that he gains access to the materials of the
knowledge of God."

Smith, Claude A. "A Sense of the Heart: The Nature of the
Soul in the Thought of Jonathan Edwards." Doctoral
dissertation, Harvard University, 1964.

Smith, Hilrie Shelton. *Changing Conceptions of Original Sin: A Study in American Theology since 1750.* New York, 1955.
Includes an excellent analysis of Edwards' doctrine of original sin, viewed in relation to the writings of John Taylor.

Smith, John E. "Jonathan Edwards as Philosophical Theologian." *Review of Metaphysics,* 30 (1976), 306-324.
In relation to his contemporaries, Edwards "was alone in his attempt to make the religious tradition intelligible in those philosophical terms first laid down by Augustine and Anselm in their enterprise of 'faith seeking understanding.'"
Smith examines Edwards' handling of three topics which "reveals his originality and critical acumen in the use of philosophical conceptions for dealing with theological issues." The three topics are Edwards' conception of the Being of God, the question of God's existence, and his notion of the "new sense" or spiritual understanding. Smith follows Elwood in interpreting Edwards as a panentheist.

Smith, John E. "Jonathan Edwards: Piety and Practice in the American Character." *Journal of Religion,* 54 (1974), 166-180.
Smith elaborates Edwards' appeal to experience in his theology, and attempts to demonstrate "how his fidelity to experience led him to connect piety and practice in a way that has had a permanent influence on all forms of religion in America."

Smith, John E., ed. *Religious Affections*. Volume II of
The Works of Jonathan Edwards. New Haven, 1959.
In his critical Introduction to this volume (pp. 1-83),
Smith indicates the historical context in which the
treatise was written, provides a somewhat overlong
analysis of Edwards' twelve signs of truly gracious
affections, and attempts to assess the contemporary
relevance of "Edwards' interpretation of heart religion."
Includes notes on the text and biographical notes on
authors cited by Edwards.
Reviews
Holbrook, Clyde A. "Edwards Re-examined." *Review of
Metaphysics*, 13 (1960), 623-641.
Moody, Robert E. *New England Quarterly*, 33 (1960),
552-554.

Smyth, Egbert Coffin. "The Flying Spider—Observations by
Jonathan Edwards when a Boy." *Andover Review*,
13 (1890), 1-19.
Smyth provides transcriptions of Edwards' essays *Of
Insects* and *The Flying Spider* with commentary.
Includes facsimiles of the originals.

Smyth, Egbert Coffin. "The Influence of Edwards on the
Spiritual Life of New England." In *Jonathan Edwards:
A Retrospect*, ed. Harry Norman Gardiner. Boston, 1901,
pp. 33-48.
Smyth speaks of Edwards as "a witness to the spiritual
life in man": in his emphasis on "its Divine origin and
attestation," in the "directness and fearlessness of his
appeal, in promoting religion, to *reason*," in that he
believed in its eventual triumph, in that he "United
Faith and Practical Piety, Religion and Morality, the
Gift and Presence of the Spirit with Training and

Discipline."

Smyth, Egbert Coffin. "Jonathan Edwards." In *Library of
the World's Best Literature, Ancient and Modern,* ed.
Charles D. Warner. New York, 1897. Vol. XIII,
pp. 5175-5188.
Smyth provides a catalogue of Edwards' major publications and numerous extracts from his writings.
    "The greatness of Edwards' character implies a
contact of his mind with permanent and the highest truth
—a profound knowledge and consciousness of God. Human
and therefore imperfect, colored by inherited prepos-
sions, and run into some perishable molds, his thought
is pervaded by a spiritual insight which has an
original and undying worth. It is not unlikely that the
future will assign him a higher rank than the past."

Smyth, Egbert Coffin. "Jonathan Edwards' Idealism. With
Special Reference to the Essay *Of Being* and to Writings
not in his Collected Works." *American Journal of
Theology,* 1 (1897), 950-964.
An influential article. Smyth finds in the early essay
Of Being the key to understanding Edwards the philosopher, theologian, and preacher. This essay, Smyth
contends, "has a special importance in relation to its
author's subsequent thinking. It expresses metaphysical presuppositions and judgments which entered into
the first definite and independent formation of his
theological opinions. It sets forth *in nuce* a view of
the universe which, so far as appears, he never lost.
It helps to a better understanding of some of his
teachings which are most repugnant to his critics. Its
idealism is a fitting counterpart to a main article of
his faith, to a leading principle of his theology, and

to an effective and permanent element of his power as
a preacher."

  Smyth attempts to demonstrate how the idealism of
this essay informed Edwards' discussion of a number of
theological topics in the *Miscellanies*. Includes a
number of extracts from the *Miscellanies*.

Smyth, Egbert Coffin. "The 'New Philosophy' against which
  Students of Yale College Were Warned in 1714."
  Proceedings of the American Antiquarian Society, new
  series, 11 (1896), 251-252.
  Smyth responds to the suggestion, generated by an
  inspired reading of Beardsley's biography of Samuel
  Johnson, that the "new philosophy" against which Yale
  students were cautioned was the philosophy of Berkeley,
  a suggestion which encouraged the theory that Edwards
  may have been acquainted with the writings of Berkeley
  in his college days. Smyth identifies the "new
  philosophy," quoting from Johnson's manuscript autobiography: "They [the students] heard indeed in 1714
  when he [Johnson] took his Bachelour's Degree, of a
  new philosophy that of late was all in vogue, and of
  such names as Des Cartes, Boyle, Locke and Newton,
  but they were cautioned against thinking anything of
  them, because the new philosophy, it was said, would
  soon bring in a new Divinity and corrupt the pure
  Religion of the Country."

Smyth, Egbert Coffin, ed. *Observations Concerning the
  Scripture Oeconomy of the Trinity and Covenant of
  Redemption*. New York, 1880.
  In his Introduction to this volume (pp. 3-18), Smyth
  recounts the public controversy surrounding the suppres-
  sion of Edwards' reportedly heterodox manuscript on the

Trinity by his literary executors, and analyzes the
manuscript in his possession that he believes to be the
one in question. As it happens, the tract analyzed and
edited by Smyth for this volume (actually item 1062 of
the *Miscellanies*) was *a* suppressed tract on the Trinity;
but it was not *the* suppressed tract referred to by
Bushnell and Holmes.

Smyth, Egbert Coffin. "Professor Allen's Jonathan Edwards,
    with Extracts from Copies of Unpublished Manuscripts."
    Andover Review, 13 (1890), 285-304.
    In a generally favorable review of Allen's volume, Smyth
    questions Allen's understanding of Edwards' conception
    of divine sovereignty as "the unconditioned, arbitrary
    will of God." In his study Allen had not dealt with
    any then unpublished material. How do Edwards' private
    Miscellanies, Smyth asks, "qualify the representation
    that Edwards' leading theological principle was that of
    arbitrary sovereignty, that his practical thought of God
    was absorbed in the conception of an immanent and uncon-
    ditioned will?" Through a series of extracts from the
    Miscellanies, Smyth attempts to illumine Edwards'
    "fuller" conception of the sovereignty of God.

Smyth, Egbert Coffin. "Some Early Writings of Jonathan
    Edwards, A.D. 1714-1726." *Proceedings of the American
    Antiquarian Society*, new series, 10 (1895), 212-247.
    Reprinted separately, under the same title;
    Worcester, 1896.
    Georges Lyon, in 1888, called for a fresh examination of
    the writings supposedly from Edwards' youth, finding it
    difficult to accept the reputed originality of these
    works and the early dating of these writings arrived at
    by Dwight. Smyth's study is written largely in response

to this challenge and focuses on the dating and possible sources of Edwards' collegiate and pre-collegiate compositions. Smyth provides transcriptions of the early essays *The Soul, Of the Rainbow, Of Being,* and *Of Colours.*

Smyth, Egbert Coffin. "The Theology of Edwards." In *Exercises Commemorating the 200th Anniversary of the Birth of Jonathan Edwards.* Andover, 1904, pp. 73-93. A study of Edwards' doctrine of God, drawing primarily upon Edwards' early philosophical notes, the unpublished *Miscellanies,* and Edwards' late treatise on God's end in creation.
   "Edwards never lost this vivid sense of God, His Reality, His Immediacy. It is the first, the fundamental thing to be taken into account in an understanding of his Theology. It is requisite to a just interpretation and valuation of his controversial treatises ...."

[Smyth, Egbert Coffin]. "Tributes to Jonathan Edwards from Careful Students of his Writings." *Congregationalist and Christian World,* 88 (1903), 458.

Sontag, Frederick, and Roth, John K. *The American Religious Experience: The Roots, Trends, and Future of American Theology.* New York, 1972. Includes a brief and somewhat superficial discussion of Edwards as a systematic theologian.
   "...[H]is both rigid and capricious God stands in stark contrast to his own discovery of the subtlety, freedom, and strange paradox present in religious affections. Edwards' true God remained unborn in his time."

Sponseller, Edwin. *Northampton and Jonathan Edwards*.
   Shippensburg State College Faculty Monograph Series,
   Vol. I, no. 1. Shippensburg, Penn., 1960.
   A popularized, largely biographical study. Sponseller
   does not treat the particulars of Edwards' thought in
   any depth, but by way of preface he suggests that the
   real Edwards was not to be located within the context
   of the revivals which marked his Northampton ministry.
       Given Edwards' gifts of intellect and spirit, notes
   Sponseller, it was inevitable that Edwards "should be
   conscripted into the services of revivalism."
   Sponseller suggests, however, that Edwards' mind was
   elsewhere. "On the full stage of the Western World the
   Great Awakening was like a sub-plot enacted in the
   wings"; and despite Edwards' central role in the
   revival, unknown to his congregation and his countrymen, "the real issues that engaged his mind were those
   of the main drama, not of the sub-plot." The main
   drama, of course, was the Enlightenment.

Sprague, William B. "Jonathan Edwards." In his *Annals of
   the American Pulpit*. New York, 1857. Vol. I,
   pp. 329-335.
   Biographical sketch of Edwards, including a list of his
   publications.

Squires, J. Radcliffe. "Jonathan Edwards." *Accent*,
   9 (1948), 31-32.
   A poem.

Squires, William Harder. "Edwards as Theologian."
   The Edwardean, 1 (1904), 129-161.
   "The metaphysical theology of Jonathan Edwards is
   certainly much out of harmony with the present, and I

suppose there is little doubt that he is the most
cordially hated thinker that has goaded the sensitive
flanks of theologians in any century."

    Squires outlines Edwards' "metaphysical theology,"
finding its cornerstone in the notion that "God is
will."

Squires, William Harder. "Edwards' Inferno." *The
    Edwardean*, 1 (1904), 162-174.
    A study of the sulphuric aspect of Edwards' thought.

    "The age believed in hell with all its horrid
accompaniments. This fact gave the preacher his theme
and his motive. That Edwards believed the symbolic
truth of his statements concerning hell, there can be no
shadow of a doubt. But the fact that the burden of so
many sermons is hell and its torments is explained by
reference to the popular belief on this subject....
Edwards, like all leaders of an age, proclaimed his
doctrines in terms of the popular convictions. His
Inferno can have no other valid interpretation."

Squires, William Harder. "Edwards' Metaphysical
    Foundations." *The Edwardean*, 1 (1903), 51-64.
    "The metaphysical foundations of Edwards' philosophy
are discovered in his doctrine of voluntarism. There
is a universal will and the world is its necessary
expression and in its entire scope identical with it."

    Squires discusses Edwards on the volitional nature
of the divine being, God's "objectification in nature,"
God's relation to man, and Edwards' doctrine of
happiness.

Squires, William Harder. "Edwards' Philosophy of History
    and Religion." *The Edwardean*, 1 (1904), 193-256.

"History is a divine process. Every event is an exhibition of the mind and purpose of deity. Nothing
transpires without being the express manifestation of
an eternal design .... History, therefore, is a religious process. A theistic philosophy of history, and
of religion, is identical in import." History is
"theistic in essence and spiritual in its ultimate
interpretation."
     This lengthy article is less an exposition of
Edwards' than of Squires' philosophy of history.

Squires, William Harder. "Edwards' Psychology of the
     Will." *The Edwardean*, 1 (1904), 84-108.
     An exposition of certain arguments in *Freedom of the
     Will*.

Squires, William Harder. "Edwards' Relation to
     Voluntarism." *The Edwardean*, 1 (1904), 109-115.
     "Edwards first developed in its full psychological and
     metaphysical scope the philosophy of voluntarism."

Squires, William Harder. "A Glance at Edwards' View of
     Reason." *The Edwardean*, 1 (1904), 116-128.
     "In Edwards' philosophy reason holds the chief place
     and determines the scope and validity of experience
     itself. The attitude of Edwards toward reason made
     his metaphysics a decisive element in the introduction
     of rationalism in America."

Squires, William Harder. "Glimpses into Edwards' Life."
     The Edwardean, 1 (1903), 4-12.
     Brief, superficial character study.

Squires, William Harder. "Jonathan Edwards as Philosopher."
The Edwardean, 1 (1904), 65-77.
"What message had he for the world, and what of it
remains still important for our vital consideration?"
Squires claims a permanent significance for the
philosophy of Edwards in the development of modern
thought, suggesting that Edwards is "the teacher of
all our modern philosophers, and not one has reached
the heights of speculative insight into the nature of
will to which he attained."

Squires, William Harder. *Jonathan Edwards und seine
Willenslehre*. Lucka, Germany, 1901. (Doctoral
dissertation, University of Leipzig, 1902.)

Squires, William Harder. "A Passage from Edwards'
Speculative Metaphysics." *The Edwardean*, 1 (1904),
175-192.
Squires examines Edwards' early philosophical
writings, comparing his insights and conclusions with
those of Kant.
"In metaphysical insight Kant is in no sense
superior to Edwards: but in the range of purely
speculative problems attacked and brought to successful issue, Kant is in advance of the New England
thinker. But it took Hume to awaken Kant from his
dogmatic slumbers: what might Edwards, with his rare
endowments for profound inquiry, have been, if he had
only had a Hume to jog his metaphysical head and
furnish him with problems to solve!"

Squires, William Harder. "President Edwards as Thinker."
The Edwardean, 1 (1903), 24-31.
"If the speculative portions of Edwards' thinking were

collected and systematically arranged, the purely
theological parts omitted, his philosophy would
speedily gain merited recognition from the coming
leaders of thought in America."
   Squires attempts to persuade scholars that Edwards
is worthy of study. This article might be read as a
call for papers for *The Edwardean*.

Squires, William Harder. "A Revival of Edwards." *The
   Edwardean*, 1 (1904), 73-83.
   Squires applauds the revival of scholarly interest in
   Edwards, and the efforts of scholars "to penetrate to
   the *real* Edwards" behind the popular caricatures and
   recognize his place in modern philosophy. Edwards,
   Squires suggests, is "the most modern of moderns."
   "Modern philosophy, genetically considered, must be
   readjusted to the works of Jonathan Edwards."

Squires, William Harder. "The Seventy Resolutions." *The
   Edwardean*, 1 (1903), 13-23.
   The text of Edwards' *Resolutions* with brief commentary.

Squires, William Harder. "Some Estimates of President
   Edwards." *The Edwardean*, 1 (1903), 32-50.
   Squires reviews a number of previously published
   remarks attesting to Edwards' greatness as a philosopher.

Stagg, John Weldon. *Calvin, Twisse and Edwards on the
   Universal Salvation of those Dying in Infancy*.
   Richmond, Va., 1902.

Stamey, Joseph D. "Newton's Time, Locke's Ideas and
   Jonathan's Spiders." *Proceedings of the New Mexico-West
   Texas Philosophical Society*, (April, 1974), 79-88.

Stamey claims a useful parallel between Edwards and Karl
Marx: "both Marx and Edwards, from a critical study of
the philosophers who influenced them, developed lines of
theory which they used both to secure a basic intellectual position and as guides to practice, practice
designed to change the societies they lived in. Each
had a conscious and self-critical theory of the role of
ideology, although Edwards did not have the term. Each
believed that the major problem of method in philosophical analysis is not theoretical or epistemological but
practical."

Starkey, Marion L. *The Congregational Way: The Role of
the Pilgrims and their Heirs in Shaping America.*
Garden City, 1966.
Includes a lengthy, readable biography of Edwards with
little discussion of his thought.

Starr, Mary Seabury. "The Home of Timothy and Jonathan
Edwards." *Connecticut Quarterly*, 4 (1898), 33-43.
A popularized and superficial discussion of the
settlement of Windsor Farms, the life of Timothy
Edwards, and the early life of Jonathan.

Stein, Stephen J., ed. *Apocalyptic Writings*. Volume V of
The Works of Jonathan Edwards. New Haven, 1977.
"The Apocalypse was the private record of his entertain-
ment and delight; his sermons and published writings
documented his increasing public involvement with the
fortunes of the church and a disposition to apply
eschatological notions to contemporary situations.
Together private reflections and public representations
formed an intriguing and complex, but sometimes contradictory, network of theological ideas."

In his Introduction to this volume (pp. 1-93), Stein
briefly documents Edwards' lifelong interest in apocalyptic themes, attempts to indicate (somewhat superficially) Edwards' place within the apocalyptic tradition,
and, in the most valuable part of his study, attempts to
correlate Edwards' private speculations with his public
pronouncements concerning the millenium. Includes the
customary notes on the manuscripts and texts, and
biographical notes on authors cited by Edwards.
Review
Gaustad, Edwin S. *Journal of American History,*
     65 (1978), 108-109.

Stein, Stephen J. "Cotton Mather and Jonathan Edwards on
     the Number of the Beast: Eighteenth-Century Speculation
     about the Antichrist." *Proceedings of the American
     Antiquarian Society,* new series, 84 (1974), 293-315.
     A comparative study of the responses of Edwards and
     Mather to Francis Potter's *An Interpretation of the
     Number 666* (1642). Stein employs this analysis to
     check the consistency of the American perspective on the
     Antichrist during the first half of the eighteenth
     century. Heimert (*Religion and the American Mind*) has
     argued that after the Great Awakening a fundamental
     change took place in the attitude of Americans toward
     Catholicism, the papacy, and the Antichrist—a change
     that supposedly began with Edwards. "If Heimert's
     analysis is correct," Stein argues, "Mather and
     Edwards should have disagreed sharply in their
     respective evaluations of Potter's work. In actual fact
     they did not."

Stein, Stephen J. "Jonathan Edwards and the Rainbow:
     Biblical Exegesis and Poetic Imagination." *New England*

Quarterly, 47 (1974), 440-456.

Stein provides excerpts from item 348 of Edwards'
manuscript *Notes on Scripture* in which Edwards uses the
rainbow as a basis for theological reflection and a
"creative exegesis" of Gen. 9:12 ff.

"Though New England did not condition him to write
poetry, Edwards' flights of exegetical fancy fulfilled
some part of the universal drive to be poetic."

Stein, Stephen J. "A Notebook on the Apocalypse by
    Jonathan Edwards." *William and Mary Quarterly*,
    series 3, 29 (1972), 623-634.
Stein introduces to scholars Edwards' notebook on the
Apocalypse, a collection of private notes on apocalyptic texts and themes. While scholars had long been
aware of the existence of this notebook, it had generally been overlooked by Edwards' interpreters. This
is not at all surprising given the fact that this
notebook was published for the first time by Stein in
1977, five years after this article appeared.

    Stein discusses the appearance and contents of this
notebook, its composition and dating, and outlines its
potential significance for Edwards scholarship and for
colonial studies in general.

Stein, Stephen J. "*Notes on the Apocalypse* by Jonathan
    Edwards." Doctoral dissertation, Yale University, 1971.

Stein, Stephen J. "Providence and the Apocalypse in the
    Early Writings of Jonathan Edwards." *Early American
    Literature*, 13 (1978-79), 250-267.
Stein suggests that "any description of Edwards'
eschatological ideas which focuses exclusively upon
millenialism runs the risk of distorting this aspect of

his thought." At least in his earliest (pre-1724)
writings, Stein argues, the concept of providence
provided a central focus in Edwards' eschatological
speculations.

Stephen, Leslie. "Jonathan Edwards." *Fraser's Magazine*,
new series, 8 (1873), 529-551. Reprinted in
Littell's Living Age, 120 (1874), 219-236; and in his
Hours in a Library. London, 1876, pp. 44-106.
One of the most influential and often quoted of the
early essays on Edwards. Edwards has suffered in general repute, Stephen observes, "from a cause which
should really increase our interest in his writings.
Metaphysicians, whilst admiring his acuteness, have
been disgusted by his adherence to an outworn theology;
and theologians have cared little for a man who was
primarily a philosophical speculator and has used his
philosophy to bring into painful relief the most
terrible dogmas of the ancient creeds." It is this
phenomenon, that of the speculative genius whose mind
"worked entirely in the groove provided for it," which
provides the focus of Stephen's analysis of Edwards'
life and thought.
    "Starting, in fact, from the Puritan assumptions,
the agony of mind which they caused never led him to
question their truth, though it animated him to discover a means of reconciling them to reason; and the
reconciliation is the whole burden of his ablest works."

Stephens, Bruce Milton. "The Doctrine of the Trinity from
Jonathan Edwards to Horace Bushnell: A Study in the
Eternal Sonship of Christ." Doctoral dissertation,
Drew University, 1970. In *Dissertation Abstracts
International*, 31 (1970), 3028A.

Stewart, James G. *Freedom of the Will Vindicated; or
President Edwards's Necessarian Theory Refuted.*
Glasgow, 1876.

Stewart, Randall. *American Literature and Christian
Doctrine.* Baton Rouge, 1958.
Discusses Edwards' doctrine of the divine and super-
natural light.

Stiles, Ezra. *The Literary Diary of Ezra Stiles, President
of Yale College, 1769-1795,* ed. Franklin B. Dexter.
3 vols. New York, 1901.
"Presid[ent] Edw[ards'] valuable Writings in another
Gener[ation] will pass into as transient Notice perhaps
scarce above Oblivion, as Willard or Twiss, or Norton;
and when Posterity occasionally comes across them in
the Rubbish of Libraries, the rare Characters who may
read & be pleased with them, will be looked upon as
singular & whimsical, as in these days an Admirer of
Suarez, Aquinas or Dionysius Areopagita."
    Stiles' *Diary* contains occasional reference to
Edwards and his writings, and more extensive discussions of Edwards' followers. This work is valuable
primarily as a source of historical information.

Stiles, Henry Reed. *The History and Genealogies of Ancient
Windsor, Connecticut: Including East Windsor, South
Windsor, Bloomfield, Windsor Locks, and Ellington.
1635-1891.* 2 vols. Hartford, 1891-92.
Includes (II, pp. 194-198) a brief section on the
Edwards family.

Stob, Henry. "The Ethics of Jonathan Edwards." In *Faith
and Philosophy,* ed. Alvin Plantinga. Grand Rapids,

1964, pp. 111-137.
An examination of Edwards' early philosophical writings.
Stob offers little in the way of interpretation.

Stokes, Anson Phelps. *Church and State in the United
States*. 3 vols. New York, 1950.
Edwards "cared little about political matters. Yet he
contributed mightily—even though indirectly, being
far from a liberal in theology—to the cause of
religious freedom."
Stokes views the Great Awakening as reinforcing the
idea of separation of church and state. References to
Edwards are brief and largely indirect.

Stokes, Anson Phelps. "Jonathan Edwards, Class of 1720,
Theologian and Metaphysician." In his *Memorials of
Eminent Yale Men: A Biographical Study of Student
Life and University Influences during the Eighteenth
and Nineteenth Centuries*. New Haven, 1914. Vol. I,
pp. 19-29.
Stokes provides a brief biographical sketch of Edwards,
testimonies to his greatness, and a transcript of a
letter Edwards wrote to his father while a student
at Yale.

Storlie, Erik Fraser. "Grace and Works, Enlightenment and
Practice: Paradox and Poetry in John Cotton, Jonathan
Edwards, and Dogen Zenji." Doctoral dissertation,
University of Minnesota, 1976. In *Dissertation
Abstracts International*, 37 (1976), 3599A-3600A.
An attempt "to illuminate John Cotton's and Jonathan
Edwards' resolutions of the paradox of grace and works
by examining the parallel Buddhist paradox of
enlightenment and practice."

Stoughton, John Alden. *"Windsor Farmes": A Glimpse of an Old Parish*. Hartford, 1883.
Stoughton provides important biographical information concerning Edwards' early years.

Stowe, [Calvin Ellis]. "Jonathan Edwards." In Herzog's *Realencyklopädie für Protestantische Theologie und Kirche*. Leipzig, 1896-1913. Vol. V, pp. 171-175.

Stromberg, Roland N. *Religious Liberalism in Eighteenth Century England*. New York, 1954.
A valuable study of Edwards' English "opposition." References to Edwards are few and generally superficial.

Strong, Augustus Hopkins. *Philosophy and Religion: A Series of Addresses, Essays and Sermons Designed to Set Forth Great Truths in Popular Form*. New York, 1888.
Includes several brief references to Edwards' theology and his philosophical idealism. Strong considers Edwards' idealism to have had disastrous consequences both for Edwards' own theology and for that of later New England theologians.

Stuart, Robert Lee. "Jonathan Edwards at Enfield: 'And Oh the Cheerfulness and Pleasantness...'" *American Literature*, 48 (1976), 46-59.
A re-examination of the Enfield sermon.
"Cut out of its original context, cited generally with major deletions—and including, typically, only the most dramatic of its passages picturing the plight of the damned—the sermon has been misunderstood for centuries." Stuart suggests that the fact that "some

of Edwards's congregation were *comforted* by the sermon
must not be ignored any longer." Stuart reviews the
reputation of this sermon, the context in which it was
preached, and examines the text "with particular attention to the elements of hope to be found there."

Stuart, Robert Lee. "'Mr. Stoddard's Way': Church and
    Sacraments in Northampton." *American Quarterly*,
    24 (1972), 243-253.
    Stuart examines Stoddard's views on qualifications for
    communion, suggesting that Edwards "was closer to his
    grandfather's position than he recognized—a fact that
    ...would have been clearly evident to him if he had
    studied [Stoddard's] *The Doctrine of the Instituted
    Churches* more carefully."

Stuart, Robert Lee. "The Table and the Desk: Conversion
    in the Writings Published by Solomon Stoddard and
    Jonathan Edwards during their Northampton Ministries,
    1672-1751." Doctoral dissertation, Stanford
    University, 1970. In *Dissertation Abstracts Interna-
    tional*, 31 (1970), 2356A-2357A.

Sullivan, Frank. "Jonathan Edwards, the Contemplative Life
    and a Spiritual Stutter." *Los Angeles Tidings*,
    11 March 1949, p. 27.
    Sullivan views Edwards as a "contemplative" in an
    active society, a conflict Sullivan finds reflected in
    Edwards' writings.

Suter, Rufus. "An American Pascal: Jonathan Edwards."
    Scientific Monthly, 68 (1949), 338-342.
    Suter finds a striking parallel between Edwards and
    Pascal in the fact that in Edwards' case, "as well as

in that of the Janssenist, a precocious early insight
into the problems of physical science was sacrificed to
the religious passion."

"The world no doubt lost in Edwards a philosopher
and possibly a great scientist. The tragedy in his
case is even more complete than in Pascal's for whereas
the religious community to which the Janssenist sacrificed his science has become defunct, Pascal's tract,
the *Pensées* still has something to offer the devout
soul. But the harrowing theology of Edwards, which
swallowed up both his natural philosophy and science,
is dead even in the Congregational churches that
nurtured him...."

Suter, Rufus. "The Concept of Morality in the Philosophy
    of Jonathan Edwards." *Journal of Religion*, 14 (1934),
    265-272.
Suter attempts to present Edwards' ethical system "in
as nearly as possible non-theological language."
    "...Edwards' ideas are exhibited in clothing which
has long since been outworn. Like all the Puritans of
his day, he believed the whole gamut of Calvinistic
dogmas, ...but the presence of these forms does not
make the kernel of his meaning archaic. It is surprising how, with a change of terminology, and with the
treating of some of these theological formulae as
metaphorical, one may invest Edwards' ideas with
freshness."

Suter, Rufus. "A Note on Platonism in the Philosophy of
    Jonathan Edwards." *Harvard Theological Review*,
    52 (1959), 283-284.
Suter draws attention to the interpretation of Edwards
advanced by William W. Fenn, whose research was never

published. According to Suter, Fenn found a "devastating tragedy" in Edwards' "inward failure as a Christian
philosopher." This consisted in Edwards' "self-
conscious awareness of being unable to reconcile his
Platonism with his Calvinism."

Suter, Rufus. "The Philosophy of Jonathan Edwards."
Doctoral dissertation, Harvard University, 1932.

Suter, Rufus. "The Problem of Evil in the Philosophy of
Jonathan Edwards." *Monist,* 44 (1934), 280-295.
Suter examines Edwards' "five different solutions"
to the problem of evil.

Suter, Rufus. "The Strange Universe of Jonathan Edwards."
Harvard Theological Review, 54 (1961), 125-128.
"To recapture Edwards' point of view requires a very
definite effort."
    Suter briefly notes certain aspects of Edwards'
thought which are not readily assimilated by the
"modern" mind: e.g., his acceptance of the literal
truth of the Bible, his conviction of the reality and
evil of sin, his "cosmo-sociological" view of the
universe.

Suter, Rufus. "The Word *Indiscerpible* and Jonathan
Edwards." *Isis,* 58 (1967), 238-239.
In a brief note Suter calls attention to the fact that
in his early scientific notes Edwards used the word
"indiscerpible," a word invented by the Cambridge
Platonist Henry More.

Tallon, John William. "Flight into Glory: The Cosmic
Imagination of Jonathan Edwards." Doctoral disserta-

tion, University of Pennsylvania, 1972.   In
Dissertation Abstracts International, 33 (1973),
3604A-3605A.

[Tappan, Henry Philip?].   "President Edwards' Doctrine of
   Original Sin, The Doctrine of Physical Depravity."
   Views in Theology, 1 no. 3 (1825), 3-104.
   An extensive examination of Edwards' doctrine of
   original sin in which Tappan (?) attempts to refute
   T.R.'s conclusion that Edwards did not hold the
   doctrine of "physical depravity," and that "it is
   perfectly consistent with his notion of tendency to
   sin that it should depend on man's external circumstances, and wholly cease by a change in these
   circumstances."

   Tappan, on the contrary, insists that in *Original
   Sin* Edwards exhibits "the original sin which he
   ascribes to mankind as a physical depravity, and that
   not in a few scattered passages merely, but uniformly
   throughout his work. All his definitions, statements,
   theories, arguments, and phraseology, appear to me so
   obviously and unequivocally to express it, as to render
   the ascription to them of any other meaning totally
   unauthorized."

Tappan, Henry Philip.   *A Review of Edwards's "Inquiry into
   the Freedom of the Will"*.   New York, 1839.
   "Let us not ask what philosophy is demanded by Calvinism
   in opposition to Pelagianism and Arminianism, or by the
   latter in opposition to the former;   let us ask simply
   for the laws of our being."

   Tappan outlines the basic arguments of Edwards'
   treatise, deduces consequences from Edwards' system
   "almost too shocking to utter," and attempts to answer

Edwards' arguments against the notion of a self-
determining will. Tappan argues that Edwards' basic
error lies in his confounding of the will with the
sensibilities: "The great point,—whether the volition
is as the most agreeable,—he takes up at the beginning
as an unquestionable fact, and adheres to throughout as
such; but he never once attempts an analysis of
consciousness in relation to it, adequate and
satisfactory."

Tarbox, Increase N. "Early Life of Edwards." In *The
Memorial Volume of the Edwards Family Meeting,* ed.
Jonathan E. Woodbridge. Boston, 1871, pp. 83-103.
Tarbox describes the physical and intellectual environment of the young Edwards and briefly comments on some
of his pre-collegiate writings. Superficial.
"If Edwards had not been the great metaphysician of
America, if another bent and direction had early been
given to his mind, he might have proved the Milton of
this new world, and sung songs which whould have been
immortal."

Tarbox, Increase N. "Jonathan Edwards." *Bibliotheca
Sacra,* 26 (1869), 243-268.
"It is not our purpose in the present Article to be
critical .... We are concerned more with the man than
with his works."
Tarbox examines at some length the circumstances
of Edwards' youth, in order to "call attention to the
manifest disparity between his early surroundings and
his future greatness." We are compelled to believe,
Tarbox observes, "that he was one whom God and not
man made great. With so little to feed the higher
literary and philosophical tastes we are driven to the

conclusion that his intellectual development
proceeded by an inward force rather than by an outward
power."

Tarbox, Increase N. "Jonathan Edwards as a Man; and the
Ministers of the Last Century." *New Englander*,
43 (1884), 615-631.
A rather vague tribute to the "greatness" of Edwards, a
greatness that Tarbox appears to locate in the fact
that Edwards "instinctively took up some of the highest
themes that can occupy the human mind;——took them up
as one self-moved and born for the purpose,——took them
up in a manner original to himself and not as a
copyist."
    Of far more interest than his treatment of Edwards
is Tarbox's discussion of Solomon Stoddard. Tarbox
relates a tradition concerning events preceding
Stoddard's "new and wonderful revelation of the gospel
scheme," which apparently led Stoddard to conclude that
sanctification was not a necessary qualification for
partaking in the Lord's Supper.

Tattrie, George Arthur. "Jonathan Edwards' Understanding
of the Natural World and Man's Relationship to it."
Doctoral dissertation, McGill University, 1973. In
Dissertation Abstracts International, 34 (1974), 6743A.
"This thesis undertakes to discover whether Jonathan
Edwards' interpretation of the natural world and man's
relationship to it contributes significantly to the
ecological debate which is now raging."

Taylor, Isaac. *Essay on the Application of Abstract
Reasoning to the Christian Doctrines: Originally
Published as an Introduction to Edwards on the Will.*

London, 1831.

"We claim Edwards as an *Englishman*; he was such in every respect but the accident of birth in a distant province of the empire."

In this essay Taylor does not discuss at any length the substance of *Freedom of the Will*; rather, as the title suggests, Taylor addresses problems and questions concerning the philosophical explanation and discussion of Christian doctrines which were being brought into focus, in part, by the criticisms and defenses of Edwards' treatise, and by the appropriation of the metaphysical arguments of this treatise by some outside the pale of the church. Taylor points to Edwards' treatise as a prime illustration of "the fruitlessness and inexpediency of this method of conducting Biblical controversy."

Taylor, Isaac. "Logic in Theology." In his *Logic in Theology and Other Essays*. London, 1859, pp. 1-76.
A "great part" of this essay originally appeared as Taylor's introductory essay to *Freedom of the Will*.

Taylor, Robert J. *Western Massachusetts in the Revolution*. Providence, 1954.
Includes a discussion of the politics surrounding Edwards' dismissal from Northampton.

Taylor, Walter F. "Jonathan Edwards." In his *A History of American Letters*. New York, 1936, pp. 29-36.
"He was the most acute logician of his time; he was potentially a great philosopher; he was at heart a poet; and he was one of the greatest mystics of the race."

Superficial comments on a few of Edwards' writings and his role in the Great Awakening.

The Theological Questions of President Edwards, Senior, And Dr. Edwards, His Son. Providence, 1822.

"The Theology of Edwards, as shewn in his Treatise concerning Religious Affections." *American Theological Review,* 1 (1859), 199-220. Reprinted in *British and Foreign Evangelical Review,* 9 (1860), 119-136.
The writer examines the doctrine of regeneration found in this treatise, insisting that "there is no part of his writings which, with greater certainty, presents his permanent convictions."

Thomas, John Newton. "Determinism in the Theological System of Jonathan Edwards." Doctoral dissertation, University of Edinburgh, 1937.

Thomas, Reuen. "Jonathan Edwards." In his *Leaders of Thought in the Modern Church.* Boston, 1892, pp. 7-24.

Thompson, Joseph P. "Jonathan Edwards, his Character, Teaching, and Influence." *Bibliotheca Sacra,* 18 (1861), 809-839.
Thompson's object is to present "a popular view of the salient points of his system in their bearing upon New England Theology, and his influence on the moral and religious life of his own denomination and that of Christendom."
"The investigating spirit, ever resolving new theorems in divinity yet ever loyal to the authority of the scriptures and to the great system of evangelical doctrine wrought out by the ages, —this characteristic feature of New England theology, is that wherein Edwards chiefly lives in his successors; and where these two traits are fairly combined in a theological instructor,

there is a school of Edwards, even though in some
respects his own phraseology may be superceded."

Thompson, Robert Ellis. "A Centenary View of Jonathan
    Edwards." *The Sunday School Times,* 3 October 1903.

Thomson, J[ohn] R. *Jonathan Edwards of New England.*
    Religious Tract Society. New Biographical Series.
    No. 63. London, n.d.

Todd, John. "The Ministry of Edwards at Northampton." In
    The Memorial Volume of the Edwards Family Meeting,
    ed. Jonathan E. Woodbridge. Boston, 1871, pp. 121-131.
    A popularized account of Edwards' Northampton ministry,
    focusing on the controversy that eventually led to
    Edwards' dismissal.

Tomas, Vincent. "The Modernity of Jonathan Edwards." *New
    England Quarterly,* 25 (1952), 60-84.
    Tomas offers a devastating critique of Perry Miller's
    claims for the modernity of Edwards, and of the methods
    by which Miller attempted to establish these claims. "I
    submit," Tomas argues, "that Mr. Miller is presenting
    Edwards not as he is 'known by nature,' in Aristotle's
    phrase, but as he might be 'known to us,' provided that
    we conceived history to be 'what the mind must perceive
    in a fashion dictated by the mind itself rather than by
    data and documents,' and if we resisted a supine
    induction from evidence, so that we might seek an inner
    coherence and a grand design."
        It is true, agrees Tomas, "that one of the *specific*
    differences between Edwards and previous Puritans is the
    presence in his thought of elements that are derived
    from Newton and Locke. But," Tomas insists, "when

Edwards is looked at in the large, and the generic and
specific characteristics of his thought are seen in
their true proportions and weight, he remains, despite
the influence of Newton and Locke, a medieval
philosopher."

Townsend, Harvey Gates. "An Alogical Element in the
Philosophy of Edwards and its Function in his
Metaphysics." In *Proceedings of the Seventh Interna-
tional Congress of Philosophy, Held at Oxford, England,
September 1-6, 1930*. Oxford, 1931, pp. 495-500.

Townsend, Harvey Gates. "Jonathan Edwards' Later Observations of Nature." *New England Quarterly*, 13 (1940),
510-518.
Townsend illumines Edwards' later interest in nature
through a study of *Images*.

Townsend, Harvey Gates. *Philosophical Ideas in the United
States*. New York, 1934.
Includes a valuable analysis of Edwards' epistemolgy,
metaphysics, and ethics.
     "The metaphysical and logical writings of Edwards
are of greater philosophical importance than all the
remainder of his work. Clergyman though he was, and
theologian (after a convention of speech), he was
above and beyond all a metaphysician."

Townsend, Harvey Gates, ed. *The Philosophy of Jonathan
Edwards from his Private Notebooks*. Eugene,
Oregon, 1955.
In his Introduction to this collection (pp. v-xxii)
Townsend provides a brief but important discussion
of Edwards the philosopher and valuable notes on the

extant manuscripts of the *Notes on Natural Science* and
Miscellanies.

"The importance of Edwards in the history of
American philosophy is to be measured... by the manifest
influence he has had and even more by the range, depth,
and security of his hold on the philosophical ideas and
methods of his own time. When judged by either of
these tests, Edwards is found to be a great American
philosopher."

Review
Miller, Perry. *American Literature*, 28 (1956), 236-237.

Townsend, Harvey Gates. "The Will and the Understanding in
the Philosophy of Jonathan Edwards." *Church History*,
16 (1947), 210-220.

Tracy, Joseph. *The Great Awakening: A History of the
Revival of Religion in the Time of Edwards and
Whitefield*. Boston, 1842.
"Edwards, indeed, had done more than any other man to
awaken the ministry and the churches in the first
instance, and to produce the movement which had now
become general. But it was a movement of minds that
thought for themselves. No one man, therefore, could
guide it."

The first extensive history of the Great Awakening,
this volume is still valuable for its inclusion of
numerous documents of the period otherwise unavailable.

Tracy, Patricia Juneau. "Jonathan Edwards, Pastor:
Minister and Congregation in the Eighteenth-Century
Connecticut Valley." Doctoral dissertation, University
of Massachusetts, 1977. In *Dissertation Abstracts
International*, 38 (1978), 5013A.

"Although renowned as a theologian, Jonathan Edwards was nevertheless a *failure* in the most essential task of the ministry—persuading his congregation to share his vision. That failure illuminates the *social* history of the man, the community he served, and the problems of many eighteenth-century New England clergymen."

Trinterud, Leonard J. *The Forming of an American Tradition: A Re-examination of Colonial Presbyterianism.* Philadelphia, 1949.
This important work provides valuable background material for the study of Edwards, and examines various aspects of the "Edwardean" theological legacy; but references to Edwards himself are few and generally superficial.

Tufts, James H. "Edwards and Newton." *Philosophical Review,* 49 (1940), 609-622.
A study of the influence of Newton on Edwards' early philosophical speculations. Tufts examines the general world view common to both Edwards and Newton and analyzes Edwards' early conceptions of solidity, atoms, and gravity in relation to the thought of Newton.

Tupper, Kerr B. "Jonathan Edwards." In his *Seven Great Lights.* Cincinnati, 1892, pp. 117-139.

Turnbull, Ralph G. "Jonathan Edwards: A Voice for God." *Christianity Today,* 2 no. 7 (1958), 8-9.
A brief note on Edwards as "a pastoral preacher who did the work of an evangelist."

Turnbull, Ralph G. "Jonathan Edwards and Great Britain." *Evangelical Quarterly,* 30 (1958), 68-74.

Brief, superficial discussion of Edwards' "contacts" with British thinkers.

Turnbull, Ralph G. "Jonathan Edwards—Bible Interpreter." *Interpretation*, 6 (1952), 422-435.

"Many have been the appreciations and studies of his life, philosophy and theology, but the preaching of Edwards has been neglected. It is time," Turnbull suggests, that Edwards is "restored as the pastoral preacher of New England. In this article we shall endeavor to see him in that context as an interpreter of divine truth through the Bible."

Turnbull attempts to outline Edwards' own conception of his task as a preacher, his belief in the sermon as an agency of conversion, his craftsmanship in writing sermons by recognized methods, his knowledge and use of the Bible, his skill as an exegete and expositor of doctrine. All in fourteen pages.

Turnbull, Ralph G. *Jonathan Edwards: The Preacher*. Grand Rapids, 1958.

"The varied operations of the mind and heart of Edwards exerted an unusual influence upon his contemporaries. He was prominent in religious revivals, and he was the center of theological controversy. In the midst of these things one essential is sometimes forgotten. Whatever he did or wrote came out of the master passion of his life—to be a preacher of the eternal gospel."

The superficial tone of Turnbull's study limits the value of this attempt "to understand and interpret the man as the pastoral preacher." It is, as elsewhere described, "a book for preachers and students of preaching."

Turpie, David. *Jonathan Edwards*. Columbus, 1893.
    Address delivered at Kenyon College, 29 June 1893.

Tweet, Roald D. "Jonathan Edwards and the Affecting
    Style." Doctoral dissertation, University of
    Chicago, 1967.

Tyler, Moses Coit. *A History of American Literature,
    1607-1765*. 2 vols. New York, 1879.
    Tyler's discussion of Edwards (II, pp. 177-192)
    provides a reliable index to how scholars of his day had
    come to approach Edwards. By far the largest part of
    Tyler's discussion is devoted to illustrating the intel-
    lectual precocity of the young Edwards as revealed in
    his *Notes on Natural Science* and *The Mind*: "It is,
    perhaps, impossible to name any department of intellec-
    tual exertion, in which, with suitable outward facili-
    ties, he might not have achieved supreme distinction."
    Edwards' youthful idealism is reviewed with awe; and
    Tyler finds that Edwards' precocity in physical science
    was "not less wonderful than his precocity in meta-
    physical science."
        Of the Edwards who lived beyond the composition of
    these notes, however, Tyler has little to say. Edwards,
    observes Tyler, engaged his mature mind with the prob-
    lems of theology: "that ganglion of heroic, acute, and
    appalling dogmas commonly named after John Calvin. To
    the defense of that theology, in all its rigors, in all
    its horrors, Jonathan Edwards brought his unsurpassed
    abilities as a dialectician."

Uhden, Herman F. *The New England Theocracy: A History of
    the Congregationalists in New England to the Revivals of*

1740, trans. H. C. Conant. Boston, 1859.

Uhden draws upon Edwards' *Faithful Narrative* to present "a copious detail" of the effects of the Northampton revival of 1734-35. The focus is on those spiritual effects that Edwards described that were "more or less wrought within" the souls of the awakened. Uhden's discussion is essentially descriptive, including lengthy extracts from the *Narrative*, and he offers little in the way of critical analysis of Edwards' observations and conclusions.

Upham, William P. "On the Shorthand Notes of Jonathan Edwards." *Proceedings of the Massachusetts Historical Society*, series 2, 15 (1902), 514-521.

Upham provides a complete translation of the shorthand notes which appear on the cover of Edwards' *Notes on Natural Science*.

"There is nothing in the short-hand here deciphered that needed special secrecy any more than other memoranda written at the same time in long-hand; and it is reasonable to suppose that Edwards, like others at that time, especially ministers, used this method of writing to save time, space, and paper."

Van Becelaere, Laurence. *La Philosophie en Amérique depuis les Origines jusqu'à nos Jours*. New York, 1904.

Van Doren, Carl, ed. *Benjamin Franklin and Jonathan Edwards: Selections from their Writings*. New York, 1920.

In his Introduction to this volume (pp. ix-xxxiv) Van Doren provides a popularized and popular contrast of Edwards and Franklin. Van Doren views Edwards as a "dim figure" from a remote past, but sees Franklin as "contemporaneous, fresh, full of vitality."

Van Doren, Carl. "The Metaphysical Messiah." New York
Herald Tribune Books, 21 September 1930, p. 7.
Review of Henry B. Parkes' *Jonathan Edwards* (New York,
1930).

Voegelin, Erich. *Ueber die Form des Amerikanischen Geistes*.
Tübingen, 1928.
Includes a discussion of the elements of Calvinism and
mysticism in Edwards' thought. Voegelin notes
resonances between Edwards and William James and
Santayana.

Waanders, David W. "Illumination and Insight: An
Analogical Study [on Jonathan Edwards]." Doctoral
dissertation, Princeton Theological Seminary, 1973.

Waanders, David W. "The Pastoral Sense of Jonathan
Edwards." *Reformed Review*, 29 (1976), 124-132.
A cursory glance at Edwards' career suggests that he had
little of the commodity in question. Waanders contends
that one "must look beyond Northampton to find Edwards'
pastoral contributions for our own time. Edwards himself is not a significant pastoral model, yet he pene-
trated to the very core of pastoral theology with his
study and analysis of religious experience. It is as
a theologian and writer that Edwards makes his most
significant contribution to pastoral theology."
    Waanders elaborates Edwards' notion of the "sense of
the heart" and the way in which Edwards used "religious
affections" in describing and evaluating religious
experience. It is a generalized study that seeks to
make Edwards "usable."

Wakeley, J. B. *The Prince of Pulpit Orators: A Portraiture of Rev. George Whitefield.* New York, 1871. Includes a brief account of Whitefield's relationship with Edwards.

Walker, George Leon. "Jonathan Edwards and the Half-Way Covenant." *New Englander*, 43 (1884), 601-614. Walker attempts to define Edwards' relation to the Halfway Covenant system, both as it was generally practiced in New England, and as it was "somewhat peculiarly administered" in Northampton following the improvements of Stoddard. Where other scholars had argued that Edwards had always been of one mind on the question of qualifications for communion, Walker insists that at some point during his Northampton ministry Edwards' views on this subject "underwent a change." The only question at issue, Walker argues, is "whether the change extended to the general half-way covenant scheme of the New England churches, or only to the special Stoddardian development of it in the Northampton Church." Walker concludes that "Mr. Edwards had already before his dismission broken with the whole half-way covenant system, and not simply with the Stoddardian development of it."

Walker, George Leon. *Some Aspects of the Religious Life of New England, with Special Reference to Congregationalists.* New York, 1897. A generalized but insightful study of New England spiritual (or intellectual) life, useful as background to the study of Edwards. References to Edwards are scattered and superficial.

W[alker], J. "Edwards' Doctrine of Original Sin."
  Christian Examiner, 2 (1825), 207-229.
  A lengthy exposition of the substance of Tappan's(?)
  article in *Views in Theology*. Walker supports
  Tappan's interpretation of Edwards' doctrine of original
  sin against that proposed by T. R.
     "Thus do we sustain the assertion, that according to
  Edwards, original sin is a physical attribute of the
  soul, —'a created attribute of its substance, inhering
  in, and contributing to make up its nature, and constitute it what it is;' and, moreover, that the soul,
  merely from its being so constituted, and independent of
  all circumstances, is, in itself, and of itself, sinful
  and deserving of punishment, in the same sense as it is
  for exerting sinful actions; and this, too, prior to
  any such actions."

Walker, Williston, ed. *The Creeds and Platforms of*
  Congregationalism. New York, 1893.
  Essential documents with valuable commentaries. Walker
  briefly discusses Edwards' relation to the Halfway
  Covenant system, insisting that Edwards came to oppose
  not only the practices of Stoddard but the Halfway
  Covenant scheme in general. Edwards' *Humble Inquiry*,
  argues Walker, "was primarily an argument against
  Stoddardeanism, that was the point under debate between
  Edwards and the Northampton council; but it contained
  ...a vigorous and consistent attack on the Half-Way
  Covenant system as conducive to a false sense of
  security and a neglect of a true seeking for
  conversion."

W[alker], W[illiston]. "Edwards's Recovered Treatise."
  Yale Alumni Weekly, 13 (4 November 1903), 106-107.

Review of Fisher's *An Unpublished Essay of Edwards on the Trinity* (New York, 1903).

Walker, Williston. *A History of the Congregational Churches in the United States*. New York, 1894.
Includes a valuable discussion of Edwards' points of departure from "historic Calvinism." Edwards, observes Walker, "aimed to raise up Calvinism, then sore pressed by the Arminian school of Whitby and Taylor; and he sought this restoration not because of any devotion to Calvinism as a system long maintained in the churches, but because the center of his own religious experience, like that of Calvin, was the recognition of the sovereignty of God. Yet he was equally convinced that Calvinism needed to be modified so that the responsibility of man should be more clearly taught. And a second aim was no less evidently his. Edwards sought to foster a warm, emotional type of Christian character, touched and vivified by a sense of immediate communion between God and the human soul."

Walker, Williston. "Jonathan Edwards." In his *Great Men of the Christian Church*. New York, 1908, pp. 341-353.
An abstract of the essay that appears in Walker's *Ten New England Leaders*.

Walker, Williston. "Jonathan Edwards." In his *Ten New England Leaders*. New York, 1901, pp. 217-263.
Excellent if brief account of Edwards' life and thought. It was Edwards' great work as a religious leader, Walker notes, "to be the chief human instrument in turning back the current for over a century in the larger part of New England to the theory of the method of salvation and of man's dependence on God which marked

the earlier types of Calvinism."

Walker stresses the spirituality of Edwards which makes him accessible today where his theological conclusions have made him more remote: "Above all his other gifts he had, and he made men feel that he had, a vision of the glory of God that transfigured his life with a beauty of spirit that makes his memory reverenced even more than his endowments of mind are respected."

Walker, Williston. *Three Phases of New England Congregational Development*. Hartford, 1893.

Ward, William Hayes. "Jonathan Edwards." *The Independent*, 55 (1903), 2321-2327.
A rather sketchy discussion touching on Edwards as "a sulphurous preacher of the doctrine of eternal torment" and the philosopher of the nature of virtue.

"I think no less of him, but the more, that he told his hearers that Hell was a fearful fate, to be avoided, and depicted it in all its horrors. I have no doubt that he did a good thing, at a good time, in a good way, which is not for our time and our way. But what I value him most for is his masterly hold on ethics, his commanding sense of the nature and obligation of True Virtue...."

Warfield, Benjamin B. "Edwards and the New England Theology." In *Encyclopedia of Religion and Ethics*, ed. James Hastings. New York, 1912. Vol. V, pp. 221-227.
A brief but useful discussion of Edwards as pastor, philosopher, and theologian. "The peculiarity of Edwards' theological work," suggests Warfield, "is due to the union in it of the richest religious sentiment with the highest intellectual powers. He was first of

all a man of faith, and it is this that gives its
character to his whole life and all its products...."
    In defining Edwards' relationship to the New England
Theology, Warfield argues a position popular among nineteenth century interpreters: "It was Edwards' misfortune that he gave his name to a party which, never in
perfect agreement with him in its doctrinal ideas,
finished by becoming the earnest advocate of (as it has
been sharply expressed) 'a set of opinions which he
gained his chief celebrity by defending.'"

Warner, Charles F. *Representative Families of Northampton.*
    Northampton, 1917.
    Includes a brief account of the Edwards family.

Waterbury, J. B. "Rev. Jonathan Edwards." In his *Sketches
    of Eloquent Preachers.* New York, 1864, pp. 151-162.

Watkins, Walter Kendall. "English Ancestry of Jonathan
    Edwards." *New England Historical and Genealogical
    Register,* 58 (1904), 202-203.

Watts, Emily Stipes. "Jonathan Edwards and the Cambridge
    Platonists." Doctoral dissertation, University of
    Illinois, 1963. In *Dissertation Abstracts,* 24 (1964),
    4180-4181.
    The first and only extensive analysis of the influence
    of the Cambridge Platonists on the development of
    Edwards' thought. Watts claims Ralph Cudworth as a
    major source of Edwards' early idealism, suggests Henry
    More as the source of Edwards' first discussions of the
    nature of virtue, argues that John Smith was a signifi-
    cant influence on his understanding of religious experi-
    ence, and cites Theophilus Gale as a possible source of

Edwards' typology and philosophy of history. This study
should not be ignored.

Watts, Emily Stipes. "The Neoplatonic Basis of Jonathan
    Edwards' *True Virtue*." *Early American Literature,*
    10 (1975), 179-189.
    Watts argues that More's *Enchiridion Ethicum* served as a
    basis for Edwards' early investigation of ethics in his
    notes on the nature of excellence in *The Mind*,
    "investigations which were eventually developed as *The
    Nature of True Virtue*."

Weber, Donald Louis. "The Image of Jonathan Edwards in
    American Culture." Doctoral dissertation, Columbia
    University, 1978. In *Dissertation Abstracts Interna-
    tional*, 39 (1978), 2281A.

Weddle, David L. "The Beauty of Faith in Jonathan Edwards."
    Ohio Journal of Religious Studies, 4 (1976), 42-52.
    Weddle elaborates the relationship between beauty and
    faith in Edwards' thought, suggesting that it is not
    Edwards' rhetoric of divine wrath but his reflections on
    the divine beauty which are most relevant to Edwards'
    view of faith: "Throughout his works, Edwards contends
    that faith is the vision of, and consent to, the beauty
    of God."

Weddle, David L. "The Democracy of Grace: Political
    Reflections on the Evangelical Theology of Jonathan
    Edwards." *Dialog,* 15 (1976), 248-252.
    Following the insights of Alan Heimert, Weddle suggests
    that the "test case for a revisionist interpretation of
    the political implications of evangelical theology is
    Jonathan Edwards. He had hardly a political bone in his

body," argues Weddle, "yet, as leader of the Great
Awakening, exemplary convert, and the most important
theologian in America, his reflections on the Awakening
established a close relation between personal religious
experience ('new birth') and political order ('new
age')."

Weddle, David L.   "The Image of the Self in Jonathan
    Edwards: A Study of Autobiography and Theology."
    Journal of the American Academy of Religion,
    43 (1975), 70-83.
    Weddle explores the relationship between "the primary
    language of 'identity' in Edwards' autobiographical
    writings, and the secondary language of 'ideology' in
    his sermons and theological treatises." The key to this
    relationship, Weddle suggests, "is a distinctive image
    of the self, coming to focus in his conversion and
    reaching clarity in his *Personal Narrative.*"

Weddle, David L.   "Jonathan Edwards on Men and Trees, and
    the Problem of Solidarity." *Harvard Theological Review,*
    67 (1974), 155-175.
    "This essay addresses the problem of the relation
    between membership and moral responsibility in the
    interpretation of the doctrine of original sin and
    atonement of Jonathan Edwards. Focusing on his image
    of a tree and its branches to typify the solidarity of
    man as sinners ('in Adam') and as saints ('in Christ'),
    I will argue that Edwards defines the 'nature' of man
    in organic and historical terms which modify signifi-
    cantly both the biological images of infection and the
    juridical terms of federal headship in Puritan covenant
    theology."

Weddle, David L. "The New Man: A Study of the Significance
    of Conversion for the Theological Definition of the
    Self in Jonathan Edwards and Charles G. Finney."
    Doctoral dissertation, Harvard University, 1973.

Weeks, John Stafford. "A Comparison of Calvin and Edwards
    on the Doctrine of Election." Doctoral dissertation,
    University of Chicago, 1963.

Wellman, J. W. "A New Biography of Jonathan Edwards." *Our
    Day*, 5 (1890), 195-219; 288-307. Reprinted separately
    as *A Review of Dr. A. V. G. Allen's Biography of
    Jonathan Edwards*. Boston, 1890.
    Review of A. V. G. Allen's *Life and Writings of
    Jonathan Edwards* (Boston, 1889).

Wendell, Barrett. *A Literary History of America*. New York,
    1900.
    Wendell provides a brief, superficial, and largely
    unsympathetic discussion of Edwards and his role in the
    history of American culture. The more notorious
    passages from Edwards' writings are quoted at length,
    and as his final comment on Edwards Wendell reads from
    Holmes' *One Hoss Shay*.
        "In Jonathan Edwards we found theoretical
    Puritanism, divorced from life, proclaiming more uncom-
    promisingly than ever that human nature is damnable.
    In such temper we find on a grand scale something akin
    to the petty enthusiasm of our own day, which now and
    again maintains that whoever takes a glass of wine shall
    sleep in a drunkard's grave.... [While] Edwards was
    preaching his unflinching Calvinism, Franklin, by living
    as well and as sensibly as he could, was demonstrating
    that, at least in America, unaided human nature could

develop in an earthly shape which looked quite as far
from damnable as that of any Puritan parson."

Werge, Thomas. "Jonathan Edwards and the Puritan Mind in
America: Directions in Textual and Interpretative
Criticism." *Reformed Review*, 23 (1970), 153-156;
173-183.
A valuable analysis of the main lines of scholarly
inquiry into English Puritanism, the Puritan mind in
New England, and current interpretations of Edwards,
particularly those of Perry Miller and Conrad Cherry.

Wertenbaker, Thomas J. *Princeton, 1746-1896*. Princeton,
1946.
Documents Edwards' involvement with Princeton.

Wessell, Lynn R. "Great Awakening: The First American
Revolution." *Christianity Today*, 17 no. 23 (1973),
11-13.
A brief, superficial essay in which Wessell attempts to
"repossess the important historical truth" that evangelical religion, and Edwards, "helped to promote the
American revolution."

West, Samuel. *Essays on Liberty and Necessity; in which
the True Nature of Liberty is Stated and Defended; and
the principal Arguments used by Mr. Edwards, and others,
for Necessity, are Considered*. Boston, 1793. Reissued
with a second part, New Bedford, 1795.

West, Stephen. *Essay on Moral Agency: Containing, Remarks
on a late anonymous publication, entitled, An Examination of the late Reverend President Edwards's Enquiry on
Freedom of Will*. New Haven, 1772.

The publication of this essay was apparently prompted by
Dana's *Examination*, but it is an independent treatise
rather than a detailed response to the criticisms of
Dana. In an appendix to the second edition of this
essay (1774) West takes particular note of Dana's
second volume.

Westbrook, Robert B. "Social Criticism and the Heavenly
    City of Jonathan Edwards." *Soundings*, 59 (1976),
    396-412.
    Responding to the often made observation that Edwards
    was a man singularly unconcerned with political or
    social theory, Westbrook suggests that what Edwards
    reveals is "not a lack of concern with society, but a
    lack of concern with imperfect society. Edwards' social
    thought," argues Westbrook, "was self-consciously norma-
    tive." The good society that Edwards envisioned was
    neither natural nor attained but supernatural and given.
        Westbrook identifies and elaborates three concepts
    basic to Edwards' heavenly city: his philosophy con-
    cerning the nature of virtue, his conviction concerning
    the kind of society this philosophy dictates, and his
    post millenial faith that history is moving toward the
    actualization of this society.

Wheatcroft, John. "Emily Dickinson's Poetry and Jonathan
    Edwards on the Will." *Bucknell Review*, 10 (1961),
    102-127.
    Wheatcroft suggests that the notion of the will held in
    common by Edwards and Dickinson was "the mainspring of
    Emily Dickinson's creative activity."

Whedon, Daniel D. *The Freedom of the Will as a Basis of
    Human Responsibility and a Divine Government Elucidated*

and Maintained in its Issue with the Necessitarian Theories of Hobbes, Edwards, the Princeton Essayists, and other leading Advocates. New York, 1864.

White, Morton Gabriel. "Jonathan Edwards: The Doctrine of Necessity and the Sense of the Heart." In his *Science and Sentiment in America: Philosophical Thought from Jonathan Edwards to John Dewey.* New York, 1972, pp. 30-54.
In this study of the various responses of American philosophers to the challenges of modern science and scientific method, White considers Edwards—"the Lockeian philosopher of evangelical Calvinism when it was the religion of theocratic New England." White provides an excellent analysis of Edwards' doctrine of the will, and examines Edwards' sense of the heart, viewed as "a device for escaping from what he thought were the limits of Locke's empiricism."

Whittemore, Robert C. "Jonathan Edwards and the Theology of the Sixth Way." *Church History,* 35 (1966), 60-75.
Whittemore challenges Elwood's contention that Edwards was a panentheist, and attempts to assess the contemporary relevance of Edwards' thought. Edwards, Whittemore contends, was not a panentheist but a Christian neoplatonist.
"The best of Edwards is his private notebooks; the remainder is, in a word, theodicy. Theodicy—and not theology. For want of this distinction most of the criticism and compliment addressed to Edwards has been beside the point. It being made, the value of his work, for those who, like himself, are servants of 'the sovereign God,' is unquestionable."

Whittemore, Robert C. *Makers of the American Mind.*
New York, 1964.
Includes a brief, superficial discussion of Edwards in
relation to the Great Awakening.

"Like Pascal, he knew that the heart has its proper
reasons, and in this 'sense of the heart' he thought to
find the essence of the spiritual life. His only
error," Whittemore suggests, "was to be a century ahead
of his time. The Boston religious mind of 1740 was not
yet sophisticated enough to grasp the psychological
subtlety of religion as change of heart."

"Why Revive Edwards?" Editorial. *Congregationalist and
Christian World,* 88 (1903), 454.

Widenhouse, Ernest C. "The Doctrine of the Atonement in the
New England Theology from Jonathan Edwards to Horace
Bushnell." Doctoral dissertation, Hartford Seminary
Foundation, 1931.

Wiebe, Dallas E. "Mr. Lowell and Mr. Edwards." *Wisconsin
Studies in Contemporary Literature,* 3 no. 2 (1962),
21-31.
A literary study of Robert Lowell's *Mr. Edwards and the
Spider,* and *After the Surprising Conversions.*

Wiggam, Albert Edward. *The Fruit of the Family Tree.*
Indianapolis, 1924.
Wiggam uses the Edwards family to illustrate the thesis
that "blood always tells." A "partial" chart of the
Edwards family appears opposite the title page of the
volume.

"From Jonathan Edwards, who married also a wonderful
woman, Sarah Pierpont, have descended 12 college

presidents, 265 college graduates, 65 college professors, 100 clergymen, 75 army officers, 60 prominent
authors, 100 lawyers, 30 judges, 80 public officers—
state governors, city mayors, and state officials—
3 congressmen, 2 United States senators and 1 vice-
president of the United States. Compare *this* with the
worthless descendants of Martin Kallikak."

Wiggam admits that factors other than heredity may
have been operative in the later success of the Edwards
line: "There can be little doubt that some members of
moderate ability attained distinguished positions
through family influence." Wiggam insists, however,
that "beyond question," heredity "has proved to be the
largest factor in giving them their positions of
distinction and power."

Willard, Malinda Kaye. "Jonathan Edwards and Nathaniel
Hawthorne: Themes from the Common Consciousness."
Doctoral dissertation, University of South Carolina,
1978. In *Dissertation Abstracts International*,
39 (1979), 6136A.

Williams, Solomon. *The True State of the Question concerning the Qualifications Necessary to lawful Communion in
the Christian Sacraments*. Boston, 1751.
A lengthy attack on Edwards' position concerning
qualifications for communion.

"All those persons whom God has taken into the
external Covenant [i.e., the visible church], are bound
to the external duties of it, except as God hath
expressly excluded; but he hath expressly excluded none
but ignorant and scandalous persons. From hence it
follows that if there be any unconverted persons in the
external Covenant besides them, 'tis their duty to

attend." Edwards responded to Williams with
Misrepresentations Corrected, and Truth vindicated
(1752).

Williamson, Joseph Crawford. "The Excellency of Christ: A
Study in the Christology of Jonathan Edwards."
Doctoral dissertation, Harvard University, 1968.

Wilson, David S. "The Flying Spider." *Journal of the
History of Ideas,* 32 (1971), 447-458.
Wilson sheds important new light on Edwards' early essay
on the flying or ballooning spider. While Edwards
scholars have created the impression that the young
Edwards was indeed a pioneering observer of nature in
this one instance, Wilson argues that this is simply not
true, and that the "observations" found in this essay
are neither original nor unique. Edwards' essay, Wilson
contends, "is one specimen only, albeit it a felicitous
and precocious one, of a well-established genre of whose
existence Edwards was probably aware...."
    Wilson establishes the genre of essays on spiders in
the literature of natural philosophy and details its
correspondences with Edwards' paper, commenting on the
"tunnel vision" of scholars who have "virtually ignored
the generic precedents for Edwards' work" for more than
two hundred and fifty years.

Wilson, James G., and Fiske, John, eds. "Jonathan Edwards."
In *Appleton's Cyclopaedia of American Biography.* New
York, 1892. Vol. II, pp. 309-311.
A brief biographical sketch and evaluation of Edwards
as a thinker.
    "He was not widely learned, and with slender
opportunities of acquaintance with the works of contem-

porary writers, it is clear that he drew his materials almost entirely from his own reflections and resources."

Wilson, John F. "Jonathan Edwards as Historian." *Church History,* 46 (1977), 5-18.
Wilson addresses the problems involved in interpreting Edwards' *History of the Work of Redemption,* and examines the various senses in which the term "historian" has been applied to Edwards on the basis of this work. Wilson criticizes the opposing interpretations of this work proposed by Perry Miller and Peter Gay, suggesting that "each failed finally to place *The Work of Redemption* properly and to understand it adequately." What characterizes this work, Wilson argues, is its apparent commitment "to work within the tradition of the 'figural' interpretation of Scripture as a rich deposit of revealed truth."

Wilson, Patricia Anne. "The Theology of Grace in Jonathan Edwards." Doctoral dissertation, University of Iowa, 1973. In *Dissertation Abstracts International,* 35 (1974), 573A.

Wilson-Kastner, Patricia. "Jonathan Edwards: History and the Covenant." *Andrews University Seminary Studies,* 15 (1977), 205-216.

Winchester, E. *A Letter to the Editor of President Edwards' lately Revised Sermon on the Eternity of Hell-torments.* London, 1789.

Winship, Albert Edward. *Heredity, a History of Jukes-Edwards Families.* Boston, 1925.

Winship, Albert Edward. *Jukes-Edwards: A Study in
Education and Heredity*. Harrisburg, 1900.
Winship contrasts the descendants of President Edwards
with the descendants of the pseudonymous "Max Jukes."
Review
[Mead, Edwin]. *New England Magazine*, new series,
23 (1900), 475-480.

Winship, Edith A. "The Human Legacy of Jonathan Edwards."
World's Work, 6 (1903), 3981-3984. An abstract of this
article appears as "The Descendants of Edwards."
Journal of the Presbyterian Historical Society,
2 (1903), 170-171.
"Fourteen hundred descendants with a wonderful history—
three Yale presidents in the list, and soldiers, public
men, professors, doctors, and ministers—the
progenitor's characteristics reproduced in successive
generations, maintaining a constant high level."
    Winship presents a "representative array" of
Edwards' illustrious descendants. In Winship's estimation, Edwards' most important contribution to the world
was his genetic structure: "The theology of Jonathan
Edwards may be dead, and his books unread, but the man
was greater than the theologian. In leaving to his
children and his children's children the legacy that he
gave, he did the best a man can do for the world."

Winslow, Ola Elizabeth. *Jonathan Edwards, 1703-1758: A
Biography*. New York, 1940.
A solidly researched work and recipient of the Pulitzer
Prize, this study is likely to remain the standard
biography of Edwards for some time to come. Beyond
writing the story of Edwards' life, Winslow does not
pretend "to do more than indicate the chronology and

general import of his ideas, particularly with respect
to his changing fortunes." Yet since Edwards is preeminently a thinker, in writing the story of Edwards
the man Winslow does in fact have a great deal to say
along these lines.

Edwards' mistake, Winslow suggests, was in choosing
to speak through the outmoded dogmatic system of
Calvinism. Edwards took "the life principle of all
religion, as he had found it in his own search, vital
and joy-giving, and shut it up in the husk of a dead
idiom." It did not occur to Edwards, observes Winslow,
"that he had in his own hand the key which would have
let himself and all his brother ministers out of
prison."

"Considering the texture of his mind, one may wonder
why he could not take the one more step to be free.
Sometimes he did take it, but not habitually. He lacked
the imagination; he lacked the mellowness and the
flexibility which would have enabled him to get outside
of the system and view it with enough detachment to
judge it. He was on too narrow a track, and the
surrounding walls were too high. For one whose thought
was capable of telescopic range, and one who exhibited
so large a degree of intellectual subtlety, his bondage
seems almost a tragic pity. More than most men he was
the prisoner of his own ideas."

Winslow's study includes an extensive description of
the Edwards manuscripts and an excellent bibliography.

Reviews

Day, Richard W. *Sewanee Review*, 49 (1941), 405-407.
Faust, Clarence H. *New England Quarterly*, 13 (1940),
723-726.
Miller, Perry. "Jonathan Edwards—Speculative Genius."
Saturday Review of Literature, 30 March 1940,

pp. 6-7.

Schneider, Herbert W. *American Historical Review*,
    46 (1941), 417-418.

Townsend, Harvey G. *Philosophical Review*,
    50 (1941), 450.

Wood, James Playsted. *Mr. Jonathan Edwards*. New York,
    1968.

A readable biography but one which offers no new
insights, recapping the now familiar events that made up
the life of Jonathan Edwards. While there is little
examination of Edwards' thought, Wood repeats the
suggestion made by many scholars that Edwards was
secretive about his personal convictions, and that there
was a difference between what Edwards himself believed
and what he taught to others. Edwards, Wood suggests,
"was a poet, a mystic, a clear eyed scholar, and—to use
a term not popularized until the next century—a
pantheistic transcendentalist. He spoke of none of
this. In fact (a prudent man concealeth knowledge) he
did his best to hide it."

Woodbridge, Frederick J. E. "Jonathan Edwards."
Philosophical Review, 13 (1904), 393-408. Appears under
the title "The Philosophy of Jonathan Edwards," in
*Exercises Commemorating the 200th Anniversary of the
Birth of Jonathan Edwards*. Andover, 1904, pp. 47-72.
Woodbridge locates and elaborates a dualism in Edwards'
thought, a dualism between Edwards the philosopher and
Edwards the theologian. "The fact is," Woodbridge
argues, "that the philosopher never became the theologian or the theologian the philosopher. It is futile to
try to understand Edwards's Calvinism from his philosophy or his philosophy from his Calvinism. In him they

are juxtaposed, not united." The explanation for what
Woodbridge considers an "extraordinary" juxtaposition of
"unrelated principles" in Edwards' thought is found in
Edwards' conversion experiences. So disrupting were
these experiences intellectually, suggests Woodbridge,
"that his philosophy and theology remained to the close
of his life almost completely divorced and unrelated."

Woodbridge, Jonathan Edwards, ed. *The Memorial Volume of*
the Edwards Family Meeting at Stockbridge,
Massachusetts, September 6-7, A.D. 1870. Boston, 1871.
(This work is sometimes referred to as *Edwards Memorial,*
which is the running title of the volume).
"... [I]f there be one thing more than another for which
a man should be devoutly grateful, it is that of being
descended from parents of great moral worth, and
integrity of character; for certainly moral qualities
are transmitted as well as intellectual and physical."
A chronicle of the Edwards family reunion.
Woodbridge provides a detailed narrative of the events
of the two day celebration that includes the texts of
the numerous speeches, addresses and remarks made by
various members of the Edwards clan (or by those who
wished they were). The volume as whole informs one more
about Edwards' descendants than about Edwards himself,
and few of the addresses delivered at this meeting can
rightly be considered as biography or criticism of
Edwards. Critical discussion and reflection was not the
order of the day.

Contents

This contents list indicates only the addresses,
remarks, or letters read at the reunion. These generally appear without formal titles in the body of the work,
and the titles below are taken from Woodbridge's Table

of Contents. Brackets enclose extended and hopefully
explanatory annotations. Only selected items are
annotated by author.

SECOND DAY

Remarks, by George Woodbridge [who suggests that "even piety is, to a certain extent, an inheritance," and notes two little known facts in the life of Edwards: seven of his children were born on a Sunday, and all were baptized on a Sunday], pp. 146-150.

Remarks, by William W. Edwards [who speaks of his grandfather, Timothy Edwards], pp. 151-154.

Remarks, by Joseph Woodbridge [who speaks of the reunion itself], pp. 155-158.

Remarks, by Frank D. Clarke [who reads a poem composed by Mary Bayard Clarke, who was wise enough not to read it herself], pp. 158-161.

Remarks [on the portraits of Jonathan Edwards and Sarah Pierrepont], by Hon. Jonathan Edwards of New Haven, pp. 162-165.

Memorial Poem, by Sarah Edwards Henshaw, pp. 165-178.

Dr. Sprague's Letter [to Jonathan Edwards Woodbridge, regretting his inability to attend the reunion. Sprague provides transcriptions of two items in his possession: an invitation to attend Edwards' ordination, from Solomon Stoddard to John Williams of Deerfield; and a letter written by Edwards and dated 13 April 1749 concerning his dispute with his congregation over qualifications for communion], pp. 179-182.

Woodward, Robert H. "Jonathan Edwards and the Sweet Life." *Fellowship in Prayer*, 15 (1964), 11-13.

Woodward, Robert H. "Jonathan Edwards as a Puritan Poet." *Exercise Exchange*, 8 (1960), 5-6.

Woolsey, Theodore Dwight. "Commemorative Discourse." In
    The Memorial Volume of the Edwards Family Meeting, ed.
    Jonathan E. Woodbridge. Boston, 1871, pp. 25-81.
    "It is not in terms of eulogy that I mean to speak of
    him. My aim is to present you an idea of the man;
    interweaving, for that purpose, the circumstances of his
    outward life, so far as they bear on that idea, but
    making his inward life, intellectual, moral, and relig-
    ious, the point towards which every thing is to be
    referred and directed."

Woolsey, Theodore Dwight. "On a Resolution of President
    Edwards." *The Quarterly Christian Spectator,*
    7 (1825), 14-17.

Wortley, George Francis. "The Status of the Child in New
    England Congregationalism from Jonathan Edwards to
    Horace Bushnell." Doctoral dissertation, Hartford
    Seminary Foundation, 1927.

Wright, Conrad. *The Beginnings of Unitarianism in America.*
    Boston, 1955.
    Wright investigates the rise of Arminianism in America
    "both for a clearer understanding of the Unitarian
    movement which emerged from it, and for a sharper focus
    on Jonathan Edwards, who was its chief opponent."
    Wright's study is fundamental for understanding the
    context of much of Edwards' work.

Wright, Conrad. "Edwards and the Arminians on the Freedom
    of the Will." *Harvard Theological Review,* 35 (1942),
    241-261.
    Wright argues that the doctrine of moral necessity that
    Edwards labored to establish in his *Freedom of the Will*

"was not the basis for the division between New England
Arminians and most New England Calvinists. And whatever
Edwards may have thought, it was not even the real basis
for the division between him and the Arminians."
Edwards, Wright contends, failed to comprehend the
Arminian position, and the Arminians in the main failed
to comprehend Edwards. "The whole controversy would
have been vastly simplified if the Arminians had recognized clearly that Edwards' treatise was not wrong but
irrelevant."

Wyckoff, D. Campbell. "Jonathan Edwards' Contribution to
    Religious Education." Doctoral dissertation, New York
    University, 1948.

Wynne, James. *Lives of Eminent Literary and Scientific Men
    of America.* New York, 1850.
    Includes a biographical sketch of Edwards.

Yale University. *Commemoration of the 200th Anniversary of
    the Birth of Jonathan Edwards.* n.p., n.d.
    Item as cited by John J. Coss (*Cambridge History of
    American Literature*) and elsewhere. Possible reference
    to above entry, "Jonathan Edwards. Yale's Commemora-
    tion..."; or to notes in *Yale Daily News*: 26 September
    1903, p. 2; 3 October 1903, p. 1; and 6 October 1903,
    p. 1.

Zenos, Andrew C. "The Permanent and the Passing in the
    Thought of Edwards." *Interior,* 34 (1903), 1274-1275.

THE PUBLISHED WRITINGS OF JONATHAN EDWARDS

Thomas H. Johnson has compiled a comprehensive bibliography of Edwards' published writings in all editions (excluding anthologies) prior to 1940 in *The Printed Writings of Jonathan Edwards, 1703-1758: A Bibliography* (Princeton, 1940). The following list of Edwards' published writings is more modest in scope. The first section lists the writings published during Edwards' lifetime, first edition only. The second section indicates works published for the first time by Edwards' literary executors in the eighteenth century, prior to the appearance of any collected editions. Most of these items were later included in one or more editions of Edwards' collected *Works*. In the third section are listed the principal editions of Edwards' collected *Works*. The fourth section details the major deposits of writings by Edwards not yet found in collected editions. No attempt has been made to indicate all of the many secondary works on Edwards that have included fragments of previously unpublished material.

I. WORKS PUBLISHED DURING JONATHAN EDWARDS' LIFETIME

*God Glorified in the Work of Redemption, By the Greatness of
Man's Dependence upon Him, in the Whole of it. A Sermon
Preached on the Publick Lecture in Boston, July 8. 1731.
And Published at the Desire of several, Ministers and
Others, in Boston, who heard it.* Boston, 1731.

*A Divine and Supernatural Light, Immediately imparted to the
Soul by the Spirit of God, Shown to be both a
Scriptural, and Rational Doctrine; In a Sermon Preach'd
at Northampton, And Published at the Desire of some of
the Hearers.* Boston, 1734.

*Part of a large letter from the Rev. Mr. Jonathan Edwards of
Northampton. Giving an Account of the late wonderful
Work of God in those Parts.* Boston, 1736. (Appended to
The Duty and Interest of a People, by William Williams.)

*A Faithful Narrative of the Surprizing Work of God In The
Conversion Of Many Hundred Souls in Northampton, and the
Neighbouring Towns and Villages of New-Hampshire in
New-England. In a Letter to the Revd. Dr. Benjamin
Colman of Boston.* London, 1737.

*A Letter To The Author Of The Pamphlet Called An Answer to
the Hampshire Narrative.* Boston, 1737.

*Discourses on Various Important Subjects, Nearly concerning
the great Affair of the Soul's Eternal Salvation, Viz.
I. Justification by Faith alone. II. Pressing into the
Kingdom of God. III. Ruth's Resolution. IV. The
Justice of God in the Damnation of Sinners. V. The
Excellency of Jesus Christ. Delivered at Northampton,*

chiefly at the Time of the late wonderful pouring out of
the Spirit of God there. Boston, 1738.

The Distinguishing Marks Of a Work of the Spirit of God.
Applied to that uncommon Operation that has lately
appeared on the Minds of many of the People of this
Land; With a particular Consideration of the extra-
ordinary Circumstances with which this Work is attended.
A Discourse Delivered at New-Haven, September 10th 1741.
Being the Day after the Commencement; And now Published
at the earnest Desire of many Ministers and other
Gentlemen that heard it; with great Enlargements.
Boston, 1741.

Sinners In The Hands of an Angry God. A Sermon Preached at
Enfield, July 8th 1741. At a Time of great Awakenings;
and attended with remarkable Impressions on many of the
Hearers. Boston, 1741.

The Resort and Remedy of those that are bereaved by the
Death of an Eminent Minister. A Sermon preached at
Hatfield, Sept. 2. 1741. Being the Day of Interment of
the Reverend Mr. William Williams, the aged and vener-
able Pastor of that church. And published at the united
Request of those Reverend and Honoured Gentlemen, the
Sons of the Deceased. As also by the Desire and at the
Expense of the Town. Boston, 1741.

Some Thoughts Concerning the present Revival of Religion in
New-England, And the Way in which it ought to be acknowledged and promoted. Humbly offered to the Publick, in
a Treatise on that Subject. In Five Parts; Part I.
Shewing that the Work that has of late been going on in
this Land, is a glorious Work of God. Part II. Shewing

the *Obligations that all are under, to acknowledge,*
rejoice in and promote this Work.   Part III. Shewing in
many Instances, wherein the Subjects, or zealous
Promoters, of this Work have been injuriously blamed.
Part IV. Shewing what Things are to be corrected or
avoided, in promoting this Work, or in our Behaviour
under it.   Part V. Shewing positively what ought to be
done to promote this Work. Boston, 1742.

The Great Concern of A Watchman for Souls, appearing in the
Duty he has to do, and the Account he has to give,
represented & improved.   In A Sermon Preach'd at the
Ordination of the Reverend Mr. Jonathan Judd, To the
Pastoral Office over the Church of Christ, in the New
Precinct at Northampton, June 8. 1743. Boston, 1743.

The true Excellency of a Minister of the Gospel.   A Sermon
Preach'd at Pelham, Aug. 30. 1744.   Being the Day of the
Ordination of the Revd Mr. Robert Abercrombie To The
Work of the Gospel Ministry In that Place. Boston,
1744.

Copies of the Two Letters Cited by the Rev. Mr. Clap, Rector
of the College at New-Haven, In his late printed Letter
to a Friend in Boston concerning what he has reported,
as from Mr. Edwards of Northampton, concerning the Rev.
Mr. Whitefield.   Communicated in A Letter to a Friend.
With some reflections on the affair those Letters relate
to, and Rector Clap's Management therein. Boston, 1745.

An Expostulatory Letter From the Rev. Mr. Edwards of
Northampton, To The Rev. Mr. Clap, Rector of Yale
College in New-Haven, In Reply to his late printed
Letter to him, relating to what he reported concerning

the Rev. Mr. Whitefield, at Boston and Cambridge and elsewhere, as from Mr. Edwards; making the Falsity of that Report yet much more manifest. Boston, 1745.

A Treatise Concerning Religious Affections, In Three Parts; Part I. Concerning the Nature of the Affections, and their Importance in Religion. Part II. Shewing what are no certain Signs that religious Affections are gracious, or that they are not. Part III. Shewing what are distinguishing Signs of truly gracious and holy Affections. Boston, 1746.

The Church's Marriage to her Sons, and to her God: A Sermon Preached at the Instalment of the Rev. Mr. Samuel Buel as Pastor of the Church and Congregation at East-Hampton on Long-Island, September 19. 1746. Boston, 1746.

True Saints, when absent from the Body, are present with the Lord. A Sermon Preached on the Day of the Funeral of the Rev. Mr. David Brainerd, Missionary to the Indians, From the Honourable Society in Scotland for the Propagation of Christian Knowledge, and Pastor of a Church of Christian Indians in New-Jersey; Who died at Northampton in New-England, Octob. 9th. 1747, in the 30th Year of his Age, and was interred on the 12th following. Containing Some Account of his Character, and Manner of Life, and remarkable Speeches and Behaviour at Death. Boston, 1747.

An Humble Attempt To promote Explicit Agreement And Visible Union Of God's People in Extraordinary Prayer for the Revival of Religion and the Advancement of Christ's Kingdom on Earth, pursuant to Scripture-Promises and Prophecies concerning the last Time. Boston, 1747.

A Strong Rod broken and withered. A Sermon Preach'd at Northampton, on the Lord's-Day, June 26. 1748. On the Death of The Honourable John Stoddard, Esq; Often a Member of his Majesty's Council, For many Years Chief Justice of the Court of Common Pleas for the County of Hampshire, Judge of the Probate of Wills, and Chief Colonel of the Regiment, &c. Who died at Boston, June 19. 1748, in the 67th Year of his Age. Boston, 1748.

An Account of the Life of the Late Reverend Mr. David Brainerd, Minister of the Gospel, Missionary to the Indians, from the Honourable Society in Scotland, for the Propagation of Christian Knowledge, and Pastor of a Church of Christian Indians in New-Jersey. Who died at Northampton in New-England, Octob. 9th 1747, in the 30th Year of his Age: Chiefly taken from his own Diary, and other private Writings, written for his own Use; and now Published. Boston, 1749.

An Humble Inquiry Into The Rules of the Word of God Concerning The Qualifications Requisite to a Compleat Standing and full Communion In the Visible Christian Church. Boston, 1749.

Christ the great Example of Gospel Ministers. A Sermon Preach'd at Portsmouth, At the Ordination of the Reverend Mr. Job Strong, To the Pastoral Office over the South Church in that Place, June 28. 1749. Boston, 1749.

Preface to Joseph Bellamy's *True Religion Delineated; Or, Experimental Religion, as distinguished from Formality on the one Hand, and Enthusiasm on the other, set in a Scriptural and Rational Light.* Boston, 1750.

A Farewel-Sermon Preached at the first Precinct in Northampton, After the People's publick Rejection of their Minister, and renouncing their Relation to Him as Pastor of the Church there, on June 22. 1750. Occasion'd by Difference of Sentiments, concerning the requisite Qualifications of Members of the Church, in compleat Standing. Boston, 1751.

Misrepresentations Corrected, and Truth vindicated, In A Reply to the Rev. Mr. Solomon William's Book, intitled, The True State of the Question concerning the Qualifications necessary to lawful Communion in the Christian Sacraments. Boston, 1752.

True Grace, Distinguished from the Experience of Devils; in A Sermon, Preached before the Synod of New-York, Covened at New-Ark, in New-Jersey, on September 28. 1752. Boston, 1752.

A careful and strict Enquiry Into The modern prevailing Notions Of That Freedom of Will, Which is supposed to be essential To Moral Agency, Vertue and Vice, Reward and Punishment, Praise and Blame. Boston, 1754.

Published Correspondence

"From Seven Rev. Pastors in the County of Hampshire." *The Christian History* (Boston), August, 1743.

"The State of Religion at Northampton in the County of Hampshire, About a Hundred Miles Westward of Boston." *The Christian History* (Boston), January, 1744.

"Letter from Mr. Edwards. To the Rev. Mr. James Robe,
    Minister of the Gospel at Kilsyth in Scotland.
    Northampton, May 12, 1743." *The Christian Monthly
    History* (Edinburgh), August, 1745.

"Mr. Edwards's Letter to his Scots Correspondent.
    Northamptoun, Nov. 20, 1745." *The Christian Monthly
    History* (Edinburgh), November, 1745.

"Extract of a Part of the Reverend Mr. Jonathan Edwards's
    Letter, concerning Mr. Whitefield's Progress, Reception,
    and Success in New-England." *The Christian Monthly
    History* (Edinburgh), December, 1745.

II. POSTHUMOUS EIGHTEENTH CENTURY PUBLICATIONS

*The Great Christian Doctrine of Original Sin defended:
    Evidences of its Truth produced, And Arguments to the
    Contrary answered. Containing, in particular, A Reply
    to the Objections and Arguings of Dr. John Taylor, in
    his Book, Intitled, "The Scripture-Doctrine of Original
    Sin proposed to free and candid Examination &c".*
    Boston, 1758. This treatise was actually in process of
    publication at the time of Edwards' death, in 1758. The
    Preface bears the date 26 May 1757.

*Two Dissertations, I. Concerning the End for which God
    created the World. II. The Nature of True Virtue.*
    Boston, 1765.

*The Life and Character of the Late Reverend Mr. Jonathan
    Edwards, President of the College of New-Jersey.
    Together with a Number of his Sermons on Various*

Important Subjects. Edited by Samuel Hopkins. Boston, 1765.

A History Of the Work of Redemption. Containing The Outlines of a Body of Divinity, In a Method entirely new. Edited by John Erskine. Edinburgh, 1774.

Sermons, On the Following Subjects: The Manner in which Salvation is to be Sought. The Unreasonableness of Indetermination in Religion. Unbelievers contemn the glory of Christ. The folly of looking back in fleeing out of Sodom. The Warnings of Scripture in the best Manner adapted to the awakening and conversion of Sinners. Hypocrites deficient in the Duty of Prayer. The future Punishment of the Wicked unavoidable and intolerable. The Eternity of hell-torments. The Peace which Christ gives his true Followers. The perpetuity & change of the Sabbath. Edited by Jonathan Edwards the Younger. Hartford, 1780.

Practical Sermons, Never Before Published. Edited by Jonathan Edwards the Younger. Edinburgh, 1788.

Christian Cautions; Or, The Necessity of Self-Examination. Edinburgh, 1788.

Miscellaneous Observations On Important Theological Subjects, Original and Collected. Edited by John Erskine. Edinburgh, 1793.

Remarks on Important Theological Controversies. Edited by John Erskine. Edinburgh, 1796.

III. COLLECTED WORKS

The Works of President Edwards. Edited by E. Williams and
  E. Parsons. 8 vols. Leeds, 1806-11. New edition,
  8 vols. London, 1817. London edition revised with a
  two volume supplement, edited by R. Ogle.
  Edinburgh, 1847.

The Works of President Edwards. Edited by Samuel Austin.
  8 vols. Worcester, 1808-09. Reissued with an index and
  Ogle's supplementary volumes. New York, 1847.
  Reprinted several times thereafter.

The Works of President Edwards. Edited by Sereno E. Dwight.
  10 vols. New York, 1829-30.

The Works of President Edwards. Edited by E. Hickman.
  2 vols. London, 1833. Reissued with Dwight's *Life* of
  Edwards and "An Essay on the Genius and Writings of
  Jonathan Edwards" by Henry Rogers. London, 1834.
  Reprinted several times thereafter.

The Works of Jonathan Edwards. General editor Perry Miller,
  succeeded in 1963 by John E. Smith. New Haven, 1957
  et seq.

This edition now in progress by the Yale University
Press is likely to become the standard edition of
Edwards' works. The extensive, scholarly introductions
to the individual volumes are important secondary
sources.

  I. *Freedom of the Will*. Edited with Introduction by
    Paul Ramsey. New Haven, 1957.

II.   *Religious Affections*. Edited with Introduction by
      John E. Smith. New Haven, 1959.

III. *Original Sin*. Edited with Introduction by Clyde
      A. Holbrook. New Haven, 1970.

IV.   *The Great Awakening*. Edited with Introduction by
      C. C. Goen. New Haven, 1972.

V.   *Apocalyptic Writings*. Edited with Introduction by
      Stephen J. Stein. New Haven, 1977.

IV.   ITEMS NOT IN COLLECTED WORKS

*Charity and its Fruits, or Christian Love as Manifested in
   the Heart and Life*. Edited by Tryon Edwards. London,
   1851.
   A collection of sermons on I Cor. 13, first preached at
   Northampton in 1738.

"The Flying Spider—Observations by Jonathan Edwards when a
   Boy." Edited by Egbert C. Smyth. *Andover Review*,
   13 (1890), 1-19.
   Edwards' early essays *Of Insects* and *The Flying Spider*,
   with facsimiles.

Images or Shadows of Divine Things. Edited with Introduction
   by Perry Miller. New Haven, 1948.

"Jonathan Edwards' Letter of Invitation to George
   Whitefield." Edited by H. Abelove. *William and Mary
   Quarterly*, series 3, 29 (1972), 487-489.

"Jonathan Edwards on the Sense of the Heart." Edited by
   Perry Miller. *Harvard Theological Review*, 41 (1948),

123-145.

Item 782 of the *Miscellanies*, "the entry most pertinent
to the rhetorical theory" of Jonathan Edwards.

*Jonathan Edwards: Representative Selections, With Introduc-
tion, Bibliography and Notes.* Edited by Clarence H.
Faust and Thomas H. Johnson. New York, 1935; rev. ed.
New York, 1962.

Jonathan Edwards' Sermon Outlines. Edited by Sheldon B.
Quincer. Grand Rapids, 1958.

"Jonathan Edwards' Sociology of the Great Awakening."
Edited by Perry Miller. *New England Quarterly,*
21 (1948), 50-77.
Excerpts from three manuscript sermons.

Letter dated Northampton, 18 May 1742, opposing lay exhorta-
tion. *The Spirit of the Pilgrims,* 6 (1833), 545-546;
and *Bibliotheca Sacra,* 28 (1871), 95-97.

Letter to Rev. Thomas Prince of Boston, dated Northampton,
27 July 1744. *The Biblical Review and Congregational
Magazine,* 1 (1846), 223-224.

Letter to Rev. Timothy Edwards, dated Northampton,
22 May 1744. *Proceedings of the Massachusetts Historical Society,* series 2, 10 (1896), 429.

"A Letter From Rev. Jonathan Edwards, to Hon. Thomas
Hubbard, Esq. Of Boston, Relating To The Indian School
At Stockbridge. Stockbridge, Aug. 31, 1751."
Collections of the Massachusetts Historical Society,
10 (1809), 142-153.

"The Mind" of Jonathan Edwards: A Reconstructed Text.
  Edited with Introduction by Leon Howard. Berkeley,
  1963.

"New Memorials of President Edwards." Edited by J. E.
  Rankin. *Independent,* 47 (1895), 1121, 1185.
  Letter to Esther Burr, dated Stockbridge,
  20 November 1757; and letter to Rev. Aaron Burr, dated
  Stockbridge, 14 March 1756. Both letters re-edited by
  Faust and Johnson in *Jonathan Edwards: Representative
  Selections* (New York, 1935).

*Observations Concerning the Scripture Oeconomy of the
  Trinity and Covenant of Redemption.* Edited by Egbert
  C. Smyth. New York, 1880.
  Item 1062 of the *Miscellanies,* thought by Smyth to be
  the unpublished tract on the Trinity referred to by
  Horace Bushnell and Oliver Wendell Holmes. In an
  Appendix to this volume Smyth provides further extracts
  from the *Miscellanies.*

"Original Letter of President Edwards." Edited by Edwards
  A. Park. *Bibliotheca Sacra,* 1 (1844), 579-591.
  Edwards' letter to Major Joseph Hawley, dated
  Stockbridge, 18 November 1754. Re-edited by Faust and
  Johnson in *Jonathan Edwards: Representative Selections*
  (New York, 1935).

*The Philosophy of Jonathan Edwards from his Private
  Notebooks.* Edited with Introduction by Harvey G.
  Townsend. Eugéne, Oregon, 1955.
  Includes the text of *The Mind,* and selections from the
  Notes on Natural Science and the *Miscellanies.*

Puritan Sage: Collected Writings of Jonathan Edwards.
Edited with Introduction by Vergilius Ferm. New York,
1953.

"The Rev. Mr. Edwards of Stockbridge to the Rev. Mr. Erskine
of Culross, April 12, 1757." In *Historical Collections
Relating To Remarkable Periods Of The Success Of The
Gospel,* edited by John Gillies. Kelso, 1845,
pp. 522-523.

Selected Sermons of Jonathan Edwards. Edited with
Introduction and Notes by Harry Norman Gardiner. New
York, 1904.

*Selections from the Unpublished Writings of Jonathan
Edwards, of America.* Edited with Introduction by
Alexander B. Grosart. Edinburgh, 1865.

"Six Letters of Jonathan Edwards to Joseph Bellamy." Edited
by Stanley T. Williams. *New England Quarterly,*
1 (1928), 226-242.

"Some Early Writings of Jonathan Edwards. A.D. 1714-1726."
Edited by Egbert C. Smyth. *Proceedings of the American
Antiquarian Society,* new series, 10 (1895), 212-247.
Includes, with facsimiles, the essays *Of Being, The
Soul, Of the Rainbow,* and *Of Colours.*

*Treatise on Grace and Other Posthumously Published Writings
by Jonathan Edwards.* Edited with Introduction by Paul
Helm. London, 1971.
Includes the two essays on the Trinity originally published by Smyth (1880) and Fisher (1903).

*An Unpublished Essay of Edwards on the Trinity, with Remarks
   on Edwards and his Theology*. Edited by George Park
   Fisher. New York, 1903.

"An Unpublished Letter of Jonathan Edwards." Edited by
   George P. Clark. *New England Quarterly*, 29 (1956),
   228-233.
   Letter of 7 May 1750 to the Rev. Peter Clark of Salem
   Village.

Park, Edwards A. "Remarks of Jonathan Edwards on the
   Trinity." *Bibliotheca Sacra*, 38 (1881), 147-187;
   333-369.
   Includes extracts from the *Miscellanies*.

Rice, Howard C., Jr. "Jonathan Edwards at Princeton: With
   a Survey of Edwards Material in the Princeton University
   Library." *Princeton University Library Chronicle*,
   15 (1954), 68-89.
   Includes eight letters and sermon notes.

Smyth, Egbert C., ed. Appendix I in *Exercises Commemorating
   the 200th Anniversary of the Birth of Jonathan Edwards*.
   Andover, 1904, pp. 1-60.
   Extracts from the *Miscellanies*.

Smyth, Egbert C. "Jonathan Edwards' Idealism. With Special
   Reference to the Essay *Of Being* and to Writings not in
   his Collected Works." *American Journal of Theology*,
   1 (1897), 950-964.
   Includes extracts from the *Miscellanies*.

Smyth, Egbert C. "Professor Allen's Jonathan Edwards, With
   Extracts from Copies of Unpublished Manuscripts."

Andover Review, 13 (1890), 285-304.
Includes extracts from the *Miscellanies*.

STUDIES IN AMERICAN RELIGION